With compliments, but
[illegible] 's.

PEACE KEEPING IN A DEMOCRATIC SOCIETY

PEACE KEEPING
IN A
DEMOCRATIC
SOCIETY

*The Lessons of
Northern Ireland*

by

ROBIN EVELEGH

C. HURST & COMPANY · LONDON

First published in the United Kingdom by
C. Hurst & Co. (Publishers) Ltd.,
1–2 Henrietta Street, London WC2E 8PS

ISBN 0-905838-10-6

Printed in Great Britain
by Billing & Sons Limited, Guildford, London and Worcester

ACKNOWLEDGEMENTS

This book was written in the summer of 1975, and it reflects my views, the state of the law and the situation in Northern Ireland up to that time. Because the troubles there go on and on, with consequent minor changes in legislation, it seemed best to draw the line at the time when my direct day-to-day involvement in the problems of Northern Ireland ended. Account is therefore not taken of developments since October 1975.

A great many people helped me with this work, both with advice and by commenting on the drafts before publication came into the question. It would be impossible to name all of them but I would like to mention specifically the help given by the following, and to record my thanks: Sir Robert Mark, late Commissioner of the Metropolitan Police; Professor Norman Gibbs of All Souls College, Oxford; Major General Frank Kitson; Dr Richard Clutterbuck of Exeter University; Mr Geoffrey Kinley of London University: Dr Keith Devlin of Brunel University; Mr Jeffrey McCann of the Legal Department, Metropolitan Police; Major Robert Williamson; Major Charles Vyvyan and Mr Christopher Hawker. The views expressed are, however, entirely my own; all responsibility for their faults and their merits lies with me.

Finally, I have the honour of dedicating this book to the officers and men of the 3rd Battalion Royal Green Jackets.

March 1978   ROBIN EVELEGH

CONTENTS

vii

Contents

PART II.   PROPOSALS FOR IMPROVING THE CONSTITUTIONAL STRUCTURE FOR COUNTERING INSURGENCY

PART III.   PROPOSALS FOR IMPROVING THE LAWS THAT GOVERN THE OPERATIONS OF THE MILITARY AND TO SOME EXTENT OF THE POLICE SO THAT THEY CAN BE EFFECTIVE IN ENDING INSURGENCY

Contents

INTRODUCTION

I was the Commanding Officer of the 3rd Battalion Royal Green Jackets, an infantry battalion of some 750 men, in the Upper Falls Area of Belfast for two tours of duty of four months, each based on the Springfield Road police station. The first tour was in the late summer and autumn of 1972 at the period that the statistics show to have been the most violent so far in Northern Ireland. The second tour was a year later in the second half of 1973, when the violence was at a much lower level.

At the time when I was in Belfast and since leaving it, I have been trying to work out why the British Government's overall campaign to restore Northern Ireland to a peacetime level of disorder was not more successful. Even if the problem of Northern Ireland is solved by some means that cannot be foreseen at the time of writing, the Government's campaign will still have been less successful than it could have been. The turbulence, the disorder, the killing, the maiming, the misery, the fear and the unhappiness have already lasted for several years. That in itself is a failure. The casualty and damage statistics are well known and speak for themselves, as does the tangible hatred between the communities. But almost as sad in their way were the little deprivations: the war-wise missile-hurling children deprived of their right to a childhood; the young girls, maturing into sullen half-educated drabs as the years of violence continued, deprived of their right to a teenage of widening horizons; the elderly couples fighting a losing battle, sometimes with a valorous determination, for their right to a peaceful old age.

What principally puzzled me at the time was that this lack of success was matched by most of the ingredients that might reasonably have been thought necessary for success. It is of course easy for an Englishman arrogantly to dismiss the Irish of all persuasions as incorrigible brawlers revelling in violence and beyond redemption. It is possible to say that the problem of Northern Ireland is insoluble by any means short of letting them cut each other's throats in unrestrained civil war till some natural and stable balance emerges from the catharsis of mutual massacre. But this denies the patent kindliness and good nature of the inhabitants of Ireland; it denies their generally law-abiding conduct in periods when political controversy has been at a low ebb; it also denies the manifest desire of the great majority of people in Northern Ireland to see an end to the troubles,

1

provided the peace terms are reasonably acceptable to them. This popular desire for peace was matched, as far as the British Government's campaign to achieve it was concerned, by intelligent, sensitive and skilled politicians, all with peace and reconciliation as their prime aim. They were prepared to pour Government money unstintingly into Northern Ireland, whenever it seemed that this might help. They were prepared to examine and consider almost any proposal put to them that seemed to offer the chance of a solution. They were supported by experienced and devoted civil servants, as well as by soldiers who, whatever other charges may be laid against them, cannot be accused of lacking courage, discipline, energy or obedience to political direction. The Police, for all the abuse flung at them, were in general extraordinarily brave, hard-working and fair. Why, then, given these near-ideal instruments, has success up to now evaded the British Government's efforts to end the disorders in Northern Ireland? My conclusion is that, even with the excellent instruments at their disposal, success in their efforts was made nearly impossible for the Government by the faults in the constitutional framework for controlling their campaign against insurrection and by the shortcomings in the laws governing the operations of their Security Forces to suppress terrorism and disorder. The constitutional shortcomings meant that the Government's campaign could not be managed effectively. The shortcomings in the laws, which laid down the operational rules for the Army and Police, meant that a grievous political price had to be paid for nearly irrelevant draconian legal powers, while the Security Forces were crippled by the lack of quite minor laws, carrying a modest political penalty, that would have made them effective. Given an appropriate organisation for managing' the Government's campaign, and laws to make the Police and Army effective against rebellion and terrorism, it might have been possible to succeed in ending these horrors. Without these preconditions it was nearly impossible to do so.

Because the current troubles in Ulster are recent, are near home and involved me personally, I have based most of my proposals on them. However, I have also tried to link these to other similar campaigns. Every terrorist-backed insurrection is to some extent an individual special case and can therefore be held to be atypical. However, this is only valid for the detailed terms of the struggle, and they all have certain general characteristics in common and tend to follow similar patterns. It therefore seems legitimate to try to draw general lessons and theories for the conduct of counter-insurgency campaigns by such an examination of one of them, that in Nothern Ireland, provided it is remembered that only the generalised conclusions will have wider validity and not the detailed examples.

The first part of the book sets out to explain more fully what were the real obstacles to the waging of a successful counter-insurgency campaign—obstacles that seem to have been little comprehended in the world at large. It begins with the constitutional vacuum for controlling the military engaged in the suppression of civil disorder within the United Kingdom. This vacuum has arisen from the wide gulf that has developed between the theory for the control of the military and the practical realities. In constitutional theory, and when they come in contact with the courts, the military are seen as having the same status as any other citizens and as intervening to suppress civil disorder on the same common law basis as all citizens who have a right and duty to do so. This means that the soldier is seen as an independent officer who is responsible solely to the courts for acting in accordance with the law on his own initiative. He is seen as only having a duty to obey his military superiors in so far as their orders do not conflict with his personal duties as a citizen, and, where they do, his civil status overrides his military one. He is seen in theory as being uncontrolled by the Government of the day and, in so far as he has a duty to respond to the civil authorities, as owing this response to the magistrates. He is seen as having a duty to come to the aid of a constable when a breach of the peace is actually taking place, but to be in no way under the command of the Police. This view is, moreover, set out specifically in written guidance to the military.[1]

In practice, however, the Army, when operating in the suppression of civil disorder within the United Kingdom, acts generally as the direct instrument of the Government of the day. It tends to think of itself as having this status, and this seems to be the status that the general public assumes it to have. The result of this yawning gap between theory and practice is that the Army has been left to operate in this role without discernible constitutional rules to guide it or a clear chain of constitutional responsibility. This has led to the Army acting with a certain aimlessness and with repeated changes of policy as it tried to respond to each new wave of pressure that washed over it in order to please everybody. It has lacked the buttress of clear and well-known constitutional rules to protect it from short-term unpopularity or from responding too readily to transient fashions. If the Army is to act confidently, predictably and firmly, there is an urgent need to close this gulf between theory and practice, and to redefine the constitutional arrangements for the control of the military to show which civil authority they should obey and within what constitutional framework they should operate.

The uncertainty of the law concerning the suppression of civil disorder is examined, together with its consequences. It is shown that this uncertainty can be in itself a source of physical conflict, because it leads to unpredictability in military and Police responses to disorder, with neither them nor the disorderly citizens nor the public at large knowing with any clarity what are the rights and duties of the different parties involved in the disturbances. Proposals are made for developing a system to declare what the law is when there is general doubt about the rights and duties of citizens, soldiers and policemen, over matters that are leading to conflict or disaffection through this uncertainty.

The proposition is developed that to counter terrorism successfully, the Government must conduct a coordinated campaign bringing into harmony its economic, political, social, legal, military, police and public relations efforts against terrorism and insurrection so that each reinforces the others. No one aspect of society can by itself be the area in which terrorism is defeated, because terrorism and rebellion is a malaise of the whole of society. Thus, while there is no purely military solution to such a problem,

there is equally no purely political or purely economic or purely propaganda solution. The case is made for organising and conducting such an
overall coordinated Government counter-insurgency campaign, to achieve
which a chain of civilian command is proposed with authority over all
aspects of the Government's efforts—military, Police and civil—based on
the British wartime system of Regional Commissioners. Indeed, to the
extent that a military tactical concept is offered at all, it is that the military
role is one that supports the rest of the Government's efforts. In other
words, military power should be exerted so as to make Police, political,
economic and social campaigns by the Government possible and effective.
Put yet another way, the military objective is to suppress disorder and
terrorism to the point where no non-military policy or activity of the
Government, whether consisting of a political settlement or the Police
going about their everyday duties, can be prevented by rioting or terrorism.
This means that when the situation can no longer be controlled by the
Police alone, the military must be able to suppress rioting, the sort of
running street disorder that has come in Northern Ireland to be called
'aggro', and illegal 'sit-ins', 'sit-downs', demonstrations and marches
quickly and certainly on every occasion. It means that, again if the Police
can no longer cope, the military must be able to arrest and achieve the
incarceration of enough important members of the terrorist organisations
to prevent those organisations functioning effectively. Any separate
military tactical concept carries with it the notion of a separate military
campaign, which is rejected. According to the Royal Commission on Police
Powers and Procedures in 1929,

The Police of this country have never been recognised, either in law or by tradition,
as a force distinct from the general body of citizens. Despite the imposition of many
extraneous duties on the police by legislation or administrative action, the principle
remains that a policeman, in the view of the common law, is only 'a person paid to
perform, as a matter of duty, acts which if he were so minded he might have done
voluntarily'.[2]

This concept can be developed to produce the military tactical doctrine
that in the suppression of civil disorder the role of the military is to do for
the Police and for every other citizen what they would have done for
themselves if they had not been prevented from so doing by the violent
power of the insurgents.
   The general legal problem of unrealistic laws for the suppression of
disorder is outlined. One of the main causes of this unrealism is the
weakness of British law when it comes to providing for the detection of
criminals. The law is well developed on how to deal with suspects once they
have been identified, and what to do with them in court. However, it seems
to expect that the suspect will simply 'emerge', and makes comparatively
little provision for finding him. Perhaps this confidence is justified in a
society such as that in England which is content with its Police and is in
general prepared to help them find criminals, but it creates formidable
difficulties in a society like the Northern Irish where widespread alienation
from the forces of law and order is backed by terrorist intimidation. A
community that does not support the Police can be policed effectively, but

it is markedly different from policing a community that helps its Police. The case is therefore made for the two fundamental measures necessary to achieve detection in a population affected by terrorism. These are: to provide for the compulsory registration and identification of the population so that the Security Forces can know who is who, what they look like and where they live; and to make the active development of informers inside the terrorist ranks by the Security Forces not only lawful but as easy as possible.

The other main cause of unrealism is that Parliament, for all its evident desire to pass the laws needed for the suppression of terrorism and disorder, often does not seem to enact these laws. The reasons for this include the propensity of British law to be imprecise, e.g. basing the right of the military and Police to use force on Section 3 of the Criminal Law Act 1967 which authorises any 'person to use such force as is reasonable in the circumstances in the prevention of crime'. The meaning of 'reasonable in the circumstances' on any particular occasion is so imprecise that it does not provide a realistic guide to what action the Security Forces are authorised by the law to take. Another reason is the haste with which counter-terrorist legislation is passed, usually in response to some recent atrocity. Perhaps the most important factor is that Parliament does not seem to have been made aware of the provisions that would in reality be effective against terrorism. To accuse Parliament of failing to support the agents of law and order by not passing the necessary laws is unfair. Indeed, Parliament on the whole seems to be generous in the substantial political price it is prepared to pay for the laws it thinks are needed by its soldiers and policemen to suppress disorder. For example, it has approved detention without trial and considered reintroducing capital punishment, both of which are measures of marginal importance to the outcome of a counter-terrorist campaign. What it has not approved are measures that really would make the Security Forces more effective, but which carry a much lower political price, such as introducing identity cards or giving the soldier the right to demand the production of driving licences and vehicle documents. Laws are therefore proposed that would make the Security Forces effective in reality when engaged in suppressing civil disorder and terrorism. The case is also made for passing a consolidating Act after careful consideration to provide emergency legislation that can be invoked if the need arises for the Army to assist in suppressing disorder within the United Kingdom, on similar lines to the reserve powers already enacted which can be invoked if troops are required to maintain essential services to the community, like the supply of food and water.[3]

In summary, therefore, this is an attempt to deduce from past mistakes the constitutional framework and operational laws that are necessary to make the military, and to some extent the Police, effective in countering rioting and terrorism in any democratic society that finds itself in a situation similar to that in Northern Ireland.

PART I: THE PROBLEM

1

SHORTCOMINGS IN THE CONSTITUTIONAL STRUCTURE FOR SUPPRESSING CIVIL DISORDER AND TERRORISM

(a) The gulf between the theoretical and the practical constitutional status of the soldier when suppressing civil disorder within the United Kingdom

The existence of the gulf between theory and practice in the constitutional control of the military when required to help in suppressing civil disorder within the United Kingdom was demonstrated the first time troops were involved in this role in Belfast in 1969. What happened is as follows.

Discussions took place in April 1969 between the Northern Ireland and the Westminster Governments about how the Army General Officer Commanding Troops in Northern Ireland should respond to a request by the Inspector-General of the Royal Ulster Constabulary for the deployment of soldiers in his aid to suppress civil disorder, if he should ever make one. The result was:

... it was made clear that the General Officer Commanding should only consider this question after consultation with London and again it was understood that there would be consultation at government level.[1]

On 3 August 1969 Mr Wolseley, the Police Commissioner for Belfast, told Lieutenant-Colonel J. Fletcher, Commanding Officer of the 2nd Battalion, The Queen's Regiment, that all Police reserves had been committed in Belfast and asked him for military assistance. Mr Wolseley received the reply from the Chief of Staff, Army Headquarters Northern Ireland, that the deployment of troops in his aid was a 'political decision'.[2] No troops were deployed, and the situation continued to deteriorate over the next two weeks. A day or two after this, the contingent request by the Stormont Government to Whitehall for military assistance was withdrawn on the basis that a negative response might inhibit the General Officer Commanding, who was left to rely on his common law powers.[3]

At 0430 on 15 August 1969, Mr Wolseley again decided to ask for military assistance to prevent intersectarian rioting between the Republican population of the Falls Road area and the Protestants of the Shankhill

Road. Not until 25 minutes after midday did the Northern Ireland Cabinet transmit a request for military aid in Belfast to the Home Office in London. Clearly, although this is not specifically stated in the Scarman Report, the Police Commissioner's direct request to the military to come to his aid had been referred for a political decision on whether it should be acceded to or not. United Kingdom ministerial approval for the deployment of troops in Belfast was given at 1510 on 15 August, but the troops did not deploy until 1830, and then in the wrong place, in the middle of the Catholic area and not on its boundary with the Protestants. It was not until 2135 that the troops ultimately arrived at the right place, which was the interface between the Catholics and the Protestants along Cupar Street.

Meanwhile the Police, exhausted with successive nights of rioting, with casualties mounting, and fearful of a general insurrection of the Catholic population inspired by the IRA, had from the early hours of 15 August virtually retired to their Police stations to defend them. They were therefore unable to disperse mobs or protect lives and property on 15 August until the Army arrived to carry out this function. Mr Bradley, the Deputy Commissioner of Police for Belfast, had assumed that the Army units would be deployed by 1000 or 1100. He had every right to make this assumption, since the military '... are bound, like all citizens, to aid the Civil Authority when lawfully called upon to do so'.[4]

From midday on 15 August onwards, persistent requests were made by priests and other members of the population of the Clonard segment of the Catholic Falls Road area to the Police for protection against a likely Protestant incursion from the Shankhill Road across Cupar Street into this area. Inter-sectarian shooting started at 1545. The Protestant mob invaded Bombay Street and burnt it out, only being prevented from doing the same to the rest of the Clonard by the ultimate arrival of the Army.[5]

This was the nearest that Ulster had, at the time of writing, come to open inter-sectarian civil war, in that the two communities had an afternoon and evening in which to battle with each other without either Police or military being present to confine them to their own territories or at least to keep them apart. The memory of this day, when, in their eyes, the Catholics were left by the forces of the British state that were supposed to protect them, to be attacked by the Protestants unhindered, to have their families terrorised and their houses burnt by a mob of their traditional enemies, was a powerful influence. 'Remember Bombay Street' was the most persistent and emotive single rallying cry for the Catholics there, as I and anyone else who has operated in the Falls Road area can testify. The 'Burning of Bombay Street' was the oft-repeated and most regarded underlying justification for the IRA's claim to be needed as the only defence force that the Catholics of Belfast could rely on in dire emergency to protect their lives and homes. The bulk of the Catholic population accepted this claim and justification of the IRA, and although many of them thoroughly disliked the bombing and murdering by the IRA, they were not prepared to cooperate with the forces of the Crown to destroy the IRA, just in case another 'Bombay Street' situation might arise, with no one but the IRA to keep the murdering Protestant mob away from them.[6]

As can be seen from the extracts from the Scarman Report, the 'Burning of Bombay Street' took place largely because of confusion, misunderstanding and delay in the arrangements for the civil authorities to obtain the assistance of the military to preserve the peace. As a result, the inter-sectarian boundary between the Falls and the Shankhill was left unpoliced for half a fateful day.

This is one example of the consequences of the confusion in the arrangements for the control of the military that results from the wide gap between the theoretical system of control and the system as it is operated, or as it is widely supposed to be. It is startling to reflect that, in strict constitutional theory, a corporal, with ten privates in a lorry, who happened to drive through Grosvenor Square in London when a crowd of demonstrators had burst through a Police cordon and were attacking an embassy, would have not merely a right to intervene and suppress the disorder with lethal weapons if necessary, but an absolute duty to do so, in spite of anyone from the Prime Minister to the senior policeman on the spot telling him not to. It is improbable that any soldier would act like that, but it is unfair to soldiers to subject them to such inappropriate rules of conduct, as well as being dangerous to liberty. This gulf between theory and practice could end in other disasters similar to the burning of Bombay Street. Perhaps attention should be paid to the words of Robert Taber:

Constitutional democracies ... are particularly exposed to the subversion that is the basic weapon of revolutionary warfare. ... Constitutional law is a further embarrassment, and sometimes may be a fatal impediment.[7]

There is no substantial disagreement between the main law books, the leading cases, or the latest parliamentary report on the matter, which was in 1908,[8] about the constitutional principles that govern the employment of the military in the suppression of internal disorder. Perhaps the best place to look at this agreed theory is the *Manual of Military Law*, for this publication is issued to the military as a guide on the law, and it is to the *Manual* that any British soldier will return, with the instinct of a homing pigeon, when faced with a legal problem, particularly an unfamiliar one. Part II, Section V of the *Manual of Military Law*, issued in 1968, is entitled 'Employment of Troops in Aid of the Civil Power', and is, in effect, the authoritative directive to the military on their duties in such circumstances.

The following extracts from this section of the *Manual of Military Law* summarise the law on suppressing civil disorder as it affects the military:

There is, however, nothing to compel a military commander to seek permission before answering a request for military support.

The common law, which governs soldiers and other citizens alike, imposes two main obligations in such cases, which are, first, that every citizen is bound to come to the aid of the civil power when the civil power requires his assistance to enforce law and order and, secondly, that to enforce law and order no one is allowed to use more force than is necessary.

When called to the aid of the civil power soldiers in no way differ in the eyes of the law from other citizens. ...

Even though the civil authority should give directions to the contrary the Commander of the troops, if it is really necessary, is bound to take such action as the circumstances [of civil disturbance] demand.

There is no mention of ministerial authority; indeed Mr Haldane in his authoritative evidence to the House of Commons Select Committee on the Employment of Military in Cases of Disturbance in 1908, stated that 'King's Regulations ... do not, and cannot, alter the common law'.[9] The Irish case of *Miller* v. *Knox* in 1838[10] established that the Police, and therefore by analogy the military, must disobey an order by the executive not to enforce the law.

Viscount Simonds, in his judgment on an appeal to the Privy Council in 1955, said:

'Their Lordships share the opinion entertained by all the judges of the High Court that the case of the constable is not in principle distinguishable from that of the soldier. ...

'Their Lordships ... repeat that in their view there is a fundamental difference between the domestic relation of servant and master and that of the holder of a public office and the State which he is said to serve. The constable falls within the latter category. His authority is original, not delegated, and is exercised at his own discretion by virtue of his office: he is a ministerial officer exercising statutory rights independent of contract.'[11]

This case, together with that of *Fisher* v. *Oldham Corporation*,[12] are often cited to support the autonomous authority of the constable when enforcing the law, and of the soldier by express analogy in the passage quoted. Although these cases give good guidance to the status of the soldier when acting to enforce the law, they did in fact concern the liability of a police authority for acts of members of the force for which it was responsible. Moreover, it seems self-evident that the status of the constable and of the soldier are normally quite different when it comes to law enforcement; indeed the soldier in the United Kingdom is more usually the recipient of the might of the law than the wielder of it—particularly at pub closing times! Furthermore, the constable has specifically taken an oath to uphold the law, which the soldier has not. It therefore seems that the soldier has exactly the same status *vis-à-vis* law enforcement as the ordinary citizen, and none of the special obligations of a constable. Indeed, this is what is usually stated to be the position.[13] But it is equally self-evident that this is not the whole picture. The *Manual of Military Law* states

... There is ... a duty to take action laid upon military commanders by Queen's Regulations which is not laid upon other citizens, except magistrates and peace officers (QR J1164).[14]

As a result of the Bristol Riots in October 1831, the Mayor of Bristol was tried for failing in his duty to keep order,[15] and two Army officers, Colonel Brereton and Captain Warrington, who had been called in to assist by the Mayor, were tried by court-martial for not fulfilling their common law duty to suppress the riots. Colonel Brereton shot himself on the fifth day of the proceedings and Captain Warrington was cashiered.[16] It was a magistrate and two Army officers who were tried and not every other citizen of Bristol who had failed to do his common law duty of keeping order. This supports the view that the military are not the same as every other citizen when it comes to the suppression of civil disorder, but that they have an exceptional duty to act which is similar to that of the constable or of the magistrate.

Perhaps the best answer to this conundrum is that sometimes the soldier has the same status regarding law enforcement as any other citizen and that sometimes he has the same status as a constable. That is to say that in normal times the soldier has no special authority to enforce the law or obligation to do so, but that he acquires both these characteristics when he is ordered to deploy to assist in the suppression of civil disorder. It would seem, moreover, that the soldier only acquires the same status as a peace officer or constable in relation to offences against public order. There is, for example, no reason for the soldier to have this status *vis-à-vis* the laws on obscenity, but there is reason for him to have it *vis-à-vis* the law on breaches of the peace. It is obvious that in Northern Ireland the soldier has had a special obligation to enforce the law that is not shared by other citizens, although it seems that the Loyalists did threaten to restore order in the 'no-go' areas on the grounds of their equal obligation with the military as citizens to enforce the law.[17] It is not difficult to foresee the unfortunate consequences if this had happened, and the threat that it might was one of the main factors that contributed to the ending of the 'no-go' areas in 1972 at Operation Motorman.

It seems necessary therefore to recognise that the soldier who is directed to suppress civil disorder as a matter of his military duty has an exceptional status when performing this task akin to that of a constable. The important thing is for this to be openly acknowledged and for it to be crystal clear when the soldier has this special status and when he does not.

This position of the constable, and therefore by analogy also of the soldier engaged in enforcing the law rather than fighting external enemies, was further developed in 1968 in the judgment of Lord Denning, Master of the Rolls, in the case of *Regina* v. *Commissioner of Police of the Metropolis Ex Parte Blackburn*:[18]

'But I have no hesitation in holding that, like every constable in the land, he should be, and is, independent of the executive. He is not subject to the orders of the Secretary of State. ... He is not the servant of anyone, save of the law itself. No Minister of the Crown can tell him ... that he must, or must not, prosecute this man or that man. He is answerable to the law and to the law alone.'

In the same case Lord Justice Salmon said in his judgement:

'Constitutionally it is clearly impermissible for the Secretary of State for Home Affairs to issue any order to the police on law enforcement.'

That this is observed in practice is confirmed in the reply of the Assistant Chief Constable of the Thames Valley Police Force to accusations that his Police had turned a blind eye to crimes at the Watchfield 'Free' Pop Festival in September 1975, on the order of the Home Secretary:

We do not act according to Home Office instructions. Chief Constables are not subject to any form of political control.[19]

The soldier is also subject to military law as well as civil law, and the

Crown as represented by Ministers may give orders deriving from its prerogative to the Chief of the General Staff, which are then transmitted down the military chain of command. However, for soldiers deployed to enforce the law in the United Kingdom, military law does not override common law unless specifically so by statute, which does not apply in this matter. Soldiers are only required to obey lawful commands under Section 34 of the Army Act 1955, and a command does not become lawful merely because it is given by a military superior to a military subordinate. Any military order, not specifically authorised by the Army Act, that conflicts with the civilian law is therefore unlawful, and a soldier need not obey it. The effect of this is that, while Ministers of the Crown may order troops to move to the scene of disorder, they have no constitutional power to use the military chain of command either to tell troops not to move to suppress civil disorder or to tell them how to enforce the law when they get there. Cabinet orders to the military not to intervene in a disorderly strike, or to permit 'no-go' areas, or to tolerate illegal processions, or not to arrest lawbreakers, or to come under the command of the Police, are therefore of no effect. Not only may the military disregard them, but it must do so if, in the personal opinion of the military commander at the scene of trouble, these orders require him to contravene the general law.

In short, the military are responsible to the courts and to the law and are not responsible to Ministers, exactly as are magistrates, Chief Constables, lesser constables and citizens, who are either summoned to aid the civil power or do so uninvited in the exercise of their citizen's duty to 'endeavour of his own authority and without any warrant or sanction of the magistrate, to suppress a riot by every means in his power'.[20] Moreover, all these potential suppressors of civil disturbances are entitled to act on their own independent judgement.

When deployed for the suppression of civil disorder within the United Kingdom, the soldier, represented by the senior military man at the scene of the trouble who continues himself to act within the law, is therefore in theory an independent ministerial authority answerable only to the law. He has a special obligation to follow, as far as possible, the requirements of the magistrates, but he need not do so. He equally has an obligation to listen to the views of other civil authorities such as the Cabinet, the Police and prominent citizens such as trade union leaders. Equally, he should heed the advice of his military superiors in distant headquarters or the Ministry of Defence. But ultimately the military commander on the spot is an independent authority himself of the same constitutional status as the others, and he must judge for himself what to do, and whose views to accept or to reject.

(b) The difficulty of discerning which is the civil authority whom the soldier should assist

In theory, then, there is an array of independent enforcers of the law, each of whom can act on his own to suppress civil disorder. Confusion could easily result and it is clear that, in the words of the Elizabethan judges in

'The Case of Arms', 'it would be more discreet for every one in such a case to attend and be assistant to the justices, sheriffs, or other ministers of the Queen in doing this.'[21] In trying to be 'discreet', as thus enjoined, and come to the aid of the civil power, the soldier meets his next difficulty, that of being able to identify the civil power that he should support. His instructions in the *Manual of Military Law* say:

The law is clear that a soldier must come to the assistance of the civil authority where it is necessary for him to do so, but not otherwise.

It also says:

The primary obligation for the preservation of order and for the suppression of disturbance rests with the civil authority.[22]

At this point the *Manual* used to have a note referring to *Queen's Regulations*, paragraph 1165 (*b*), for the definition of 'civil authority'. However, this note has recently been cancelled due to the deletion without replacement from *Queen's Regulations* of the definition of 'civil authority', although the new paragraph in *Queen's Regulations* says:

Assistance will normally be requested by the Chief Officer of Police and should be confirmed in writing. Where a request is received from a source other than the Chief Officer of Police, the Service Commander on the spot is to refer the request to the Chief Officer of Police and report it to his superiors.[23]

What is defined in this frequently rewritten paragraph is only the channel of request for military help, not the 'civil authority'. The 1972 predecessor to the current wording mentioned military assistance being requested by 'the Police or local civil authorities'.

The soldier is therefore left to decide for himself who are the civil authorities that he should support. The problem is unlikely to arise if only one civil authority, such as the Police, presents himself as the authority to be supported, because in such a case the soldier would probably fall on the one civil authority's neck with relief. The problem arises, if several conflicting civil authorities present themselves, of choosing one to support—or, more probably, if none presents itself, of rooting out one on which this burden can unequivocally be laid.

The Police are clearly a civil authority of some sort and the duty of citizens, including military citizens, to come to the aid of a constable quelling a breach of the peace was established in the case of *Rex* v. *Brown* in 1841.[24] However, in summing up in this case, the Judge, Baron Alderson, said to the jury:

'It is necessary you should be satisfied of three particulars—first, that the constable actually saw a breach of the peace being committed by two or more persons.'

A constable may demand the assistance of a citizen to end a breach of the peace which is actually taking place, but this rule does not confer on the constable a right to mobilise citizens on a continuing basis in a force under his command, or indeed to demand their aid in anticipation of a breach of the peace which has not yet been committed. As any devotee of Western Cowboy films will realise, the right to impress a *posse comitatus* or a peace-keeping force of citizens rests with the Sheriff and his equivalents the Mayor, the Bailiff and the Justice of the Peace. The authority of the constable to mobilise his fellow-citizens to suppress disorder is much more limited.[25]

When Parliament last examined the matter in 1908,[26] the civil authority was described as being responsible for the preservation of the peace and having at its disposal the Police forces. Moreover, it was stated in evidence to the Committee by the Permanent Under-Secretary of the Home Office that the Chief Constable of the local force would have no special authority over the military deployed to suppress disorder unless the Chief Constable also happened to be a magistrate.[27] Thus Viscount Colville of Culross, at the time a Junior Minister at the Home Office, made a wrong implication when he said in the House of Lords in January 1974 about the deployment of troops at London Airport:

In operations of this sort, as ... Lord Wigg has said, the police are in overall control; and they were on this occasion. They specify the task which they wish the military to perform and the military commander then directs his troops to carry it out.[28]

He was wrong in implying that the troops at London Airport had to obey the orders of the Police. There is no constitutional way in which the military can be put under the orders of the Police or of any other civil authority, with an absolute duty to obey those orders, short of an Act of Parliament specifying it. This certainly cannot be achieved by ministerial pronouncements.

In constitutional theory, the civil authority for the suppression of disorder is the magistrate. Such was envisaged from medieval times through such enactments as the Riot Act of 1714 right up to the present day. For example, *Stone's Justice's Manual* (1973), when discussing 'Riot and Affray', states:

If it should be found that the civil power is insufficient the military may be called upon by the magistrates to act.[29]

It then defines with more precision exactly who those magistrates are in the metropolis, counties and boroughs. For London it states that the Commissioner or Assistant Commissioner of the Metropolitan Police is the civil authority for this purpose, although this is presumably now out of date, since these police officers ceased to be magistrates on 1 April 1974.[30] This change has removed the only policeman who could theoretically be considered as the civil authority for calling for military assistance. Moreover, as these Commissioners are not sworn in as Constables, they appear to have no authority at all to call for military aid.

The role of the Chief Constable as defined in 1908 appears to be confined to co-ordinating the requests of the magistrates for military assistance and transmitting these to the Army. In evidence the Chief Constable of Nottingham told the Parliamentary Committee in 1908 that he would not forward to the military requests by magistrates for assistance that he considered unjustified, although he did not have lawful authority to withhold such requests in this way.[31]

The Royal Commission on the Police in 1962 stated:

The importance of the historical subordination of the constable to the justice is this.

It was the legal form of control over the police favoured by Parliament in enacting the 19th Century statutes which still govern their constitutional position; but it is a control which in this century has virtually fallen into disuse. The law and practice are consequently at odds, with the result that there is now uncertainty as to the control of the police, the Chief Constables asserting a large measure of independence and the police authorities appearing to exercise some, at least, of the powers formerly exercised by justices.[32]

This situation with the Police then seems a close parallel to the current situation with regard to the Army and the civil power. In theory the civil power to which the Army should primarily look for guidance in England lies with the magistrates and not the Police.

The position in Scotland is probably that the Army should respond to the magistrates in a burgh and to the sheriff elsewhere, for Section 17 (3) of the Police (Scotland) Act 1967 says,

In directing the constables of a police force in the performance of their functions the appropriate chief constable shall comply with all lawful instructions (whether general or special) which he may receive—
(a) as respects any place in a burgh, from the magistrates of the burgh, and
(b) as respects any place not in a burgh, from the sheriff having jurisdiction in the place:
Provided that in relation to the investigation of offences the chief constable shall comply with such lawful instructions as he may receive from the appropriate prosecutor.
In this subsection 'sheriff' does not include a sheriff-substitute.

The police in Scotland are more clearly subordinate to authorities other than the Chief Constable than is the case in England. It is, however, illuminating to read the comment in *Current Law Statutes Annotated* on this section when it first appeared as Section 4 (3) of the Police (Scotland) Act 1956:

Subs. (3) is also a compromise. The position was that, in burghs by s. 86 of the Act of 1892, the magistrates might give instructions to the chief constable. In counties, by s. 6 of the Act of 1857, the chief constable was required to obey the lawful orders of the sheriff or of the justices of the peace: should the orders of the sheriff and of the justice conflict, those of the former were to prevail unless or until the Secretary of State should decide otherwise. The Consolidation Committee suggested that the chief constable should comply with orders given by the Secretary of State or of the Lord Advocate and, in the case of burghs, the magistrates, or, elsewhere, the sheriff. After discussion, however, it was agreed to drop the provision enabling the Secretary of State or Lord Advocate to give directions to the chief constable. Accordingly in burghs the chief constable must conform to directions given by the magistrates and in other places to directions by the appropriate sheriff principal. The proviso also gives the prosecutor the right to give instructions in matters relating to the investigation of offenders.[33]

In Northern Ireland the civil authority for purpose of the maintenance of public order became the Minister of Home Affairs under the Civil Authorities (Special Powers) Act (Northern Ireland) 1922, Section 1 (2). This role was taken over, after the prorogation of the Northern Ireland Parliament, by the Secretary of State for Northern Ireland. However, the establishment of a Police Authority for Northern Ireland under the Police

Act (Northern Ireland) 1970 brought the constitutional control of the Royal Ulster Constabulary into line with the English position, and the Secretary of State for Northern Ireland cannot give orders on law enforcement to the Chief Constable of the Royal Ulster Constabulary any more than the Home Secretary in England can give orders to the Chief Constable of, for example, the Thames Valley Police. The magistrates are left out of the question of law enforcement in Northern Ireland except in so far as they are members of the Police Authority. The Summary Jurisdiction and Criminal Justice Act (Northern Ireland) 1935, Section 3, removed the responsibility of the lay magistrates in Northern Ireland for most activities and transferred these to the Resident Magistrates, who are permanent paid judges in the magistrates' courts.

The gulf between law and practice referred to by the Royal Commission on the Police in 1962 is wide. It is very probable that the majority of private citizens, policemen and soldiers believe that, when civil disorder has to be suppressed in the United Kingdom, the Army has to obey the orders of the Government and that the civil authority responsible for keeping the peace is the Police. They would undoubtedly also say that the Army would operate in suppressing civil disorder in support of and under the command of the Police, and that soldiers could not operate independently. An example to support the view that this general opinion on the matter is the correct one was provided by the appearance on Independent Television News on 1 November 1974 of Commander Christopher Payne, then newly appointed Head of the Airport Division of the Metropolitan Police. He stated that the Police would be in charge of security at Heathrow Airport, and of the soldiers deployed there. Another example is the statement of Major P. F. Steer, representing the Junior Division of the Staff College, at the Royal United Services Institute for Defence Studies seminar on 4 April 1973:

We must also remember an essential difference between soldiers and policemen and that is in their command. There is no clearcut chain of command within the police forces. Station Sergeants do not 'command' the constables of that station, and Chief Constables are autocratic within their own areas of responsibility, whereas in the Army we have a clearly defined chain of command from the Army Commander who is in turn governed by directives from the political masters in an internal security situation, down to the patrol commanders. I feel that it would be wrong to turn a soldier into a sort of special constable, nor would I like to see every fourth man controlling a riot a soldier.

However, if the majority of soldiers and policemen did reply on these lines, they would only be reflecting practice as it has grown up over this century.

The law on the suppression of civil disorder and the control of the military in this role has hardly developed since the end of the eighteenth century. At that time there were no regular or efficient Police, just a few ineffective parish constables, and the military were constantly engaged in aiding the local civil power, i.e. the magistrates, to enforce the law and even the customs regulations. The fastest means of transport or communication was the horse and arrangements had to be made for the military to act in suppression of disorder without reference to London because if they did not, their intervention would probably be too late. The law concerning the control of the military acting in aid of the civil power has taken little if any account of the establishment of the whole elaborate system of regular Police, of modern communications and transport, and of the development of modern Cabinet government, and the consequent loss by the magistrates of their role as the local Ministers of the Crown. Nor has the law reflected the development of modern local government, which followed from the Municipal Corporations Act 1835.

However, even if the law has not kept pace with these developments, practice has done so to some extent. The changes began in earnest in 1910 in the Tonypandy riots, which occurred only two years after Parliament had reaffirmed the old doctrines. These riots resulted from a strike in South Wales by miners against the colliery owners. The magistrates concerned were mostly appointed from among the directors or shareholders of the Cambrian Collieries Company, whose collieries were involved in the dispute. The local Police tended to be employed as a strike-breaking force operated for the benefit of the coal-owners. Thus the local civil authority and the local Police were parties to the dispute causing the civil disturbances. The Home Secretary at the time, Winston Churchill, was not prepared either to put the military in support of the local magistrates or to leave the Police under their control. Moreover, he did not wish to repeat the separation of control between the civil and military authorities that had caused problems on other similar occasions. Churchill therefore sent Major-General Nevil Macready from the War Office to act as the representative of central Government and to take command of both the Police and the military in suppressing the disorder. Thus the constitutional theory was turned upside down.[34]

It is interesting to observe how more or less the same process was repeated in Ulster when disorder grew too much for the Royal Ulster Constabulary in August 1969. They were thought to be partisan on behalf of the Protestants—probably wrongly with regard to their actions, whatever may have been their thoughts.[35] The Royal Ulster Constabulary went the same way as the Glamorgan police at the time of the Tonypandy riots, and the following communiqué was issued by the British Government on 19 August 1969:

It was agreed that the General Officer Commanding Northern Ireland will with immediate effect assume overall responsibility for security operations. He will continue to be responsible directly to the Ministry of Defence but will work in the closest co-operation with the Northern Ireland Government and the Inspector-General of the Royal Ulster Constabulary. For all security operations the General Officer Commanding will have full control of the deployment and tasks of the Royal Ulster Constabulary. For normal police duties outside the field of security the Royal Ulster Constabulary will remain answerable to the Inspector-General, who will be responsible to the Northern Ireland Government.

In Ireland between 1919 and 1922 the Police were not placed under military command, but both the police and the military acted as the instruments of the British Cabinet working through the Chief Secretary of

Ireland in Dublin Castle. There was no question of their supporting or being able to support a local civil authority.[36]

In the Ulster troubles since 1969, the Army has acted as the instrument of Central Government rather than as independent officers of the law aiding the local civil authorities. This is confirmed not only by the communiqué quoted above but also by the observable facts. Lord Widgery, in his report on 'Bloody Sunday' at paragraphs 10 to 12, describes how the Bogside and Creggan areas were allowed to become 'no-go' areas in which 'the law was not effectively enforced' and 'the terrorists were still firmly in control'.[37] This did not happen by chance or by the *force majeure* of an insurrection, but as the result of an agreement made in the autumn of 1971 between the General Officer Commanding Northern Ireland, Lieutenant-General Sir Harry Tuzo, and a self-appointed group of prominent citizens from the Creggan and the Bogside. The 'no-go' situation was well known and must have been authorised by the Cabinet. There is a plethora of evidence for it in the press, including pictures of IRA control points with armed sentries at the entry roads to the 'no-go' areas. I myself was attached to a battalion operating in Londonderry for a few days in March 1972 and can confirm that the military had strict orders not to enter the Bogside and Creggan although frequent shots could be heard emanating from these areas, one of which hit the Wall of Londonderry just below my head as I peeped above it, causing me to fall over backwards with fright. There was also persistent and open rioting and stone throwing taking place beneath the eyes of the soldiers. The Commission under the chairmanship of Lord Diplock reported in December 1972:

In Belfast and in Londonderry the IRA terrorist groups operate from those areas which are Republican strongholds. For a long time these were 'no-go' areas into which neither the police nor the army entered.[38]

Thus for nearly a year, between August 1971 and Operation Motorman on 30 July 1972, the Army accepted orders not to enforce the law in Londonderry. Although I have spelt out this most glaring example of the Army acting against the law on the orders of the Cabinet, it was only one among many such examples. There were other 'no-go' areas, and orders to operate in 'low-profile' could only mean orders not to enforce the law, since orders to operate 'normally' or in 'high profile' could not conceivably mean that more than the law was to be applied. All battalion commanders in Ulster received and passed down to their subordinates a stream of orders on when and where the law was to be enforced or was not to be enforced. These would include orders not to interfere with illegal marches or funerals with marchers wearing uniforms and firing volleys over terrorists' graves. The examples of this sort of order are legion, but perhaps one illustration will suffice: namely the order to the military to ignore the 3,500 Ulster Defence Association men who paraded at the funeral of Tommy Herron, their assassinated leader, on 19 September 1973 in 'drab pale green and yellow uniforms'.[39] Such parading was illegal under the Public Order Act (Northern Ireland), 1951.

In Lord Widgery's Report on 'Bloody Sunday' he records that although 'parades and processions had been prohibited throughout Nothern Ireland by law since 9 August 1971, ... the final decision, which was taken by higher authority after General Ford and the Chief Constable had been consulted, was to allow the march to begin but contain it within the general area of the Bogside and the Creggan Estate. ...'[40] A further example of the Cabinet (whether Stormont or Westminster is not clear) directing the military to permit an open breach of the law.

It may be thought that in accepting such orders and carrying them out, the military and indeed the Police were merely exercising a power of discretion in law enforcement analogous to that under which a constable lets a minor offender off with a 'caution' rather than invariably prosecuting. It seems, however, that Ministers and officials do not have an unlimited right to use their own discretion as to when to enforce the law and when not to. The Petition of Right in 1628 objected to the King that,

... divers of your officers and ministers of justice have unjustly refused or foreborne to proceed against such offenders according to the same laws and statutes. ...

The Bill of Rights in 1688 included the passage:

And therefore the said lords spiritual and temporal and commons ... declare: That the pretended power of dispensing with laws or the execution of law by regall authoritie as it hath beene assumed and exercised of late is illegal.

In *Regina* v. *Commissioner of Police of the Metropolis Ex Parte Blackburn* in 1968[41] and Mr Raymond Blackburn's similar case in 1973,[42] it was confirmed that a Chief Constable had wide discretion whether to prosecute in any particular case, but very narrow discretion on how far to deviate from enforcing the law as a matter of general policy. For example Lord Denning, when giving judgment in the former case, said:

Suppose a chief constable were to issue a directive to his men that no person should be prosecuted for stealing any goods less that £100 in value. I should have thought that the court could countermand it. He would be failing in his duty to enforce the law.

Clearly a discretion of this very limited order open to the Police—and, by analogy, to the military—cannot cover such open and continuing breaches as the Londonderry 'no-go' areas which, although part of a British city, were allowed for nearly a year to lie outside the area governed by the British Crown, its courts and its officers, and abandoned to the rule of other peoples, self-appointed and disaffected. Yet the Army permitted this. In the circumstances of Northern Ireland, where the Army has acted throughout as the direct instrument of Ministers in London, this permission must have derived from instructions to the Army by the Cabinet in Whitehall. It would be naive to think that the Army allowed this on its own independent common law authority.

It may be thought that such indulgences to citizens to disregard the law were in some way an exercise of the Royal Prerogative to pardon. The Crown undoubtedly enjoys the Prerogative to pardon any offence against the criminal law, before or after conviction, but this does not make the acts legal. All it does is relieve the perpetrator of a crime from the legal consequences of that crime. As recently as 1948 the then Lord Chief

Justice, Lord Goddard, objected, in a speech in the House of Lords, to the automatic use of the Royal Pardon to reprieve those condemned to death while an Act to abolish capital punishment was being debated in Parliament. He objected that such a wholesale use of the Royal Pardon came near to the exercise of the suspending and dispensing powers claimed by the Stuart Kings and forbidden by the Bill of Rights.[43]

It seems, therefore, that the gulf between theory and practice in the Constitutional control and responsibility of the military acting to suppress civil disturbance is dangerously wide. In theory the Army is supposed to act on the initiative of the local military commander responsible only to the general law of the land and answerable only in the civilian courts. It is supposed to pay great attention to the magistrates, but little if any to the elected Government and its Ministers at Westminster, or indeed to military superiors outside the immediate area of disorder. In practice, it can be seen that throughout this century the Army has tended to act as the directly controlled instrument of the Central Government, ignoring the require-ments of the law, at least in a negative sense, where these conflicted with the orders of the Cabinet. As far as the local civil authorities are concerned, the military have generally ignored the local magistracy, and either supported the local Police, or, equally often, taken the Police under military command so that they too would act as the instruments of the Central Government.

The question must then be asked whether this gulf matters, and the answer must be that it does for two reasons. The first reason is that it is wrong in itself to permit such a divergence between theory and practice. The second is that this gulf leads to a situation in which the law and its enforcement become a flexible factor in the overall relationships of the civil disturbance, instead of being the known constant providing a solid framework within which all other parties have to manoeuvre, implicit in the concept of the rule of law.

Since the method by which the military are controlled, namely by orders from the Cabinet, is unrecognised, there has been no formalisation of this control. There can be few limits set to a system of control which is not acknowledged by the law as even existing, and there can be little opportunity for the practices of Government within such a system to be effectively challenged either in Parliament or in the courts. A citizen who is aggrieved by the actions or decisions of Government can secure the assistance of the courts to ensure that Ministers and their officials follow the rules laid down by statute or by the common law. Where a Minister or his officials have a discretion to decide a particular question, the courts cannot compel them to decide one way or the other, but they can compel them to obey the rules and to act reasonably in coming to the decision they have a duty to take. For example, in the case of *Padfield* v. *Minister of Agriculture* in 1968, Lord Upjohn, giving the judgment of the Court of Appeal, said:

But the use of that adjective [unfettered discretion], even in an Act of Parliament, can do nothing to unfetter the control which the judiciary have over the executive, namely that in exercising their powers the latter must act lawfully, and that is a matter to be determined by looking at the Act and its scope and object in conferring a discretion on the Minister rather than by the use of adjectives.[46]

But how can the judiciary ensure that Ministers act lawfully in giving orders to the military on how they are to suppress civil disorder, when the courts do not recognise the right of Ministers to give any such orders at all?

An example of the sort of abuse to which such an unacknowledged system of controlling the Security Forces in a campaign against civil disorder is liable is provided by the 'Reprisal' policy of the Lloyd George Cabinet which was applied to Ireland in the summer of 1920. This is an example which has many special factors, but it is an awful warning of the possible results. The Cabinet encouraged the Royal Irish Constabulary and their auxiliaries—the Cadets and the 'Black and Tans'—to take 'unauthorised reprisals' on areas where there had been terrorist activity. 'Unauthorised reprisals' meant sending parties of Police to the offending villages to burn, destroy and shoot at will without any lawful sanction in order to discourage any who might be disposed to help the rebels. The most notorious incident was the Police riot at the village of Balbriggan on 20 September 1920 when two civilians were gratuitously killed. The Police were told by their superiors that they would not be made to suffer for crimes they might commit in the course of these reprisals, although of course such a guarantee would have been valueless if any of them had been brought to trial. General Sir Nevil Macready, the Army Commander-in-Chief in Ireland, was a man of strong constitutionalist views and considerable moral courage. He managed to keep the Army more or less out of these lawless excesses, but it is easy to see the road the Army might have taken with a man of a different stamp as Commander-in-Chief.[45]

An effect of the military being controlled by an unacknowledged system is that it reduces the extent to which Ministers can protect themselves behind a barrier of constitutional rules. For example, when under pressure in early 1975 to release the 'Shrewsbury Two' who had been jailed for violent strike-enforcing, the Home Secretary Mr Jenkins was able to reply: 'The law must take its course'. He could point out that the 'Shrewsbury Two' had been tried and sentenced under the recognised and accepted law of the land, and that it was not for him to interfere with these processes, although it was of course always open to Parliament to change the law. Ministers have no such firm framework within which to operate where control of the military is concerned, because clearly the military will respond, more or less without question, to whatever orders the Cabinet gives them. Since therefore Ministers undoubtedly have power to control with precision how the military enforce the law, they are inevitably compelled to do so by the pressures put on them through the democratic process in Parliament. Although they should be able to do so in theory, in practice the gulf means that Ministers can no longer reply that in suppressing disorder the military will simply enforce the recognised law without fear or favour. This removal from the politicians of their protection from responsibility for the law enforcement operations of the military has been largely the cause of the disastrous development of flexible law in

Northern Ireland. If the politicians could respond to strong popular pressures, they had to do so. Such is, after all, their business. If, however, they had been unable to respond without going through the slow processes of altering the law, they would have been under less immediate pressure to react at once to the feelings aroused by the 'most recent atrocity'.

(c) The consequences of flexible and unpredictable law enforcement

Flexible law has many synonyms. It is variously called 'showing political sensitivity', or 'restraint', or 'winning hearts and minds', or 'low profile'. But whatever it is called, it always has the characteristic that the extent to which the published law will be enforced is uncertain to both the law breakers and the law enforcers. My experience in Ulster leads me to believe that a substantial proportion of the cases in which the Army there failed to enforce the law and suppress disorder occurred because, in the face of flagrant breaches of the law, the troops were uncertain whether they were supposed to enforce the law, and, if they did, the extent to which they would be supported in doing so.

I had great sympathy with the disaffected section of the population in the face of flexible law. They never knew where they stood. One illegal procession would be permitted and another, apparently similar to it, would be stopped. One week vigilantes would be allowed, and the next week firmly suppressed. On 4 December 1974 the Court of Appeal in London criticised the Director of Public Prosecutions in the case of *Regina* v. *Arrowsmith* in the following terms:

The court felt that because the Director of Public Prosecutions had decided to take no action against her [Miss Pat Arrowsmith] when she distributed similar leaflets at an Army camp in Colchester last year she might have thought that she could continue with immunity doing what she had done previously.[46]

Many a person convicted in Belfast could have made the same defence, namely that the offence he was charged with had been openly condoned on previous occasions and he had no idea that a turn of the law enforcement pressure valve now meant that this condonation had ceased.

Like all such matters, the Ulster Policy of flexible law developed over many years from small beginnings. The situation is described by Bernadette Devlin in her book:

One thing of political significance which I remember from my childhood was my father wearing a lily in his buttonhole on Easter Mondays. We all knew what this meant; he was commemorating the Easter Rising of 1916. Officially it was illegal to commemorate the Rising, but being Irish, the authorities tolerated what they had banned and lots of people wore Easter lilies.[47]

Flexible law was a hardy growth in Northern Ireland, but perhaps the moment the dam burst was in Londonderry at 1915 hours on 14 August 1969. The story can perhaps best be told by extracts from Chapter 12 of the Scarman Report:[48]

By the morning of 14th it was obvious to the senior police officers that their men were too few and too tired to restore order in the face of Bogside resistance. Severe static rioting continued all day in the William Street/Rossville Street area. ... They knew that it was no longer possible for them to restore law and order to the Bogside or peace to the city. In the course of the day the Ulster Special Constabulary were brought on to the streets and the decision to call upon the Army was made and implemented. By 5 pm the police were on the defensive in William Street, a sectarian riot was in progress in Bishop Street, and the Bogside was alive with rumours that the 'B' Specials were coming. At this moment a company of the 1st Battalion of the Prince of Wales Own Regiment arrived in Waterloo Place under the command of Major Hanson. A barrier of wire was put across the roads leading into Waterloo Place, a gap being left through which the police could be moved out of sight and this was done. He asked for a fire engine to deal with the fires burning in William Street. A little later Mr P. L. Doherty, Mr Cameron and Mr Stanley Orme, M.P., called on the battalion Commanding Officer, Lt.-Colonel Todd, at the Victoria Barracks: the colonel agreed to withdraw the police behind the army lines, thereby modifying his original plan for a joint police-military operation.

At the same meeting Colonel Todd tried unsuccessfully to persuade Mr Cameron and Mr Doherty to allow his troops to enter the Bogside. In the absence of their agreement, the Colonel did not insist and (with the exception of one accidental intrusion) his men did not enter the Bogside at any time up until the battalion's departure on 19 August.

The law is quite clear. In the words of Lord Chief Justice Tindal's charge to the Bristol Grand Jury in 1832:

..., the military subjects of the King, like his civil subjects, not only may, but are bound to do their utmost, of their own authority, to prevent the perpetration of outrage, to put down riot and tumult, and to preserve the lives and property of the people.[49]

On 14 August 1969 the established civil law enforcement officers, the Royal Ulster Constabulary, had been thrown out of the Bogside by a riotous mob. It was the clear and unequivocal legal and constitutional duty of the military to use every weapon and resource necessary, whether lethal or not, to restore that civil authority to the Bogside on their own authorisation. Whether the civil authority in the shape of the Royal Ulster Constabulary was unpopular or partisan did not matter; the Royal Ulster Constabulary were the constitutional civil authority charged as constables under the Crown with enforcing the law. Yet the Army acquiesced in this defeat of the civil authority and permitted another régime to hold sway in the Bogside.

It is inconceivable in the era of telephonic and radio communication that Colonel Todd would have acted as he did without reference to his military superiors, or that they would have directed him as they must have done without reference to Ministers. Ministers must therefore have ordered the Army to ignore the law and to accept the overthrow of the civil authority by riot. In these circumstances Colonel Todd had no option but to act as he did. Thus was made a mighty breach in the doctrine of the rule of law and the constitution as a firm framework for the control of the military engaged in suppressing civil disorder.

Bernadette Devlin, who participated in these events, wrote:

... These people [the Catholics of Derry] out of fear, could never go back to the situation before August 12th, 1969. ... In fifty hours we brought a government to its knees, and we gave back to a down-trodden people their pride and the strength of their convictions.[52]

Describing the event from a different viewpoint, she confirms that the authority of the state was overthrown irretrievably, or at least for many subsequent years, by the failure of the Army to execute its constitutional duty and restore the authority of the state over its rebellious subjects without reference to or permission from anyone.

These events in Londonderry on 14 August 1969 and the indication they gave that the forces of the state had lost the resolution needed to fulfil their constitutional duty led both the people of Northern Ireland and the men in the Police and the Army to draw certain conclusions. The people of Northern Ireland concluded that the enforcement of law, even by the military, was subject to political direction and therefore to pressure on politicians. Riots, demonstrations and uniformed marches produce this political pressure; therefore such activities pay off. As a consequence they have been resorted to interminably by any section of society wishing to free itself from constitutional and legal restraints, or wishing to redress a political balance that seemed to be tipping against it. Since most such manifestations are followed by concessions, this deduction has been amply justified by events.

The soldiers and policemen drew the conclusion that they could no longer be sure of the support of their professional or political superiors, or of the legal system, if they enforced the law impartially, without fear or favour. Thus the Army and Police have ever since been looking over their shoulders wondering what was required of them, sometimes exceeding the law, as exemplified by the illegal practice of 'interrogation in depth',[51] and sometimes falling short of it, but neither of these amplitudes seemed to matter as long as what they did reflected the day-to-day attitudes of Ministers and the media.

14 August 1969 marked a key point in the collapse of the general framework of constitutional legality in Northern Ireland, but its individual role must not be exaggerated. It was an important step but only one of a long series in which the fixities of constitutional legality were abandoned and overridden in favour of illegalities that seemed at the time advantageous, but have been disastrous in their combined effect in the discrediting of the rule of law in Northern Ireland.

The development of flexible law left the Army adrift on the troubled waters of Northern Ireland without the engine, rudder or course that constitutional certainty should have provided. Hence the Army wallowed aimlessly, its direction liable to be changed by each puff of wind or buffet of the waves.

(d) Differences between the law in England and Wales, Scotland, and Northern Ireland

There is another constitutional problem that needs to be recognised when the military are deployed in support of the civil power within the United Kingdom. This problem is that there are substantial differences between the law of England (together with Wales) and those of, respectively, Scotland and Northern Ireland. Whereas English law is based in the Anglo-Saxon Common Law, that of Scotland is based in Roman Dutch law. Although Northern Irish law is based in English Common Law rather than Roman Law, it has nevertheless developed substantial differences. For example, the 'Judges Rules' which guide the Police on their proper conduct when taking evidence from suspects differ in Northern Ireland and England.[52] For someone accustomed to the English courts it is surprising to find that in Ulster witnesses are allowed to remain in court to hear the evidence of witnesses who precede them. At least in Scotland it is possible to discover what the law is, for legal reference books exist for Scots law, but in Northern Ireland there appear to be no comprehensive legal reference books, and the peculiarities of their law are embodied as a 'skilled mystery' in the heads and memories of its practitioners, supported by local precedent. The *Manual of Military Law* does not indicate to soldiers that the law differs from one part of the United Kingdom to another, and there seems therefore to be a need for it to be standarised throughout the country for the employment of the military in aid of the civil power.

(e) What is the law concerning civil disorder? The results of this difficulty

If the military are, like the constable (in the words of Lord Denning), 'answerable to the law and to the law alone', then it is important that they should have some authoritative means of finding out what the law is. Indeed in 1803 Chief Justice Marshall in the Supreme Court of the United States of America, giving judgment in the case of *Marbury* v. *Madison*, said:

It is emphatically the province and duty of the judicial department to say what the law is. ... If two laws conflict with each other, the courts must decide on the operation of each.[53]

It is true that the Supreme Court in the United States has a special duty to declare what the law is, but the principle expressed is nonetheless valid for this country as well.

The stock answer of the lawyer to the complaint that the law is unknown is that a case should be brought, whereupon the courts will declare the law when they decide the case. This is adequate for finer points of law (concerning, for example, breathalyser tests in the Home Counties of England), but it does not suffice in the circumstances of civil disorder such as have prevailed for several years in Ulster. This is because, if they are to be answerable to the law, the Security Forces must know in advance what the law is, since their actions may involve killing people and other serious derogations of the normal rights and liberties of citizens. If the Army misunderstands the law, many citizens may be killed, injured or wrongfully imprisoned, and many soldiers may lay themselves open to convictions for murder, manslaughter and lesser assaults, while some individual leading case takes the usual year or more to make its way through the full legal process of the trial of an individual until its final decision.

The soldier needs to know whether the orders he has received are lawful before he complies with them. He needs to know whether his operating methods are lawful; for example, was the 'Yellow Card', which told him in twenty-three paragraphs the circumstances in which he might shoot to kill, a correct statement of the common law? The need for such definitive guidance on his rights and duties in the use of firearms was clearly brought out by the words of the Lord Chief Justice of Northern Ireland, Sir Robert Lowry, giving judgment in the case of *Regina* v. *Donald Ernest MacNaughton* at the Belfast City Commission on 5 September 1974:

There was, of course, at the same time in existence what is called the yellow card; something the contents of which, it seems, are largely dictated by policy and are intended to lay down guidelines for the security forces but which do not define the legal rights and obligations of members of the forces under statute or common law.[54]

He also needs to know what state of civil disorder exists—whether, for example, the circumstances justify martial law or whether an insurrection is taking place. Equally the ordinary citizen, who feels that the military are exceeding the law or failing to enforce it in general rather than in any particular case, needs a system to challenge their behaviour. Moreover, like the soldier, he needs a system that is readily available to the ordinary person. In this context it is worth recalling the judgment of Lord Justice Salmon in the earlier Blackburn case:

It seems to me fantastically unrealistic for the police to suggest, as they have done, that their policy decision was unimportant because Mr Blackburn was free to start private prosecutions of his own and fight the gambling empires, possibly up to the House of Lords, single-handed.[55]

There is an exposition of why the ordinary processes of civil or criminal actions through the courts were not effective in Northern Ireland in correcting illegalities, and indeed more or less fell into disuse, in a book by three Belfast lawyers.[56] They ask this question:

But the failure of the civil rights leaders to make any sustained attempt to obtain a legal remedy for their grievances also requires some explanation. It is a primary task of law and lawyers to deal with basic grievances of this kind before recourse is made to direct action, with all the risks of riot and disorder which that may bring in its train. Why was it that in Northern Ireland this essential safety valve of legal redress was not there to avert the confrontation which developed?[57]

Their conclusion is as follows:

First, it is doubtful whether the British style of legal decision-making, in which cases were dealt with on the basis of very precise and often highly technical points rather than the broad issues underlying the dispute, was appropriate in civil rights litigation. This approach was perhaps more attractive to the judges, in that it enabled them to sidestep the main issues. But all too often it meant that the courts did not fulfil their main function of dealing with those main issues in so far as they were subject to legal adjudication. When the guarantors of civil rights take refuge in technicalities, aggrieved complainants are more likely to take to the streets.[58]

A soldier is only required by Section 34 of the Army Act, 1955, to obey lawful commands. His first duty is to the general law, and, as has already been noted, mere military orders, unless specifically authorised in a statute, cannot override the common law. Lord Haldane, before the House of Commons Select Committee of 1908,[59] confirmed that a contradiction between the military orders and civil duties of a soldier engaged in aid to the civil power may require him to disobey a military command. This type of contradiction is usually seen in the legal reference books as an immediate one, where the soldier is ordered, as in the case of *Regina* v. *Smith* in South Africa in 1900,[60] to shoot someone and has to obey or disobey on the spot. The rule here is that the soldier is protected from an unlawful act in these circumstances unless the order was 'manifestly illegal'. In this sort of situation there is no option; the soldier must either immediately obey or immediately disobey, as he thinks right, and hope to be vindicated by the courts later if he is subsequently charged with an offence. However, in a situation such as that in Northern Ireland, orders, which perhaps a soldier ought to disobey, are usually of a more general nature, and usually offer a time-lag before a final choice of obeying or disobeying them has to be made. The sort of orders meant are ones to permit 'no-go' areas, or not to interfere with barricades across the highway, or orders not to arrest members of the Official IRA suspected of offences because to do so might upset delicate negotiations, or orders to carry out 'interrogation in depth', or orders to treat members of one religious sect differently from those of another as regards searching of their homes. Example of these types of orders were given by R. T. Paget, Labour M.P. for Northampton, during the House of Commons debate on the Northern Ireland (Emergency Provisions) Bill of 5 July 1973:[61]

This kind of thing has effect right through in the question of arrests and getting them. This is an impression of the troops. I again quote from letters.

> Commanders will not allow arrest of suspects if they can avoid it. Tough interrogation is forbidden. We must avoid a row. Do not do anything that might annoy the other side. Keep the way clear for a political solution.

That is not the way to deal with a guerilla movement. A letter from the Grenadiers says:

> There were periods of two or three days during our last tour when we were given clear orders not to arrest anyone [the next part is underlined] whether or not they were on the wanted list, in case an arrest provoked hostile action.

They go on to say:

> On more than one occasion when guardsmen arrested men for whom they had been searching for months they were made to let them go because of a blanket order of no arrests.

I shall read a passage that impressed me greatly, written by an officer who has been on a number of tours to Northern Ireland. He says:

Like Keats' small boats they are 'borne aloft or sinking as the light wind lives and dies'. Ever since I came to Derry in 1969 I have watched them keep the tragedy alive by blowing hot and cold. We could easily finish it in two or three months. Every soldier knows this. But he will not keep coming back to be a duty target or an acceptable casualty. While my battalion ... was in Derry we had to stand by while the IRA fired Armalites over the grave of one of their terrorists. Later one of our guardsmen was shot by the same sort of weapon in the Creggan. What explanation do I give to my soldiers? Every day my men saw Reg Tester in the Creggan. He is known to have helped murder Ranger Best. We cannot arrest him because we have a truce with the Official IRA.

A further example of what appear to be orders of dubious legality given to troops was provided in a letter to the *Daily Telegraph* from Captain Lord Richard Cecil on 7 January 1974:

I have recently left the Army after my third Ulster tour. ...

This year, in Londonderry, my battalion had to stand by and watch while the IRA fired Armalite rifles over a grave. A week later a guardsman in my brother's platoon was shot by one of those weapons.

Daily in the Creggan our troops come face to face with men who are known to have murdered British soldiers. They are not allowed to arrest them because the Government has a truce with the Official IRA.

Confirmation of this sort of order was provided by R. J. Maxwell-Hyslop, Conservative M.P. for Tiverton, in the House of Commons on 28 November 1974:

We all know that at funerals in Northern Ireland members of the IRA have been recognised by the security forces and the police, but they have been instructed not to do their duty and arrest those men.[62]

The case of the order not to arrest Seamus Twomey that appeared in the press in August and September 1975 seems to be an example of the same sort of thing. Mr Ian Paisley produced a copy of an intelligence report prepared by the Marine Commandos in Andersontown in June 1975 which contained the paragraph:

Seamus Twomey, Chief of Staff Provisional IRA, aware that he is no longer a wanted man, was seen this week in his house [address quoted] and has been relatively open in his movements.[63]

The Army admitted that this was a genuine document. It is hard to see how any construction can be put on it other than that soldiers had been ordered not to arrest a man who at the same time was acknowledged to be Chief of Staff of a proscribed organisation, membership of which was a scheduled offence under Section 19 as amplified by Schedules 2 and 4 of the Northern Ireland (Emergency Provisions) Act 1973.

It seems therefore that the courts should be prepared to hear challenges of their orders by soldiers and to rule on their legality; such an arrangement could be as valuable to the Commander-in-Chief, as exemplified by General Sir Nevil Macready's problems in Ireland between 1920 and 1921 in keeping to a lawful course, as it would be to the most junior private who might be forbidden for some reason to fire even in defence of his own life, or to give the people of such and such a street a 'rough time' whenever he patrolled it.

On 21 January 1975 at Belfast City Commission, Mr Justice McGonigal, trying the case of *Regina* v. *Riley and Rimmer* which had arisen from events on 25 October 1973, commented adversely on the practice of 'headchecking' by soldiers in houses in Belfast. He said that after studying the Northern Ireland (Emergency Provisions) Act 1973, which authorises the circumstances in which the military may enter dwelling houses to search for munitions or suspects, he could find no authority for the practice of 'headchecking' and that the military authorities should either stop it or seek statutory authority to continue with headchecks.[64] The finer differences between a 'friendly visit', a 'headcheck' and a full-scale 'search' need not concern us here. The point is that fifteen months elapsed between the possible malpractice taking place and it coming to the notice of the courts through prosecution of two individuals on a charge of theft. Meanwhile the practice had continued and it can be assumed that there had been thousands, if not tens of thousands, of 'headchecks' in the intervening period. During this period, and indeed before it, the legality of 'headchecking' had been questioned from time to time as a result of complaints by members of the public that it was unlawful. These came to nothing because after desultory arguments and counter-arguments, no one, neither the complaining citizens nor the military, had come any nearer to a decisive conclusion as to its legality. The practice therefore continued, with the Army half pretending that it did not. What was needed was a quick and authoritative ruling by a court on whether 'headchecking' was lawful or not. If it had been pronounced lawful, the practice could have been continued openly without embarrassment. If it had been declared unlawful, the Army would have had to stop it, unless they could have persuaded Parliament to pass enabling legislation.

This shows the inadequacy of the normal criminal prosecution or civil process for deciding on the legality of Security Forces' operating methods in the context of civil disorder. It seems that a system is required whereby individual citizens, perhaps sometimes represented by community leaders, could challenge Security Force operating practices that they suspect are illegal, within a week or so of incidents occurring. A parallel can be drawn with normal times by looking at the contradictory and uncertain state of the law on removing 'squatters' from houses that was aired in the press in July and August 1975.[65]

The need to obtain authoritative legal rulings on operational methods was well exemplified by the question of soldiers operating in civilian clothes. The ability of the terrorist to merge into the urban population gives him an overwhelming tactical advantage over the soldier in Army uniform or in a military vehicle, both of whom stand out sharply from the urban background. Maria McGuire, who circulated among the top Provisional IRA leadership, wrote:

The British soldiers were very vulnerable, as are any uniformed force in a guerilla war. Our Volunteers could recognise them; whereas they could never be sure who amongst the civilians around them was friend, who enemy. ... But in areas like Andersonstown, they were very clear targets, a sniper could fire a single shot with a modern weapon like an SLR or an MI carbine from a bedroom window a hundred yards away or more and then take cover and withdraw, or even stand up above a garden wall and pick off the last man in a patrol. A Volunteer once told me it was like aiming at the moving ducks in a fairground shooting gallery.[66]

Indeed, the local nickname for Army foot patrols was 'duck patrols'. Maria McGuire's description was right, and the great majority of British Army casualties in Ulster were caused by the simple fact of the soldiers being in uniform or in military vehicles. No quick reaction, no prowess in marksmanship, no tactical manoeuvring by the soldiers could compensate for their inherent vulnerability on a public road or street. The same handicap applied when the soldiers tried to attack the terrorists with precision. The leading terrorists—say Provisional IRA Company officers and above or especially accurate snipers—had scouts who moved a few yards ahead or behind them on the street or acted as sentries if they were in a house. If one of these scouts saw a soldier or a military vehicle, he would open a newspaper, scratch his head or make some other signal, and the wanted man would dive into cover and make his getaway. Three hundred yards' notice of the approach of a soldier or military vehicle was ample warning for a wanted man to escape the military. This meant that it was almost impossible for uniformed troops to close with precision on a wanted man to arrest him even if they knew what he looked like and where he was—a big uncertainty in itself. Denied by their uniforms and military vehicles the possibility of acting with tactical precision, the military had no choice but to go in for widespread search, arrest and screening operations, hoping that by chance a wanted man or two would thus be caught. Yet it was these widespread imprecise operations that so strongly alienated the section of the population that were not involved with the terrorists but were inevitably treated as though they were. Nothing could have been more calculated to drive the non-committed part of the population into the arms of the terrorists from a sense of personal outrage and humiliation. It all turned on whether or not the military could operate freely in civilian clothes, which was the only way for the military to wrest the tactical initiative from the terrorists. In another terrorist campaign, the disadvantages endured by soldiers who have to operate in military vehicles and uniform are well illustrated throughout *The Memoirs of General Grivas*. Of a British attempt to catch him, he writes:

Just before dawn I saw a convoy of British trucks moving up the road from Milikouri; once more the enemy had given us notice of his intentions! We set off at once for the heights. ...[67]

If those British troops in 1956 in Cyprus had been in civilian vehicles, let alone in civilian clothes, they would have stood at least some chance of closing with Grivas and catching him—in military vehicles they had none.

It was obvious to me that with, say, fifty soldiers in my area in civilian clothes and civilian vehicles, I could have controlled the terrorists without much difficulty, whereas it was only just possible to achieve this with great effort and much less effectively than one would have wished with the more than 400 uniformed soldiers available. Of course coping with riots and street disorder is not a role for plainclothes men, but requires a substantial number of soldiers in uniform. The proportion of soldiers that should operate in civilian clothes depends largely on the extent to which the military are acting as substitutes for the Police. If the military are merely in the background, to cope for example with a major crowd that might overwhelm the Police, then only a few soldiers need to operate in civilian clothes so that they can observe the situation without making it worse by aggravating the crowd through a display of military uniforms. If the other extreme is reached—as in the Republican Areas of Northern Ireland where the Police have hardly operated at all for years—then the military, if they are to be effective in policing, need to have roughly the same proportion operating in civilian clothes as a normal Police force.

For example, the Metropolitan Police in December 1974 had 18 per cent of its strength in plain clothes. There is no intrinsic objection to some compromise being reached whereby the Police might provide the plain-clothes element of the Security Forces and the military only operate in uniform. The Security Forces will be ineffective unless they have a proportion of some 20 per cent of their total strength in the terrorist-affected areas operating out of uniform. Moreover, there must be no separation between the uniformed and the plainclothes elements of the Security Forces. The uniformed part provides the framework on which the plainclothes part can base its precise terrorist-observing and -destroying activities. Perhaps this amounts to little more than saying that when the Army is required to act like a Police force, it should also be organised like one. An operational objection to soldiers operating in plain clothes is that in a physical confrontation they may not be recognised by other soldiers or by civilians. This is a valid objection, but it can be neutralised if the plainclothes and uniformed troops work in close harmony. If confusion then arises the uniformed troops, in substantial numbers, can secure the area immediately and discover at leisure who is a genuine member of the Security Forces and who is not. Some risk has to be accepted in this area of plainclothes operations in return for the advantages of a substantial force that can merge into the background. Equally, of course, terrorists can pretend to be uniformed troops, as appears to have happened in the murders in South Armagh on 31 July and 25 August 1975.[67]

Most of the vital arrests, identifications and locations of terrorists were largely due to the tiny number of soldiers who were permitted to operate, under heavy restrictions, in plain clothes, although the actual execution of an arrest was normally carried out by uniformed soldiers. This being the case, why did the Army not operate more in civilian clothes? As in all these matters, there were a number of contributory reasons. It was thought that the political price of increasing the scale of plainclothes operations by soldiers would be heavy. There were doubts about their control. However, the main cause of the denial to the Army of this highly effective mode of operation lay in legal uncertainty. It was thought to be possibly unlawful, and hence politically unacceptable, for soldiers to operate in civilian clothes. There seemed to be an illogical extension of the principle that soldiers in a war against an external enemy should be in uniform, into the situation of soldiers coping with internal terrorism. The matter came to a head after the 'Four Square Laundry Murder', and I personally experienced an example of it. On 27 September 1972 I was interviewed for BBC Radio about the shooting of Daniel Rooney in St James's Crescent, Belfast, by a plainclothes army patrol the previous night. The interview was transmitted on BBC radio the same day. During the interview (this part was not broadcast) the interviewer, Nicholas Woolley, asked me why the Army had been acting illegally by being in plainclothes. I said that there was no law against soldiers being in civilian clothes in the United Kingdom. This appeared to be a new idea to him, but after further discussion, while agreeing that this might be the strict law, he said that it nevertheless seemed to him quite improper.

The IRA knew very well how important it was to their safety and operational freedom for soldiers to be kept in uniform and in unmistakable khaki vehicles. They therefore mounted a sustained propaganda attack on soldiers in plain clothes, based largely on the implication that this was an illegal practice for soldiers. Articles on these lines have appeared frequently in the press over the last few years. Typical was one by Robert Fisk in *The Times* on 3 March 1973 about protests in Northern Ireland against Army plainclothes operations. It mentioned that the terrorist propaganda machine seemed particularly active against Army units and tactics that were especially effective against them. The terrorists in Northern Ireland had considerable success in their propaganda campaign against Army plainclothes operations and succeeded in raising the political penalty to be paid for increasing these to a level which prevented the expansion of them which was necessary. Although some plainclothes operations have been permitted at most times, they have been very few and have involved a tiny proportion of soldiers compared to the total military force in Northern Ireland and have been subject to crippling operational restraints.

Yet the whole problem could have been solved both legally and politically if either the Army collectively, a soldier individually, or a citizen either approving or aggrieved, had been able to approach a court and obtain a declaration on whether soldiers could operate lawfully in civilian clothes and vehicles. If the answer had been 'yes', then all restraints could have been removed. There should be little political penalty involved in doing what is lawful. There would no longer have been any need to cover up or restrict activities declared lawful, and the effectiveness of the Army in dealing with terrorism would have been immensely increased. If the answer had been 'no' then the practice would have had to cease unless the Government could have made a good enough case to obtain statutory authority for it from Parliament. At least such a course would have crystallised the issues, which would in any case have been preferable to the lame way such operations were actually conducted. However, there is little doubt that the courts would have approved this practice as lawful. There is no specific law requiring soldiers to wear uniform on duty in the United Kingdom. The issue regarding the Police (in this context they are analogous to the military) was decided in 1833 when Parliament approved the Police operating in civilian clothes.[69] The purpose of a uniform is for the soldier to be recognisable as such—originally by his own side but later, under the Geneva Conventions, to entitle its wearer to the status of a prisoner-of-war if captured by the enemy. In short, uniform was an advantage and protection to its wearer. Its purpose has never hitherto been to make its wearer an easier target for the enemy.

A similar uncertainty and a similar need for a clear declaration on the law arises from the common law consequences of the various 'states' of disorder that it recognises. The common law is in general clear enough as to the rights and duties of the Crown, officials and the Army that proceed automatically from increasing states of civil disorder within the United Kingdom. The problem is to know when these 'states' are deemed to exist. The common law concept of martial law provides a good illustration of this need for clear declarations of what state of disorder has been reached in the eyes of the courts.

There is a tendency for the books on common law to declare that martial law is unknown to Britain, but then to go on and outline a notion of the prerogative right of the Crown to use the military in suppressing extreme disorder without legal restraints that is difficult for the layman to distinguish from the concept of martial law. What does not exist in Britain is a system of statutorily constituted courts staffed by the military for trying terrorist or rebellious offences. Something similar to this was established in Ireland by the Restoration of Order in Ireland Act 1920, but as this example of martial law was declared by statute, it was fundamentally different from the common law concept. We should perhaps now look at some authoritative statements on the common law concept of martial law.

In February 1921 Chief Justice Molony, in a judgment in the King's Bench Division of Ireland in the case of *Rex* v. *Allen* concerning possession of arms in the south-west of Ireland a month before, said:

'... It is impossible not to come to the conclusion that at the time of the Lord Lieutenant's proclamation a state of war actually existed and continued to exist at the time of the arrrest of John Allen and since then down to the present time.'[71]

In the case of *Ex parte D. F. Marias* in 1902 the Lord Chancellor, in a judgment for the Judicial Committee of the Privy Council, said:

'... But once let the fact of actual war be established, and there is a universal consensus of opinion that the civil courts have no jurisdiction to call in question the propriety of the action of military authorities'.[72]

In the case of *Rex (Garde)* v. *Strickland* in 1921, Chief Justice Molony again said:

'... We desire to state, in the clearest possible language, that this Court has the power and the duty to decide whether a state of war exists which justifies the application of martial law'.[73]

Professor S. A. de Smith, in his book *Constitutional and Administrative Law*, writes:

Levying 'war' against the Queen in her realm is both treason and treason felony. The civil power primarily responsible for containing and suppressing an uprising must be the Government in office. ... The Crown acting through its advisers, has moreover a prerogative power to direct the disposition of the use of the armed forces.[74]

The common law allows for the exercise of martial law by the military in effect 'if not in name within the United Kingdom. The common law provides that when war or insurrection are raging inside the Kingdom, the Crown may, and indeed must, order the military to use all measures necessary to suppress the rebellion including executing rebels without civil trial if need be. It is true that, after the insurrection has subsided, the military may be called to account in the civil courts for actions in suppressing the rebellion that were excessive or unreasonable. The problem for the military is to know authoritatively whether a state exists that justifies the application of martial law in advance of applying it. The position of the soldier, thinking such a state existed and consequently hanging some rebels without civil trial would, if he were subsequently found by the courts to have thought wrongly, be unenviable. Martial law was introduced in Southern Ireland in 1920 and 1921, but proved largely ineffective because of the legal problems engendered by introducing it through a declaration authorised by a statute,[75] rather than by following the proper constitutional course and letting martial law derive from the fact of insurrection. The judgement of the Irish King's bench in Allen's case, quoted above, indicates that, had it been left to itself, the law would probably have worked round to martial law had this become necessary.

However, the courts cannot in reason have it both ways. While claiming, quite properly, to be the judge of whether a state justifying martial law exists, they cannot then decline to make this judgement until it is too late. The conditions in South-west Ireland described to the court by the Commander-in-Chief General Sir Nevil Macready, which were held by the court to have amounted to a state of war, were as follows:

The scheme of the said warfare does not entail fighting in distinctive uniforms, or in accordance with the laws of war, but under a system of guerilla attacks, in which inhabitants, apparently pursuing peaceful avocations, constantly come together and carry out guerilla operations which often result in the death of or serious injuries to members of His Majesty's forces and police at the hands of the people who are posing as peaceful citizens.[76]

That seems to describe the IRA's campaign in recent years in Northern Ireland. When I arrived in August 1972, to take command of the Upper Falls Area of Belfast with my battalion just after the British Army had re-entered the 'no-go' areas at Operation Motorman, the IRA governed the area, which had been effectively alienated from British rule, and the British forces made armed incursions into or through this rebel-held territory. If a state of war justifying martial law existed in South-west Ireland in 1921, then a comparison with that situation seems to reveal that in 1971, 1972 and part of 1973 such a situation existed in the Republican areas of Belfast and Londonderry and that it not only existed then but still exists in South Armagh at the time of writing.

It may be that the system of 'flexible law' remarked on above is no more than martial law exercised by the Government as it sees fit, as it is perfectly entitled to do in a low-profile manner, in an area given over to insurrection. It may be that the Army is being used in Northern Ireland as a direct instrument of the Government under the Royal Prerogative to impose as much or as little order as the Government sees fit, under whatever authority the Crown chooses to place its military forces. It seems, however, that the employment of troops under the Royal Prerogative in this way within the borders of the United Kingdom is unlawful while the courts are able to sit, this being the basis of the constitutional settlement of 1688 and of the doctrines on the employment of the military in the suppression of civil disorder that developed during the eighteenth century. If the control of the Army in Northern Ireland has been an exercise of the Prerogative right to enforce martial law where no other law exists, then this should have been clearly said, because other consequences derive from such a position, particularly in connection with the subjection of the military to the civil courts while engaged on anti-terrorist operations. States of war have apparently existed in various areas of Northern Ireland since 1969, but the military have continued to be subject to the civil laws as if there had been no insurrection.

It may equally be thought that nowadays the whole common law concept of martial law and duty to use the force necessary to suppress rebellion is repugnant and outmoded. If that is the case, then let Parliament say so and alter the current law by statute.

The Security Forces' need for the courts to declare the 'state' of the civil disorders applies not only to martial law but also to whether a series of continued street disorders are 'riots' or 'insurrections'. The need for an authoritative ruling is explained by the following extract from Chapter V of Part II of the *Manual of Military Law*:

17. An insurrection differs from a riot in this—that a riot has in view some enterprise of a private nature, while an insurrection savours of high treason, and contemplates some enterprise of a general and public nature. An insurrection, in short, involves an intention to 'levy war against the Queen', as it is technically called, or otherwise to act in general defiance of the government of the country.

18. For example, a determined mob assembling to pull down or burn a building belonging to their civil employers with whom they have a dispute, are engaged in a riot as soon as they have actually commenced to execute their purpose. If the object were to attack a barrack with a view to arming themselves and making war against the government they would be in a state of insurrection.

19. The observations made above with respect to the duty of suppressing riots apply still more strongly to insurrections or 'riots which savour of rebellion'. In such cases the use of arms may be resorted to as soon as the intention of the insurgents to carry their purpose by force of arms is shown by open acts of violence, and it becomes apparent that immediate action by the use of arms is necessary.[77]

It thus seems that most riots and days of 'aggro' and rioting in Northern Ireland have been insurrections, and that on 'Bloody Sunday' there was an insurrection, at which the 1st Battalion The Parachute Regiment were guilty of failing to enforce the law rather than of exceeding it. It seems that, if soldiers had been able to obtain declarations on appropriate occasions from the courts that insurrections were taking place, then disorder could have been suppressed within hours. Any soldier can in theory disperse a riot or end street disorders and 'aggro' within a few minutes by using lethal fire. What is needed is legal authority to use the force necessary to end rioting, not ministerial authority. This does not mean that soldiers should 'mow down' rioters with lethal fire at the slightest excuse. It means rather that the knowledge that they can and will do so with the backing of the law, plus perhaps one or two exemplary 'whiffs of grapeshot', would normally induce rioters to desist before the need for lethal fire had developed. Had such legal authority as to the fact of an insurrection taking place been obtainable from the courts over the last few years in Northern Ireland, there might have been fewer occasions when British soldiers felt they had to remain inactive while being stoned, attacked and defied by rioters, thus unfortunately showing that the forces of law were ineffectual. What the troops lacked was not physical courage or weapons, but legal confidence to do their duty and suppress disorder.

This is no new problem in England, as it was in evidence at the time of the Gordon Riots in 1780:

The frequent failure of the agencies of control was not so much one of strategic action, which was often well conceived and carried out, but in the ineffectiveness of troops on arrival in the riot area, and this of course stemmed from the unfortunate legal ambiguity discussed above. It is true that the appearance of troops, although it angered one crowd, could be enough to disperse another, but a mob, especially one engaged in food rioting, often showed fight, and officers and men were uncertain of their powers. Such vacillation and delay was always regarded as weakness, and increased the violence and sense of elated power often noticed in crowds. During the riot at the King's Bench prison on 10th May 1768 it appeared at the subsequent trial that the soldiers threatened to fire several times, kneeling and presenting their firelocks, but to no purpose; the excitement of the crowd increased greatly as a result, and the soldiers were bombarded with stones so as scarcely to be able to keep their ranks. A captain's threat to fire was treated as bluff. Similar occurrences in 1780 convinced the Gordon rioters that they had nothing to fear from the troops, and their violence increased accordingly. The disastrous result is that counter-measures, when eventually resorted to, have to be proportionately more violent.[78]

I had a good deal of sympathy with the view which was often expressed in the Upper Falls by the more moderate Catholics when they would ask: 'Why don't the soldiers keep away from these areas? There is never any trouble when they are not here'. Essentially this ridiculous but more or less true situation derived from the policy of 'restraint', which itself derived from lack of legal certainty. If there were disorders, the troops had an absolute duty to suppress them. If there were no disorders, the troops should indeed have kept away. But by appearing in the presence of disorder and then doing nothing about it, the troops stimulated breaches of the peace by their mere presence, providing the disaffected with a quiescent target on which to vent their wrath and work themselves up into a hysteria of violence. Against this must be set the advantages of having uniformed troops in a disorderly area to report on events as they develop. In his report on the Red Lion Square Disorders of 15 June 1974, Lord Justice Scarman says:

When the I.M.G. [International Marxist Group] asssaulted the police cordon there began a riot, which it was the duty of the police to suppress, by force if necessary.

Every other person present in the square was, as a matter of law, under the duty of assisting the police.[79]

Had the military been able to obtain from the courts in Northern Ireland some such declaration of their duty under the law, they would have recovered the legal confidence that comes from knowing what is expected of them, and would not have had to continue to permit street disorders in Northern Ireland.

One battalion serving in Northern Ireland for a tour of four months had ten soldiers killed and forty-eight wounded. My battalion had 2,500 rounds of ammunition fired at it in an area of two square miles during the first six weeks of its tour in 1972, apart from a plethora of bombs of various kinds. In South Armagh, the area containing Forkhill and Crossmaglen, the ratio of deaths between the two sides at the time of writing is forty-three soldiers killed to one IRA member, and he was killed by his own side.

Yet the Army has never officially been on 'active service' in Northern Ireland. A number of important consequences for the internal administration of justice in the Army derive from being on 'active service'. On this subject the Army Act 1955 says:

In this Act the expression 'on active service', in relation to a force, means that it is engaged in operations against an enemy. ... [and] 'Enemy' includes all persons engaged in armed operations against any of Her Majesty's forces or any forces cooperating therewith, and also includes armed mutineers, armed rebels, armed rioters and pirates.[81]

There are special provisions for active service to be declared to exist outside the United Kingdom in circumstances involving a lesser degree of conflict than described above—as in Berlin for the past thirty years. However, it seems that inside the United Kingdom 'active service', like martial law, is a state of fact and not of ministerial or military declaration. It seems therefore that in denying that the military in Northern Ireland were on active service, the ministerial and superior military authorities were probably exercising a power which they not only did not possess according to the Army Act, but which directly contravened a provision of that Act. It appears that, if called upon to decide, the courts would have directed these authorities to comply with the statute in the matter of 'active service'.

The essence of the problem outlined above is that both ministerial and military authorities, usually with the best short-term intentions, ignore and override the common and statute law habitually and with impunity. They can do this because there is no realistic machinery available to the individual soldier or citizen to ask the courts to direct these authorities to comply with the law. If such a system had existed, the 'reprisal' policy of Lloyd George might have been stopped very quickly, as might 'interrogation in depth' without (in the latter case), having to wait for the shame of a press *exposé*.

(f) The lack of an effective Government public relations policy to support its counter-insurgency campaign

In Northern Ireland the principal controlling factor over Security Force actions—both the extent to which they enforced the law and the means they used—was the thought of what would appear in the news media, and hence the effect on public opinion. It is true that there were four distinct groups of public opinion to be considered, the Northern Irish Loyalists, the Northern Irish Republicans, the mainland British, and the rest of the world. Usually, the effect on one group had to be traded-off against that on another, since it was clearly impossible for the Security Forces to please everyone. So the reactions of each of these groups had to be evaluated and an aggregate public reaction predicted. In my experience, this prediction over-rode all the other factors when a decision had to be made on how the Security Forces would act. Sometimes the importance of public relations in deciding Security Force actions was admitted, but it was often allowed to have its overriding effect while the decision was rationalised in ways that were emotionally more acceptable to the takers of military and Police decisions.

The evidence for this does not lie just in one man's observations, but in the observable conduct of the military over the years in Northern Ireland. The following is quoted from the Northern Ireland Community Relations Commission research paper *Intimidation in Housing* of February 1974,

Nevertheless ... views on the negative role of the Army and Police must be taken as fairly representative of a significant minority of the population of the Province. An article by Desmond Wilson, entitled 'Descent into barbarism', is an indictment of the inconsistency of the Police and soldiers who 'have often watched gangs of youths beating men in the streets and breaking into homes without doing anything to help. They do not want to get into more trouble than they have to and will avoid rescue operations unless given clear orders and reinforcements.'

There is documentation of individual and community groups which, faced by intimidation crises, have appealed for help directly to army units and army command. There are instances where this help has been refused or delayed. ...

During the course of our researches into these areas we found evidence of a number of instances where the Army did not protect the property of intimidated families, failed to arrest intimidators, allowed barricades to remain, and came to terms with paramilitary groups in order to avoid a head-on clash.[82]

While it would be impossible ever to prove why the troops reacted like this, my own experience assures me that such inactivity will probably have been caused by two factors: the less important factor is uncertainty among the soldiers as to their legal right to interfere and as to how far the law would support them if they used the force needed to suppress these disorders; much the more important factor is the fear of adverse publicity whether they acted lawfully or not. If they dealt severely with the intimidators, the soldiers could be certain of press allegations of military brutality, which would in their turn spark off political inquiries into what they had done, followed by Police inquiries. This might bring down on them the disapproval of their military superiors. Soldiers, even the worst-behaved among them, usually like playing the rescuing hero, particularly if there is a chance that some grateful damsels will be among the rescued—their natural reaction would therefore be to rush round and 'sort out' the bullies and intimidators. That they have often failed to do so lies in their near-certainty that such positive action to enforce the law will result in heavy adverse publicity, and that there will be little if any effective effort to present their side of the story to the public through the media. The effect of this fear of adverse publicity on the Security Forces contributed significantly to the successful use of intimidation to drive between 30,000 and 60,000 people out of their homes in the Belfast urban area in the period covered by the above-quoted research paper.

It was the factor of public relations that so frequently induced the British Army to stand inactively by while illegal uniformed marchers paraded the streets and while at funerals of extremists illegally armed parties fired volleys over the coffins of their dead comrades within a few yards of the troops. This was the factor that led so often to the British Army not entering a crowded bar where a wanted gunman was known to be. This was a contributory factor that led to troops standing helplessly in rows letting themselves be stoned by rioters without response. This was the factor that led to troops being forbidden to go inside post offices to guard against armed robberies by being stationed inside the post offices, when this was the only effective way to achieve that end without the troops being excessively vulnerable or considerable military effort being wasted. This was the factor that led to troops being permitted to use the more dangerous but more effective plastic anti-riot bullets only in dire emergencies and then only on the authority of a Brigade Commander, when these plastic bullets, unlike the rubber ones, had sufficient power to keep stone-throwers out of range. This was a significant factor leading to the Army's most effective forces, the plainclothes and civilian vehicle-borne groups, being kept tiny in size and severely restricted in scope. This was the factor that led to two adverse words in a newspaper article being made the subject of a rigorous and wide-ranging Military Police investigation carried out immediately, whereas the death of a soldier would produce a few stylised messages of condolence from on high and perhaps a couple of pages of cursory Military Police investigation completed months after the event.

This sensitivity to public relations was based in sound reasoning. A terrorist campaign is essentially a battle of political calculation into which terrorism is flung by one side to redress the power of established state authority on the other. 'Armed propaganda' is the stock phrase of the urban guerrilla from Carlos Marighella onwards. The physical damage that the terrorist is able to inflict is seldom mortal and indeed is comparatively slight relative to the time taken to inflict it. Similarly the casualties he inflicts are less than those that arise from any other sort of armed conflict, again relative to the length of the struggle. For example, 750 people were killed in Belfast in a German air raid on the night of 17/18 April 1941;[83] and in the Royal Victoria Hospital off the Falls Road casualties caused by civil disturbances formed only a small proportion of the total of emergency admissions, even in the worst years of the troubles. The accidents and disasters of everyday life accounted for the vast majority. The exact percentages of civil disturbance casualties were 2.39

per cent of the total emergency admissions to the hospital in 1971, 5.39 per cent in 1972, and 2.58 per cent in 1973.[84] It was always surprising to the newcomer to Northern Ireland how normally life continued even in the centres of such supposedly devastated cities as Belfast and Londonderrry, and at the height of the terrorist bombing campaign. The terrorist's method of fighting is to spread the impression that because of his acts of terror the Government can no longer govern, that whole areas are out of Government control, that the Government forces face inevitable defeat, that the counter-terrorist effort is useless, and that the wisest course for the Government and its supporters is to negotiate from the terrorists the best terms possible as quickly as possible. In short he wishes to create the 'climate of collapse'. Acts of terror are carefully planned to achieve the maximum publicity due to their target, their location or their timing, rather than the actual casualties or damage they cause. Indeed, the latter can be counter-productive for the terrorists as when, on the afternoon of 21 July 1972, the Provisional IRA killed eleven people and injured 130 in an orgy of bombing in the centre of Belfast.[85] The effect of this was to swing public opinion away from the Republican cause, which it had supported since 'Bloody Sunday' in Londonderry on 30 January 1972, in favour of the Government's efforts to suppress terrorism. Operation Motorman on 30 July 1972, when the British Army re-entered the Republican 'no-go' areas, only became politically possible after this shift in public opinion, particularly international public opinion. It was the concept of 'armed propaganda' that lay behind the practice of the Provisional IRA of giving warning of their bombs to avoid casualties, and in planting them in such dramatic places as cross-border trains and the Europa Hotel in Belfast, where most of the press stayed. These bombs were propaganda exercises rather than acts of physical offence in themselves.

The terrorists' acts of terror back up a stream of interlinked propaganda which the terrorists put out, and must put out if they are to succeed in demonstrating their power and justifying themselves. In Ulster this propaganda included television appearances, press statements after incidents, and a stream of handbills pushed through letter-boxes. While the terrorist propaganda campaign on television and in the press was very clear in its targets and its purposes, the handbill campaign combined with such local newspapers as *The Republican News* was less generally appreciated on the Government side. The great strength of the latter was that it dealt with local issues of the conflict. By local, I really mean local: the issues that affected one of the areas consisting of only a few streets, such as 'The Rodney' or 'The Old Beechmount', that had a definite corporate village identity and would act more or less as one community.

One of the curious effects of civil disturbances and terrorist activity is that perspectives become shortened in time and distance. In normal times even local political issues are seen in relation to their effects over years; they are seen in such terms as where the new comprehensive school will be built, or when the new by-pass road will be opened. In disturbed times there are so many crises that the neighbouring suburb of Andersonstown, let alone Derry, seems a world away from the Upper Falls. Few think beyond next week's protest march, or tonight's bomb threat, or last week's

atrocity. This means that local propaganda, or rather propaganda interpreted into local terms, becomes all-important in winning or losing the
support of the population in the disturbed areas. Let us suppose that a
Catholic was shot in the Springfield Road by a presumed Protestant
gunman. The IRA would not see this as the terrible assassination of one of
their kith and kin, but as a heaven-sent chance to win a propaganda
victory, as an opportunity to be exploited in public relations terms. They
would therefore, without troubling to check any of the supplementary facts,
probably put out an immediate statement that the Army had connived at
the shooting because the victim was a Catholic, or, if it had not actually
been involved in the murder, that the Army had at best been criminally
negligent of Catholic lives compared with its high concern for Protestant
lives. This statement would be telephoned to the press and television but,
more important, a sheet of typescript presenting their version would be
duplicated and quickly pushed through the letter-boxes of people in the
area likely to be emotionally upset by the murder. Ministers making
statements in London or Stormont about 'The Irish Dimension' or religious
leaders calling for restraint have no effect on this sort of issue. The
compliance, if not the loyalty, of the Catholic population in the immediate
vicinity of the shooting would be lost to the Government if the Army could
not immmediately show, in precise local terms, who was doing what at
what time, and what its performance had been in relation to the
intersectarian conflict, to prove that it had done its best to prevent
Catholics from being murdered. What is more, the Army's answer would
have to be pushed through the same letterboxes as the IRA's handout, and
read out to the protest-delegation of Catholic women that would be sure to
arrive at the Springfield Road Police Station within the hour. It is natural
that a public relations exercise of this kind should be parochial in its
content and in its objectives. If the citizens to be persuaded think in
parochial terms, then it is in parochial terms that they have to be
persuaded. Over-centralisation in this area is doomed to ineffectiveness. A
set of rules should set out clearly the scope and limits of local propaganda
efforts by Government representatives. No ministerial statements that 'the
Army are pursuing an impartial policy' or twenty-second news flash on
television showing a Commanding Officer telling the world what a good
job he and his chaps are doing can take the place of the detailed local
answer to the detailed local terrorist propaganda.

Moreover, this local propaganda effort must be continuous. There will
be an event tonight and another tomorrow morning and another tomorrow
night, year in and year out. The propaganda battle in an insurrectionary
campaign is like a tug of war with public opinion as the tell-tale
handkerchief in the middle of the rope. If either side relaxes or stops
pulling, the handkerchief will flash to the opposite side, and it may never
return. Propaganda, like intelligence in a counter-terrorist campaign, is
seldom a question of 'scoops' and 'coups' but one of working hard and
incessantly to gain and keep the support of public opinion, a sort of war of
attrition of little fights and little victories that add up in the end to overall
victory or defeat. Law in a democracy depends largely on public
acceptance. In his report on the Red Lion Square disorders Lord Justice

Scarman says: 'It cannot be said too often that our law assumes that people will be tolerant, self-disciplined and willing to co-operate with the police'.[86] Civil disorders of the magnitude of those in Northern Ireland do not arise unless a large section of the population has opted out of that proposition. That section will, moreover, be subject to a stream of propaganda stating the rebels' case. It is erroneous to think that the majority of citizens in such areas will give their support to the Government forces, or even withdraw their opposition to the Government, unless the Government actively, continuously and in the local terms of its audience persuades them to do so. Loyalty is not automatic; it has to be won. Inevitably the measures which the Security Forces must take to counter the rebels will inconvenience, frighten, annoy and humiliate ordinary people. It is impossible to search people, their cars and their houses without doing this. The sufferers will tend to be thrown into the arms of the extremists unless they can be persuaded that the actions of the Government and its Security Forces are reasonable, necessary and in their own long-term interests. After all, a Government exists for the people, not the people for the Government. The Government must persuade the people of its case exactly as an advocate sets out to persuade a court. Indeed this is what Mr Wilson's Government did in the summer of 1975 with a publicity campaign costing £2,000,000 to secure public support for its anti-inflationary policy. The Cabinet did not expect trade unionists and the rest of the population to accept the need for a strict limit on wage rises without having the arguments for it fully explained to them. This campaign to gain support for the Government's economic policy included a leaflet carrying a facsimile of the Prime Minister's signature being sent to every household individually, as well as press advertisements and television talks.[87] If such a public relations effort was necessary to win public support for the fairly mild pressure of a policy to reduce the rate of wage increases, surely it is obvious that something similar is required to persuade the public of the need for the harshness, inconvenience and loss of liberty that must inevitably accompany any campaign to end terrorism and disorder on the scale that has arisen in Northern Ireland.

While the arrangements for ministerial statements of policy and responses to events in Northern Ireland were satisfactory, the Security Forces lacked an effective civilian machinery for expounding the Government's case continuously and at all levels. This is largely what brought the Army—unwillingly—into the information policy field and led to the frequent appearance of Army officers in the media. To this reason was allied the peculiar nature of television news.

News conveyed by radio and newspapers contains much more information than does television news. In radio and newspapers there is an opportunity to state both sides of an argument and set any matter in perspective. Words can be used wherever they come from, and therefore press releases at ministerial level, or after approval by high authorities from press desks, can be considered and incorporated in radio and newspaper news. Television news, by contrast, conveys relatively little information, and has virtually no time for balanced argument. It sends out a narrowly focused but exceedingly vivid image, a brief moment extracted from a much more long-drawn-out matter, with little sense of context.[88] Television news, being visual, has to be created at the scene of the event or by the participants or by onlookers. Considered and anodyne statements released by a public relations officer on television are usually unimpressive because they lack that special vital quality which only the man on the spot, with his own first-hand evidence, can impart.

In a city such as Belfast television news travels quickly. All television reporters have a network of informers who, in return for cash, alert the television news teams by telephone. Thus not only is television news made on the spot, but it is made within a few minutes of the start of a shooting or some other event.

Anyone who becomes involved with the media quickly learns that the advantage of the first news reports being favourable to one's own side is overwhelming. The first reports are usually the ones generally believed, and it is very hard to reverse an unfavourable first report. The example of 'Bloody Sunday' is a case in point. There was an unlawful march which involved a riotous attack on the forces of the Crown. When these forces advanced to carry out their inescapable legal duty of arresting the rioters, they were fired on. In firing back, the Army killed some rioters. Whether or not these rioters were armed matters little to the British law when a riot savouring of insurrection is being suppressed. The Security Forces were generally exonerated after an exhaustive enquiry by the Lord Chief Justice of England. Yet the world believed then, and still believes, that the troops behaved wrongly on 'Bloody Sunday'. This was an example of the effect of first reports. The television and news reports on the evening of 'Bloody Sunday' were almost all unfavourable to the Army. It seems that no one put the Army's case clearly and forcefully to the media at Londonderry within a few minutes of the shooting. Those who were opposed to the Army's actions were only too ready to give their views. It appears from *The Times* of 31 January 1972 that the official Army version was not put out until late that night a considerable time after the event, and then in a press statement issued from Lisburn by the General Officer Commanding in Northern Ireland after consulting the officers concerned. But by then it was too late and the world has never paid any significant attention to this reply or the evidence to support its version that has emerged since.

Hence the Government must be prepared to put its side of a story to television at the scene of the incident within ten minutes of the event. The Army's involvement with information policy and television appearances in Ulster came about because no one else would, or perhaps could, meet this vital need. Nevertheless, it seems constitutionally undesirable that the Army should be used as the Government's spokesman in this way. The current rules contained in *Queen's Regulations*, paragraph J897, issued in January 1974, do not differ greatly from their predecessors:

Official communications to the Press [which includes TV for this purpose] will normally be made by Public Relations staff. They may, however, be made by other duly authorised personnel in British Commands, ships, units and establishments, e.g. the Commanding Officer or his representative, when the information given is factual and relates solely to the Command, ship, unit or establishment concerned and when this is in accordance with separate instructions. They must avoid comment on issues of a politically controversial nature.

This ignores the reality of a counter-insurgency campaign, and, as matters stand at present, unless the Army states the Government's case on television, no one else will do so with any effect, and the rebels will win a propaganda victory by default.

A secondary but none the less strong reason for the Government to pursue an active information policy is to maintain the morale of its own forces. This need is often forgotten by civil officials and politicians who tend to assume, until too late, that their military and Police forces are impervious to any sort of abuse. These forces are formed of human beings who thrive on praise and appreciation like anyone else, and wilt under abuse and denigration. The effect of this lack of concern for the morale of the Government forces can be clearly seen in the demoralisation of the Royal Ulster Constabulary (R.U.C.) and their reduction to near-ineffectiveness. This was caused mainly by the wave of abuse, blame, inquiries and critical reorganisation to which they were subjected in 1968 and 1969. Yet, as was shown by the Cameron and Scarman Reports, the regular R.U.C. had on the whole behaved well and acted with fairness. The effect of this was illustrated in a conversation I had in the autumn of 1973 with an experienced R.U.C. officer, who explained why the R.U.C. would not go back into the Republican areas of Belfast, although they could probably have done so at that time, given sufficient determination. The following represents his words in general terms, and is not verbatim:

Before 1969 we were a proud, efficient and confident Police force; we enforced the law throughout Ulster whatever the danger to ourselves. In 1969 we met the threat of rebellion and in the course of meeting it had half our total strength injured. We were prepared to go on to restore the law whatever the cost to ourselves. Then followed the propaganda attacks on the Royal Ulster Constabulary. Everything was said to have been our fault. All we had endured and risked and achieved was denigrated. Even our own Government, and Ministers to whom we looked for support, joined in this chorus. We were then disarmed in the face of armed and murderous terrorists after the Hunt Report. We had our own senior officers removed and Sir Arthur Young from the City of London Police forced on us, and were invited to police the Falls Road as if it had been a Surrey market town. The result of this is that we no longer care. If our previous efforts were treated by our own masters as they were, why should we bother? Let them find someone else to sort out the Ballymurphy until we can return there without any trouble at all. We are never again going to make the effort we made before, or try like we tried before, or take the risks we took before, because of the way we were let down.

This understandable reaction to unanswered propaganda has led to an insoluble policing problem in Ulster, and it is ultimately attributable to the Government failing to counter the propaganda attack on the R.U.C. in 1969, and assuming that the members of the R.U.C. would continue to act as they had always acted regardless of the abuse and however little public projection there was for their side of the case. Mere statements of support without making the case are not enough.

The discipline, restraint and morale of the British Army in Northern

Ireland has been widely praised. The maintenance of this performance has been largely due to the generally favourable press and television view of it projected in Britain. Soldiers, like other people, care deeply what is said about them, and especially what their own families read about them in the papers and see of them on the television. It is of tremendous importance to their morale that they should receive a favourable press; that the name of their battalion should be well thought of, and that allegations of misdemeanours should be effectively answered.

The Army was dragged into the propaganda war in Northern Ireland because the alternative was to lose the campaign. But what of the position of the individual soldier or officer? Political factors interweave with everything that the military do in a counter-insurgency campaign, right down to the tone of voice used by the most junior soldier in talking to civilians on the street. Therefore the proposition that soldiers should confine themselves when confronted by the media to facts and avoid politics collapses in reality as soon as it is stated. In *Queen's Regulations* the political area forbidden to soldiers when speaking to the media is defined as follows: 'A politically controversial issue is one which is, has been or is clearly about to be a matter of controversy between political parties in this country'.[89]

In Ulster the terrorists were backed by violently opposed political parties and therefore this definition embraced not only the acts of the Army but its very presence there. For example, I was asked by a BBC interviewer after the shooting of the notorious gunman James Bryson: 'Are you happy that he has been shot?' The political traps awaiting an answer of either 'yes' or 'no' are obvious, and would undoubtedly have been exploited had it not been possible to avoid replying by expressing some generalised views on the whole problem.

Are soldiers obliged to tell the truth to the media, even if this would be damaging to the Government's cause? Before speaking to the media in Ulster a soldier was always, as far as I know, told by his superiors the line he was to take to the media. Were these lawful commands and what would have happened if a soldier had taken, say, the opposite line to that prescribed? It seems that a soldier can lawfully be ordered not to say anything to the media, or on the other hand to adopt a particular line. *Queen's Regulations* says: 'It is an offence against the Official Secrets Acts for a person to divulge, whether during or after a period of service with the Armed Forces, official information acquired by him during such service unless expressly authorised to do so'.[90]

The Army Act, 1955, obliges a soldier to obey a lawful command, which is defined in the notes as being 'for the execution of a military duty'. It has been ruled that to be lawful a command must have some military purpose.[91] To say something to the media which will further the anti-terrorist campaign seems to have a 'military purpose' or be 'military duty'. It therefore seems that a soldier appearing before the press and television must obey both an order to conceal an unpalatable truth and an order to tell a palatable lie. It is important that this should be understood by both the press and the public.

Putting the Government case cannot simply be left to the media. It is not after all, the media's job. If one party fails to say anything at all, the media are not obliged to fill this gap; the absence of any comment is all they need to report. Therefore, if the official side says nothing, its case will go unheard and only the terrorists' case will be put out by the media. Many of those on the Government side in Northern Ireland failed to grasp this truth. If something unfavourable happened, they thought that if they kept an official silence nothing would be said by the media. Of course, the exact reverse would inevitably happen, and wide publicity would be given to the terrorist view. Again there is a belief that to put the Government's case must involve lying and deception. This is a misunderstanding. The facts will not speak for themselves, and the ones favourable to the Government will only be heard if they are highlighted and proclaimed.

A case is sometimes made for censorship of the media in a terrorist situation linked to demands that terrorist leaders should not be allowed to appear in television interviews. The trouble with any sort of censorship is that, like most forms of dishonesty, its advantages are short-term while its disadvantages are long-term and soon completely overwhelm whatever good has been done. The key question concerns the credibility of Government spokesmen. It does not matter what someone says to the press or shows on television if no one believes him. Any form of censorship must undermine the credibility of what the Government says, or indeed of what is said on the media by anyone, since there is by implication something that is not being said. If the media are uncensored, then presumably all that is to be known is known, apart from a few specifically clandestine activities of both sides. The Government must be prepared to make a better case to public opinion through the media than the terrorists are able to do. If the reverse happens, it is no more than a welcome indication that it is time for the Government to change its policies.

There is perhaps a case for the Government to embargo a particular item of news that could spark off a riot in an inflammable situation for, say, five hours but on balance the matter is probably best left to the good sense of reporters and editors, since such a rule would be wide open to abuse by the Government and evasion by the media. I found it politic on riotous evenings in the Upper Falls to move around the area with a small transistor radio in my flakjacket pocket tuned to the BBC so that I would have some warning of a change of mood in the crowds that might result from any particular news item.

One aspect of the media in a counter-terrorist campaign that is often forgotten or not understood is the vulnerability of reporters and cameramen to intimidation. They have to expose themselves to terrorist action in order to see and report what is going on. There are, therefore, strong pressures on them not to be so unfavourable to the terrorists that the latter decide to erase them. I knew of a number of television and press reporters who were warned to get out of Northern Ireland for being unfavourable to the terrorists and had to do so.

During the afternoon of 26 August 1973 there was a riot outside the Springfield Road Police Station. After it was over, various newsmen were interviewing people in the crowd. I approached these newsmen and asked them if they would come into the Springfield Road Police Station to hear the Army version of the day's events, to counter the version then being given to them by the people who had been involved in the riot. Macdonald Hastings of Independent Television News agreed to accompany me, whereupon the crowd turned on him with abuse, jostling and racialist jeering. He was visibly unnerved.[92]

On the evening of Friday 4 October 1974 a television programme was presented on BBC 2 to mark the fiftieth anniversary of broadcasting in Northern Ireland. A senior reporter, talking of the dangers of doing his job when covering inter-sectarian conflict in Northern Ireland, said: 'If you meet hostility and are told to go, you go.' This confirms (what was obvious to those in Northern Ireland) how easily the media can be intimidated. The personal threats to media reporters must, unless they are brave to the point of foolhardiness, tend to induce them to soften their strictures on terrorist activities. This is an additional reason why the Government has to be determinedly vociferous in publicising its side of the question.

The greatest fear of the press or television reporter is that his sources of news may turn silent on him. Thus it was that the *Guardian* reporter Simon Winchester records that he wrote an apology to the General Officer Commanding in Northern Ireland, Lieutenant-General Sir Harry Tuzo, much against his inclinations, because the Army had punished a supposed breach of confidence on his part by denying him access to Army press briefings.[93] Except in an occasional case like this, there was little the Government could do to deny information to reporters, however unfavourable or unfair their writings.

The terrorists have a much stronger hand in this respect, and if a reporter is unfavourable to them, they will deny him information as to their doings. His colleagues will then get the scoops and he will get none. There is really no effective sanction that the press can apply to the terrorists in return for such treatment, since inside information from the terrorists is always news, and to ask other pressmen to eschew it would be like asking an alcoholic to eschew drink. The first aim of pressmen is, after all, news that sells newspapers or makes people watch television. There is plenty of evidence that the media do get access to terrorist organisations on the undestanding that they do not 'tip off' the Security Forces or write unfavourable articles. The best-known example of this was when Joe Cahill, at the time a Provisional IRA leader, held a large press conference in Saint Peter's School, Belfast, together with other Republican leaders when all were men whom the Security Forces very much wanted to arrest.[94]

A terrorist campaign is largely a battle of will between the rebels and the Government rather than a direct physical battle. To sustain their resolution, the Governments need the political strength derived from the support of public opinion. It will not have this, and what it has will disappear, if the Government does not actively, continuously and at all levels from the Cabinet to the street, support its counter-terrorist campaign by publicising its case and denigrating that of the rebels. The events in Northern Ireland have shown that the machinery for doing this on the one hand and the constitutional framework to set limits to this activity on the other are both inadequate. This can result in too little being done and the campaign being lost, or the wrong organisation—the Army—doing too much and appearing unintentionally as a political faction with views of its own.

This section can be fittingly concluded with a professional comment on the failure of the United States Government to carry the nation with it in its Vietnam policy:

In Vietnam, we were never successful in creating public understanding of our policy or its execution, and public opposition simply forced the Government to abandon its program. Vietnam is the classic case where public opinion, public reaction, in due time forced a major reversal in Government performance, in Government action, for better or worse, depending on your outlook ...[95]

—and with the view of the chief of army public relations in Northern Ireland in 1972 and 1973, Colonel Maurice Tugwell:

A major lesson soldiers engaged in counter-insurgency must learn is that if they cannot fight an enemy in a way that public opinion at home, and fair-minded opinion overseas, find tolerable, there is little point in fighting. To endeavour for any length of time to conduct a campaign in the face of really hostile public opinion may cost more than just a lost battle.[96]

It is, surprisingly, Governments and politicians who are most in need of this political lesson, rather than soldiers. Public opinion is not static, and it can be won over by those prepared to make the necessary effort.

In summary, then, the terrorist can win by propaganda supported by acts of terror. He cannot win by terror alone, because the physical damage and deaths he can inflict and the inconvenience he can cause are insignificant compared, for example, to the effects of aerial bombing. He can win by convincing his enemies and public opinion that his success is inevitable and the failure of his opponents is already written in the stars. He can do this if he can convince them that his power is irresistible, that he has most informed and worthwhile opinion as well as natural justice and morality on his side, and that his opponents are militarily, morally and politically bankrupt. If his propaganda can thus convince his enemies and public opinion, then resistance to the terrorists will collapse from internal failure in the face of his relatively puny physical power.

The Government forces, on the other hand, cannot win by propaganda, but they can lose by it. They can only win by taking the appropriate physical action to expose and root out the terrorists. However, they can only take these measures if the climate of public and political opinion is prepared to endorse their authority. The necessary measures will not be authorised or accepted by the population unless the Government is able to convince them of their correctness.

For the terrorists propaganda is therefore positive, being their main route to success, but it is negative for the Government forces, as failure in this area can prevent them from taking the measures that will bring victory to the state. In a counter-terrorist campaign, therefore, the Government must realise this and establish an appropriate constitutional mechanism to conduct effective propaganda. It is essential if they are to be victorious.

(g) Shortcomings of British Government machinery to counter civil disorder and terrorism; the lack of a Government organisation to manage the efforts of the whole of society as a coordinated campaign against insurgency

'Competition in government' was the essence of the counter-terrorist operations in Northern Ireland. Most of the population of the Republican areas of Northern Ireland did not particularly wish to be British. They felt Irish and Celtic; they would refer to themselves in conversation as 'We Gaels'. Therefore, they would only acquiesce in British rule if they were offered something in return that would reconcile them to a situation which contradicted their natural patriotism. Due to many factors, of which the principal was the patchwork distribution of Protestant and Catholic communities, they could not be offered the obvious prize that would bring them in behind the Government, namely independence. This was the political prize that had contributed significantly to securing popular support in the defeat of the Communists in Malaya and of the rebels and Indonesians in Borneo. What could be offered to the Catholics of Northern Ireland if not independence? They could only be offered a much higher standard of government than they could have obtained without British rule. Much was said of the benefits to the Catholics in Northern Ireland of British social security, unemployment pay and health services, all of which were far superior to anything that the Republic of Ireland could provide. The value of British subsidies to Northern Irish industry was also frequently referred to, although it seems that this mostly benefited Protestants rather than Catholics. These material factors did appear to reconcile some Catholics somewhat to British rule. Good government, however, means more than subsistence level handouts issued by post from an office. It means that the whole system of society should be well organised, from policing to bus services, electricity supply, housing, employment, and even personal help with personal problems. It was good government of this sort that the Republican areas of Northern Ireland so noticeably lacked, although it existed more or less in the Protestant areas. This failure arose from incomprehension among civil Government officials of what was wrong, of how the situation differed from normal, and of how the problem could be solved. This was compounded by the reluctance of Ministers and civil servants to learn at first hand the situation in the Republican areas, and their tendency rather to base their views on written and verbal reports, which they then interpreted to themselves in 'normal' terms, which no longer existed.

Another factor that made normal civil Government ineffective was the shortening of perspective in terms of both time and space produced by a terrorist campaign. This has been referred to above in connection with the need for continuous day-to-day local propaganda by the Government in support of their counter-terrorist campaign, but it applied equally to overall Government. In peacetime, civil Government tends to be concerned with plans, investment and development in terms of years, but in a counter-terrorist campaign a week or a month is a long time. A Northern Ireland

Community Relations Commission (CRC) research paper of February 1974 stated that there existed in Belfast 'in neighbouring estates, overcrowded schools and schools with half their 1969 population; streets with vacant houses and streets where 10–12 people in a house is not uncommon; welfare services geared to situations which no longer exist'.[97] Demographic movements which in normal times happen over periods of many years can take months or even weeks during an insurrection, as happened in August 1971. Civil Government, if it is to provide the good government that will make it acceptable to the people, needs to shorten its perspective to keep up with such a mobile and volatile situation.

That there is a competition in government cannot be doubted. The CRC report referred to above emphasises that in many areas with both public and private housing, the allocation of accommodation was in the hands of either the IRA or the UDA. To cite an example from my own personal experience, the New Beechmount was a fine council estate a few hundred yards from the Springfield Road Police Station that was being built and progressively completed during both my tours in the area. As soon as the houses were finished they were allocated by either the Provisional IRA housing officer, or the Official IRA equivalent, whose names were well known. No attention whatever was paid to the Northern Ireland Housing Executive or to their established system in the allocation of these houses. This, as the CRC report shows, was a general pattern throughout Ulster. There was widespread squatting, controlled by the UDA or the IRA, combined with equally widespread failure to pay rent. In large areas the Housing Executive had no idea who was in its houses and was unable to visit them to find out. Any thought of enforcing a court order to evict the wrongful tenants and insert those entitled to the houses according to the official system was out of the question because the terrorist organisations who controlled the housing estates would physically have prevented such a thing happening. The CRC report describes this situation vividly:

During the 18 months since August 1971 their [the Housing Executive's] representatives in a number of instances have been unable to gain access to survey public housing property because of the security situation. Representatives of the Housing Executive, in terms of collecting rents and assessing occupancy rates in its property, are often faced by civil commotion and by great hostility. Rapid tenancy changes can occur which can make any assessment out of date overnight. In these circumstances it is almost impossible for the Housing Executive to operate effectively. ...

The Provisional IRA, for example, have a measure of control over what family gets which house in Lenadoon, Twinbrook and some other housing estates in West Belfast. The UDA have assumed a major role in the allocation of housing in parts of Rathcoole, Shankill and parts of East Belfast (including Cregagh). The housing authorities have been unable to maintain control over housing allocation in many estates in Lurgan, Portadown and Derry. In these circumstances, the needy often suffer most and houses are allocated on criteria which often have little to do with the needs of the homeless.[98]

Since that report was written, the Government's ability to govern has deteriorated much further, not merely in housing but in all its functions. Already in mid-1975, the Government had lost all effective control and influence over its functions in large areas of Belfast, which were in effect governed either by the Official IRA and Provisional IRA, or by the UDA and Ulster Volunteer Force, depending on the religion of the area. Effective authority belonged to the officers of these organisations rather than Government officials or elected representatives who were not coincidentally members of the organisations. This was because only the terrorist organisations had the will and the means to enforce their decisions, and in the end government is a matter of taking decisions and seeing that they are carried out. The British Government might make laws and regulations, but these had no weight because the will and increasingly the means to enforce decisions is so manifestly lacking. The inadequacy of the Police to enforce the will of the Government was illustrated by the ease with which large numbers of them were intimidated into not reporting for duty at the Ulster Workers' Council strike in May 1974. The only remaining instrument of the Government which could get anything done was the Army because in the end it could act by force of arms. However, when the power of the Army was curtailed and restrained with each successive cease fire or period of 'low-profile', so increasingly the effective authority of Government slipped away into the hands of those prepared to offer some semblance of order and decision (in other words, 'government') however tyrannous and unjust. The official British Government was increasingly left in a vacuum of authority comically resembling the Lon Nol government in Phnom Penh, which appointed a Minister of Tourism the day before it was overrun by the Khmer Rouge.

This competition in government was enacted before me like a play on the evening of 15 November 1973 in Iveagh Street just off the Catholic Falls Road. At 1730 a Protestant car bomb exploded outside the Pidgeon Club in this street. The blast made six or seven houses completely uninhabitable and another hundred were severely damaged. Frightened families were on the street. It was a cold, wet night. A large number of people needed temporary housing and food that night, while their houses were repaired. Whoever provided best for their needs would have demonstrated to the people of the Upper Falls their capacity to govern best. The Army kept out of it, because a new civilian reorganisation of the Health and Social Services had taken place which offered at least the possibility that representatives of civil Government with authority to help the homeless would appear on the scene. When a similar bomb had exploded two weeks earlier on 1 November 1973 outside the Beehive Bar on the Falls Road, itself damaging 140 houses, there had been no one who could represent the civil Government except for the local Army Company commander who had arranged rehousing in collaboration with the Catholic priest and a local Councillor, who was an ex-internee and self-acknowledged officer of the Official IRA. The contestants in the 'best government competition' in Iveagh Street on 15 November were the Provisional IRA, the Official IRA, the Catholic Church and the British Government. The Provisional IRA failed to house anyone and showed their ineffectiveness as administrators, losing much support in the area by this failure. The Official IRA showed some administrative capacity and fitness to govern. The British Government was represented by the District Health Administrative

Officer and the District Social Services Officer. During the previous four years, no senior representatives of civil Government had been present at the scene of such incidents, at least in the Catholic areas. These two provided blankets and offered accommodation, but were handicapped by being of equal status with the result that coordination had to be by agreement, and by having no authority over the other official services, such as the repair teams from Belfast City Corporation, or the Fire Service's own repair organisation. The undisputed winner of the 'competition' was the Catholic Church, which actually arranged for most of the homeless to be billeted in parishioners' houses or in religious houses and arranged feeding. The Catholic Church was able to show who could govern most effectively; it was coordinated under one authority and its members would follow central direction. A year later, the Catholic Church in the area still owed some of its support to the administrative capacity it had shown that evening. In fact, that support could have been won by anyone capable of demonstrating superiority in the art of government. It was a major failure of the British Government that it repeatedly failed to win the 'competition in government' in the Republican areas, usually through not being present where it was wanted, but often, when it was present, through sheer incompetence and confusion over responsibilities.

The experience of the 1st Battalion the Queen's Own Highlanders in Ballymacarett, in Belfast, in December 1971, has been described in an article published nearly three years after the event.[99] At this time the Provisional IRA had been cleared out of this Republican area. There was however no machinery of civil Government capable of moving into Ballymacarett at this crucial moment with assistance, aid and benefits for these Catholics who had been newly liberated from the rule of the IRA. The Army attempted to supply this need, but very ineffectively because of their inexperience of civil Government. This was the moment for civil Government to move into the area to repair and redecorate damaged housing, restore facilities such as street lighting, and help people with their individual problems—above all, to show that they cared. As it was, the civil Government took no action whatever. There was therefore no reason for the people of the area to prefer British rule to IRA rule. Six weeks later, the Provisional IRA had been able to re-establish themselves in Bally-macarett on the theme that they were the only ones who even tried to do anything for the people of the community there.

I myself had similar experiences, perhaps the most notable of which was the administrative vacuum that followed the smashing of E Company, 2nd Battalion Provisional IRA in 'The Rodney' by December 1972. This had been one of the most powerful IRA Companies which had enforced a virtual 'no-go' area in 'The Rodney' long after such areas were officially ended in July 1972. Starting with an initial success by the Army, they were in ruins by December 1972, but no civil action was taken to seize that moment, and before long the Provisional IRA were able to resurrect themselves in the area. Such failure of civil Government to act in coordination with the military campaign was a recurring theme of complaint by the Army in Ulster. The Army felt repeatedly that it had crushed the extremists on both sides to the extent that they could no longer prevent civil action, but then civil Government repeatedly missed these opportunities.

So it is clear that a campaign against a terrorist-backed insurrection such as has occurred in Northern Ireland is not a military campaign alone: it is possible for the military to repress an area into a sort of calm, but trouble will burst out again as soon as their pressure is reduced. Such a campaign is also not only political. However neatly the politicians erect their solutions and compromises, these will collapse like card-houses if the terrorists are strong enough to veto whatever they do not like in them. Since it is in the terrorists' interests to keep their terror alive as long as possible, and since all such political compromises must involve a degree of yielding to the other side's point of view, it is inevitable that the terrorists will always destroy such compromises as long as they have the military strength to do so. Such a campaign is not only an economic one either. Improving employment by itself will not solve all the problems in Ulster. Nor is such a campaign a question of social services, welfare or housing. In a counter-terrorist campaign, the battle runs across every level and every activity of society. Thus the conflict must be seen by the Government in terms of coordinating the whole social system to counter the insurrection.

The rebels' war is, in the words of General Giap, 'a war by the entire people, a total war',[100] and the Government must counter in the same terms. If the Government sees its campaign in terms of security, or employment, or political initiatives, it will lose. If it sees it in terms of all these together as one whole coordinated system, it just might succeed. A fictitious but realistic example will help to illustrate this theme. Imagine a Republican housing estate with high unemployment. The youths in this estate throw stones at soldiers because they have little else to do of any interest. The nearby factories are Protestant-dominated and their shop stewards will not permit any more Catholics to be engaged. There are however new factories in distant suburbs with vacancies and, hitherto, no sectarian problems. However the bus routes to these factories run through Protestant areas and any Catholic worker who travels regularly on them is a likely target for an inter-sectarian murder group. Therefore the Catholic youths cannot get to the jobs so they stay on their estate and throw stones at soldiers. In the end a soldier and a youth are both killed, relationships worsen, and more and more young men join the terrorists. Yet it can be seen that at the centre of this mythical problem lies the ability to re-route the buses so that they go from the estate to the factories without passing through militant Protestant areas. It is in such a way that a civil administrative problem and the security problem interact and cannot be considered apart.

The British Constitution assumes that there will be local civil authorities as well as Police to whom the military can give their support. A hundred and fifty years ago these local civil authorities were the magistrates. Today they are the various district and county councils which have existed with more or less efficiency in the Protestant areas of Northern Ireland. The Police have not operated openly in the Republican areas since 1969, except for a few contrived activities to support the fiction that they were still an effective presence in these areas. The local elected authorities were equally ineffective in the Republican areas, largely because extremists of one complexion or another were often elected to these offices and saw them as positions from which to carry on the struggle rather than as posts of administrative responsibility. However, in order to avoid partisan use of local authority power, which was one of the problems of Northern Ireland before 1969, these local authorities had, as the result of the MacRory reforms,[101] substantially fewer powers than their English equivalents.

It was due to these factors that the Army was dragged unwillingly into representing the civil Government in the Republican areas. This phenomenon was most acute in the period between the introduction of internment on 9 August 1971 and the appointment of Civil Affairs Advisers. Civil Affairs Advisers were first appointed for the Catholic Areas of West Belfast in the Autumn of 1972. All Commanding Officers and, even more, their Company Commanders received from their areas of responsibility a stream of delegations and met a plethora of ad hoc committees of local citizens on such varied matters as Security Force actions, road safety, street lighting, physical cleaning of the area, vigilante groups to give warning of raids by the other sect, access to churches, provision of recreation facilities, safe passage of workers to and from a factory, and so on. In my role as *de facto* civil authority, I was asked by a mother to advise on the most moral 'disco' at which to let her young son have his first night out, and by a clergyman to 'harass' some of his congregation back to his church from the clutches of a heretical mission.

This situation arose partly because there was no one else to visit for people who wished to make contact with the Government below the Secretary of State; partly because, at the height of the troubles, it was obvious that the only organisation that could enter the Republican areas—for example, to mend a gas main—was the Army; and partly because the only officials at a low level likely to show any real interest in the needs and problems of the Catholics were the military commanders responsible for their areas.

In this context the story of the New Barnsley Sewer is worth recounting because it happened in January 1975, during a ceasefire, at a time when such matters were supposed to have improved, and six years after Catholic grievances had erupted into violence. On the morning of Friday 3 January 1975 the sewer in the Catholic New Barnsley Drive burst, and faeces flowed down into the Catholic New Barnsley Parade. The Army, to whom the people of the area had come for help, contacted the Department for Sewers. This Department replied that no action could be taken as it was the weekend and anyway workmen would not go into that area because of vandalism. In Northern Irish terms this was the same as saying that they would not enter it because it was a Catholic area, but that something would be done on the following Monday. On Monday 6 January, the sewage was still pouring into this Catholic estate, as it had done all through the weekend, but in spite of further telephoning by the Army nothing was done to repair the sewer. On Tuesday 7 January the Commanding Officer of the battalion in the Springfield Road Police Station rang the Lord Mayor of Belfast's Department, which replied that it was nothing to do with them. The Commanding Officer then rang the Permanent Secretary of the

Department of the Environment, who said he would do something, but hours passed and nothing happened. Therefore later on 7 January the Commanding Officer rang Mr Paddy Devlin of the Social Democratic and Labour party and a member of the Northern Ireland Assembly. Mr Devlin rang the Permanent Under Secretary of the British Northern Ireland Office. Half an hour later workmen turned up to repair the sewer. This anecdote illustrates the role that the Army tended to play as the only credible representative of civil Government in the Catholic areas. It also illustrates the insensitive attitude of the official machine in Northern Ireland to the need to provide good government for the Catholics in order to retain their neutrality. What possible reason was there for Catholics to support a Government that could treat them in this way?

From August 1969, when the Army took over the policing of the Republican areas of Northern Ireland, until November 1972, the people of Republican districts were effectually left to conduct the business of civil Government on their own. After much pressing by Brigadier F. E. Kitson, at that time commanding the Army Brigade in Belfast, a single civil servant was appointed in September 1971 as civil representative to the Army in Belfast. In October 1971 it was agreed that more would be appointed. These were Northern Ireland civil servants, and it seems that it was originally intended that they should be accredited to Royal Ulster Constabulary Police divisions. However, I was in post at the Springfield Road Police Station when the first of these Civil Affairs Advisers arrrived in the main Republican area of West Belfast in October 1972. They were, strangely, accredited to military Commanding Officers as their advisers on civil affairs; indeed one was accredited to me, as if in tacit acknowledgement of the role as Civil Governors of their areas that had devolved on Army Commanding Officers. In the event Commanding Officers did their best to make the position of these Civil Affairs Advisers independent. This suited the civil servants concerned, and they quickly slipped into their natural role as the representatives of civil Government in the Catholic areas. However, although they worked hard, they did not succeed in acquiring the *de facto* civil authority of the military for two reasons. First, there were too few of them—originally two and later four for 250,000 citizens in West Belfast. Secondly, their position within the administration of Northern Ireland carried no authority.

It is instructive to consider exactly what representatives of civil Government and Government offices were available to these 250,000 Catholic citizens in West Belfast at one particular point in time. In January 1975 there were six sub-post offices, two Police stations, four Civil Affairs Advisers (two in an Army fort and two in the Springfield Road Police Station), a public cleansing yard in the Whiterock Road, a welfare office in the Iveagh School, and a Housing Executive Repair Yard in Turf Lodge. It is therefore not surprising that the Republican citizens of West Belfast felt out of contact with civil Government which, it sensed, had no interest in them if this was the sum total of its representation in their areas.

The Civil Affairs Advisers suffered from lack of authority. They could not order anyone to do anything and were in no position to get their voice heard at the top of the Northern Ireland administrative machine. The

Ministry of Community Relations, to which they belonged, was a peripheral department, and other more powerful departments did not need to comply with its wishes if they felt disinclined to do so. Thus activities of marginal relevance were pursued in Stormont with vigour such as the 'cosmetic campaign' of Autumn 1972 to improve the appearance of Belfast, while the real needs of the Republican areas were ignored. In my battalion area of the Upper Falls containing at least 50,000 and probably as many as 70,000 Catholics, there was not a single generally available municipal playing field. Plans for creating one dragged bureaucratically on from year to year, and, with nothing else to amuse them, the bored and unemployed youths of the area found their recreation in throwing stones at soldiers. Corrigan Park Stadium on the edge of the Ballymurphy was reserved for higher level competitions and league games. The other playing field, off Mica Drive, belonged to one of the schools and could therefore only be used by anyone who did not belong to the school out of term-time. There was just nowhere for boys to 'kick about'.

A further factor that exacerbated the unwanted civil role of the military in the Republican Areas was the organisation of civil Government into such functional activities as Health, Social Services, Housing, Transport and Electricity. Although coordination was possible at Stormont, there appeared to be no machinery for coordination at the lower levels. Presumably this coordination into plans that could be implemented at a local level, is carrried out in normal times by local authorities, but for the Republican areas these local authorities were effectually non-existent, and anyway were far too slow and cumbersome to be able to cope with the shortened perspectives of an insurrection. As a military Commanding Officer I spent a fair proportion of my time trying to achieve some coordination of the affairs of Government in terms that would make sense to the people of the Upper Falls. This uncoordinated Government is well illustrated by a passage from the February 1974 Community Relations Commission Report:

Assessment
(1) *Compartmentalisation:* In investigating the role of the various Ministries it became apparent that the various schemes and benefits to aid intimidated families were divided amongst a number of different Ministries and other agencies. Some of the different departments within different agencies had merely a 'fringe' involvement in aiding or compensating victims of intimidation. Other departments of other agencies were more directly involved. Some resources were allocated from one Ministry through another Ministry. Certain voluntary agencies administered funds provided by certain Ministries under certain statutory and extra-statutory schemes. The mechanism of the administrative machinery for emergency relief services has become compartmentalised and fragmented to such a degree that the needs of the individual or family seemed almost to become a secondary consideration.

(2) *Degree of flexibility and complexity:* There are a number of outstanding examples of flexible and efficient co-operation between various agencies and Ministries. For example, the close liaison between the Ministry of Development and the Belfast Housing Aid in the provision of emergency house purchase grants. Many of the schemes in operation are bound by rigid rules concerning which people do, and which people do not, qualify for emergency assistance. An intimidated mother or house-holder faced with an emergency, fearing for the safety of the children and

the prospect of losing everything, often faces confusion, frustration and delay. The individual fills in numerous application forms, is directed from one department or agency to another department or agency, each of which is intent on operating its own scheme, without regard for other agencies within the total structure.

Enquiries reveal some remarkable structural and procedural complexities involved in the way in which different Ministries and branches within ministries and agencies have organised themselves to discharge their social service functions. As far as can be determined, for example, the Emergency Relief Fund is channelled from the Ministry of Finance through the Ministry of Community Relations to the Ministry of Development and the Ministry of Health and Social Services. Money is allocated for emergency relief of intimidated families from this fund under separate schemes for redundancy payments (MHSS), cross-channel transport (Belfast Council of Social Welfare), removal costs and rent subsidy (Housing Executive through the Ministry of Development), house repairs (Ministry of Development), and miscellaneous funds (churches and other agencies).

(3) *Delays*: A major feature emerging from family case studies and agency interviews, and from investigations into the role of Government agencies, is the recurrent theme of delays—delays in re-housing intimidated families; delays in hearing the claims of victims; and delays in receiving compensation (there are still unsettled cases arising from the 1969 and 1971 disturbances—see family case studies G1 and G4).

(4) *Emergency*: The problems of intimidation arising out of the social situations which have existed in many housing estates in Northern Ireland since August 1969 have not been treated by most of the Agencies with the degree of urgency required for effective emergency relief or on the basis of the collective needs of a family. Speed and a comprehensive system of aid are often not the primary considerations in the provision and the reorganisation of emergency relief.[102]

Great annoyance was caused to the Catholics of the Upper Falls, and presumably elsewhere, until the matter was put right in early 1973, by the length of time it took for the Government to compensate them for damage to their homes caused by Army searches. The cost of such damage was usually in the £5–£10 bracket, but it would take months and sometimes years before the compensation was paid out. One of the prime reasons for this delay was that if the damage had resulted from a pre-planned search, then the Northern Ireland budget paid the compensation, whereas if it resulted from the 'hot pursuit' of a wanted man who had been spotted, payment was the responsibility of the Ministry of Defence in London. The householder had no means of telling why the soldiers had searched his house, and the soldiers would certainly not enlighten him, thus giving away what they knew. Equally, the individual junior soldier might well not know the precise reason for the order to him to search that particular dwelling. Yet there were different application forms for the householder to fill in, according to the reason for the damage. Even if he at last sent off the correct form, the two Ministries would argue away with each other for months as to why the damage had been done and therefore which of them should pay for it. They would also try to send professional estimators to view the damage—as if these officials could have crossed the barrier of the Peace Line into the fanatically Republican Clonard, let alone survived there for half an hour. Meanwhile the householder had a broken back door for months and received no compensation. Is it surprising, therefore, that he might be disinclined to help the Government and the Army? Yet these were the people whose 'hearts and minds' the Government and its armed forces were supposed to be winning!

Such were the results of organising administration in terms of its functional inputs—Housing, Health, Social Services—rather than in terms of its output, that is to say overall good government for the disaffected areas. In the competition for good government, any competitor functionally- rather than customer-oriented was fatally handicapped. The Government repeated this error with dreary regularity and despite its huge resources, its performance lagged time and again behind that of its competitors, the Catholic Church, the IRA or the UDA, who offered government in terms of its recipients.

This functional separation of the organs of Government and the consequent lack of coordination between them also led to one of the most persistent complaints of Army officers in Northern Ireland: namely, the lack of a coherent security plan or policy with defined objectives towards which they could work. Instead, every event tended to be treated as an isolated affair that had somehow generated itself and would not affect other events, and which could and should be finished with and forgotten as soon as possible. It was generally ignored that each event in itself was merely a component of the whole campaign arising from what had gone before and affecting what would come later. Short-term points therefore tended to be pursued rather than long term policies.

The list of examples of uncoordinated government in Northern Ireland is limitless. It stretches from the years it took to obtain the authority to demolish a derelict building which offered a fire position to a sniper, to the extraordinary situation that allowed juvenile terrorists to abscond year after year from St Patrick's Training School. 'St Pat's', as it was known, was the remand home and institute for correction for Catholic youths below the age at which they could be sent to prison. It had no bars, and was run by monks without any warders or policemen. It lay on the edge of Catholic Andersonstown. In 1973 there were 128 escapes from 'St Pat's' and in 1974 there were 99. On 11 November 1973 a youth named Bernard Taggart, aged 15, who was suspected of being an Army informer, was removed from 'St Pat's' and murdered on the following day. I myself caught a 15-year-old boy planting a bomb at a petrol pump on the Springfield Road on 9 October 1973. He was remanded on bail to 'St Pat's', and immediately escaped. He was not seen again until early in 1975 when he voluntarily went into the New Barnsley Police Station, confident in the cover story and alias under which he had presumably been living in the meantime while carrying on his terrorist activities. Fortunately he was recognised and was sentenced on 17 June 1975 to seven years imprisonment. He was only one of many such cases. The situation whereby they caught juvenile terrorists who immediately escaped through 'St Pat's' was a theme of recurrent Army complaints from 1971 onwards. The Diplock Commission in December 1972 commented on the lack of security at the training school, from which offenders could not be prevented from absconding.[103] It went on to say:

We are frankly appalled at the apparent lack of any sense of urgency. The need is immediate for a secure unit capable of accommodating up to 100 young persons aged from 14 to 16 years on remand and after sentence. We find it difficult to credit that temporary accommodation of this kind could not be prepared in a matter of weeks rather than years.[104]

It was not until 31 July 1974 under the Northern Ireland Young Person Act that this state of affairs was ended. Meanwhile dozens of juvenile terrorists, arrested at great danger by the Security Forces, had escaped to plant more bombs and commit more murders.

One of the more bizarre effects of uncoordinated Government was provided by the situation over the Royal Victoria Hospital in Belfast. This major teaching hospital was situated at the junction of the Falls Road and the Grosvenor Road, at the heart of the IRA-dominated Republican area. The wards were separated from the Falls Road by a glass swing door. There were plenty of other hospitals in Northern Ireland, yet it was to this completely vulnerable hospital that terrorist prisoners, whether convicted and under sentence, awaiting trial or in detention, were sent. The Prison authorities did not regard it as their job to alert anyone when they delivered a prisoner to this hospital for treatment. They seemed to believe that their responsibility ended as soon as they had delivered the prisoner to the hospital door. This hospital was in my area of responsibility and many were the times when my battalion was telephoned by the receptionist at the hospital to say that some prison warders had arrived, delivered a prisoner into her inadequate hands and disappeared, and could we do something about it. There were, inevitably, escapes from this hospital. To prevent escapes, as well as to protect the staff, sick policemen, sick soldiers and terrorist victims also patients in the hospital, the permanent Army guard on it sometimes needed to be more than 40 soldiers. At the same time it seemed that soldiers were not allowed to guard prisoners under treatment, but only terrorist victims or members of the Security Forces in the hospital. This meant that policemen too were supplied to mount a twenty-four hour guard on prisoners under treatment—once it had been revealed to the Security Forces that they were in the hospital. The soldiers, however, were required to guard the policemen who were guarding the suspects. For me this muddle was only redeemed by the welcome I used to receive from the incredibly brave, devoted and resilient nurses in the hospital who used to supply me with the most delicious chicken and shellfish sandwiches I ever tasted.

This was the sort of effect that a discoordinated civil Government machine, functioning separately from the needs and perspectives of a counter-insurgency battle, produced on security operations. As Richard Clutterbuck has written of Malaya,

The civil problem was to retain the thread of government control in each village through an unintimidated police post and a local administration with the strength and will to enforce decisions of the central government. Otherwise, the central government could have done no more than 'legislate in a void', as the French described it in Vietnam.[105]

By withdrawing the Police from the Republican areas in 1969 and by failing to make a serious attempt to govern them, the British allowed the thread of Government to be severed and such a void created. What the Northern Ireland Prime Minister or the Secretary of State enacted or pronounced at Stormont mattered not a 'tinker's cuss' in the Ballymurphy because there was no machinery at the disposal of these Ministers with which their decisions could be implemented. The Army alone could enforce a semblance of compliance on these areas and thus became not only their Police but also their Government, for neither of which tasks the Army was trained or in post long enough to be efficient.

Constitutional machinery is needed to ensure that the thread of government is maintained throughout the United Kingdom and that the Army is never again forced into the position of becoming a substitute civil authority because of the collapse of the proper civil authority.

On 12 March 1975 Mr Merlyn Rees, then Secretary of State for Northern Ireland, said in the House of Commons: 'Over the last five years the Army have taken the lead in well nigh everything', and that the Government needed to reverse the position 'so that the police take the lead'.[106] If he had said '... so that the police *and the civil administration* take the lead', he would have reflected the whole need. One may suspect that he did not say this, because even he had no idea of the extent to which the Army had taken the lead in all aspects of civil Government in the Republican Areas, and not only in policing.

2

SHORTCOMINGS IN
THE LAWS CONTROLLING
COUNTER-INSURGENCY OPERATIONS

*(a) The lack of appropriate legal powers to make the security
forces effective in suppressing civil disorder*

The Army and the Police can only be as effective in the suppression of
terrorism and insurrection as the laws, which are their operating rules,
allow them to be. Insurrection and terrorism are abnormal, and, in order to
cope with them, the laws governing its own enforcement have to be
appropriately adjusted from their normal state. Frank Kitson wrote of the
campaign against the Mau Mau in Kenya that the greatest problem of the
Security Forces was how to deal with Mau Mau without breaking the law.
He relates a story of Police Inspectors advising their constables to run
away if they encountered the Mau Mau rather than to shoot at them and
risk the probable legal consequences to themselves if they killed a
terrorist.[1] Sir Michael Blundell, who became a minister in the post-
independence Kenya government, related that 'witnesses were murdered or
so intimidated that they dared not go into court, the magistrates were
overworked and the long mechanisms of the appeals process removed any
visible signs of the action of the law from innocent and guilty alike.' In a
notable case '... nineteen oath administrators had been found guilty of
oath-giving in the Lower Court and were awarded suitable punishments.
All the sentences were quashed by the Court of Appeal, not on the
judgment of the magistrate, with which the Court of Appeal agreed, but on
a small clerical error in the charge-sheet of one of the accused. The
terrorists learnt from this and other instances to exploit to the full the
cumbersome British legal system, which was never evolved to deal with
full-scale revolt in ... Africa.'[2]

The dilemma facing a democratic society is that the means needed to
defeat terrorism and suppress insurrection are the very ones needed to
enforce a tyranny. The methods that defeated the Communist terrorists in
Malaya are those that sustained the Gulag Archipelago. The methods of
the Gestapo and of the Swedish Special Branch, which was reported in
1973 to have operated a secret intelligence group that kept close tabs on
left-wing members of the ruling Social Democratic Party and the trade
unions, are of the same nature. Indeed all the practices of these different
internal security services, while of very different intensities and with very

different limits, are basically the same because they are the only methods by which a society can protect itself against organised citizens within itself who wish to destroy their own polity. In Northern Ireland this situation was complicated because a substantial portion of the Catholic population simply did not wish to be part of the British state or under British rule. Their patriotism was given to Celtic Ireland, and they could in the final analysis only be governed by force of British arms, albeit tempered by political subtlety and material benefits.

This meant that law enforcement in the Republican areas of Northern Ireland was more akin to that in a colony than to that in a self-governing independent state. Ultimately these Catholic areas could only be governed by the British by the methods, however mollified, that all occupying nations use to hold down all occupied territories. The logical deduction from this was either to rule the Catholics by naked force or to let them rule themselves, but such simple solutions were prevented by the curious patchwork demography of Northern Ireland, as exemplified by the Springfield Road. The houses on the North side of this city street were Protestant and law enforcement on that pavement was in principle the same as in England, namely one of self-policing by the community. The houses on the South side were Catholic and law enforcement on that pavement consisted essentially of imposing alien rule on an unwilling people. One evening in November 1973, I guided an experienced Queen's Counsel round the Catholic areas of the Upper Falls in an armoured car. As it happened we saw some 'aggro' and were stoned. Afterwards the Q.C. said: 'Now I see. The idea of an acceptable Police Force in this area is fantasy. It can only be policed by a thoroughly unacceptable gendarmerie, who are prepared to enforce the law whether the community likes it or not.'

There exists an age-old contradiction between the desire of citizens for liberty and the order in which to enjoy it, and the constraints needed to ensure that this desire will be satisfied. However, this contradiction presents itself in a particularly acute form in Northern Ireland, because the terrorists there can only be defeated and unwilling subjects kept from rebellion by considerable erosions of the liberties considered normal in a Western democracy. Some readers may be surprised, when they come to the special laws for this situation recommended below, to find that they are more in the nature of administrative proposals than recommendations for torture, hanging, etc. Herein lies a further contradiction. It seems that legislators and public opinion can only think in terms of 'all or nothing' when it comes to the deprivations of liberty needed to combat terrorism and insurrection. Once they have overcome their initial repugnance to eroding liberty in any way at all, they then seem quite ready to accept unnecessarily massive erosions. For me, detention without trial was an unnecessarily massive erosion of liberty in Northern Ireland, and as a security operator in the Upper Falls, I would happily have traded it for compulsory identity cards showing photograph, fingerprint and signature. There may be a good case for a small number of top terrorist organisers, and snipers and bomb-makers of exceptional skill, to be detained without trial, but, beyond this, detention is unnecessary provided that the law makes detection of the terrorists and their conviction in court reasonably likely. British law and British legislators in Parliament take enormous pains over court procedure and the minutiae of describing offences, but make comparatively little provision for the law to be enforced by detecting the criminal and finding the evidence needed to convict him. That this error is a general one and not confined to terrorist problems is illustrated by a ridiculous instance quoted in the *Criminal Law Review*:

The Litter Act, 1958, ... contains no provision whatever for enforcement, and the police officer who sees an offence committed under this Act is completely powerless. He may ask the offender for his name and address, but this information may be refused, politely or otherwise, and the officer can do nothing.[3]

The attitude of Parliament can be discerned from the Official Report of the House of Commons debates and committee proceedings for the Northern Ireland (Emergency Provisions) Bill in the Spring of 1973. This Bill resulted from the Diplock Report and eventually became the Northern Ireland (Emergency Provisions) Act of 1973. It was supposed to enact measures to remove the need for internment without trial. The main reason for internment was usually given as the difficulty of securing convictions in court of terrorists, due to prejudiced juries and intimidation of the public and of witnesses. It might therefore have been expected that the debate would be mainly concerned with overcoming some of these problems. Yet the entire Report Stage was taken up with considering capital punishment, which was not even mentioned in the Diplock Report; no word was spoken of how to find the terrorist. Whether or not he is to be hanged, he first has to be found. In the Standing Committee on the Bill, more than four out of the ten sittings were concerned with the mode of trial on indictment of scheduled offences. On 22 May the Standing Committee devoted a substantial part of its deliberations to the obscure possibility of a man who might have been sentenced to probation for a scheduled offence, and then appealed against it, making himself liable to automatic re-imprisonment while the appeal was pending. Yet the same committee spent only fifty-three minutes on 12 June 1973 on the whole question of juvenile terrorists. This was the sole discussion of the subject throughout the House of Commons debates on the Bill, and concerned exclusively such matters as visits by parents to the reformatory and the religious aspects of the inmates' training. The question which the Diplock report had stated as so urgent, of how to keep these juvenile terrorists incarcerated at all, was ignored by Parliament. Would they, for example, have expected that a magistrate's direction would so frighten the 16-year-old Provisional IRA gunman who wounded five of my soldiers in 'The Rodney' on the night of 8 December 1972, that he would never dare to walk out of the unguarded, unlocked St Patrick's Training School? For more than a year after this debate, and for more than 18 months after the Diplock Report, juvenile gunmen and bombers were all remanded on bail from court to 'St Pat's' from which they regularly escaped. If only a fraction of the attention that has been paid to court minutiae were devoted to the problems of crime detection and law enforcement, the increase in crime might possibly be reversed and terrorism suppressed.

There are five fundamental requirements for the laws that govern the operations of the Police and Army engaged in the suppression of insurrection and terrorism.

(a) The Security Forces, whether Police or Army or both, should know who is who, what they look like, and where they live. In a phrase—population surveillance.

(b) The Security Forces should have informers inside the subversive organisations.

(c) The law on the suppression of street disorder should be clear enough for the Security Forces and the disorderly to know with clarity what is permitted to, and what is required of, each other.

(d) If soldiers are employed as policemen, they should have the necessary powers to fulfil Police tasks relative to the suppression of terrorism.

(e) The system used to preserve the discipline of the military when suppressing civil disorder should be effective and appropriate.

My experience in Northern Ireland showed me that the law does not meet these requirements, and indeed hardly seems to recognise the need for some of them.

(b) Identification and surveillance of the population in an insurgent-affected society

The English law is based on the principle of self-policing by the community, on the concept that the community knows who among its members has done wrong and should itself produce them for trial. Historically the constable emerged as the officer of the community who carried out the mechanics of this task. In the words of the Report of the Royal Commission on the Police in 1962:

The office of constable in England and Wales is very ancient. It is associated with the village, perhaps the oldest area of local self-government in England. The constable was the executive agent of the village or township, and also its representative. As such, he was required to make quarterly reports known as 'presentments' at courts leet, or [later] at petty sessions. ... Thus no police system as such existed, and law enforcement was a matter for each local community in which all citizens were expected to join in the 'hue and cry' after felons.[4]

A legacy of this tradition is an assumption in the English law that law enforcement officers will know who is who, where they live and what they look like. It seems to be assumed that if they do not know these things, the answers can be found out by asking around in the community among which will be citizens well disposed to the authorities and willing to give this information. Indeed there is still a certain validity in this assumption in Great Britain and to a much lesser extent among the Protestant population of Northern Ireland. Police surveillance is maintained, more or less, in these areas because the Police can move and live among the community. They know the faces of the trouble-makers, often from their first clashes with the law in their 'teens', and they can enter the shops and pubs and ask around. However, as D. A. Thomas writes on the necessity for the law to provide power to arrest in respect of any offence, however trivial, as a last resort, 'in a modern urban society the police officer cannot possibly know the name of every possible offender, and the possibility of enforcement in the present situation depends on the co-operation of the alleged offender. ... ' Thus 'It is clearly self-defeating to enact legislation which carries no possibility of enforcement.'[5]

In well disposed areas the Police can carry out the task of general surveillance because they know, or can find out with little difficulty, who is law-abiding and who is likely to help them. Indeed they will usually be right if they assume that citizens in certain posts and of certain standing, such as County Councillors, will feel an especial duty to help the Police, and will themselves have a wide range of contacts. Such a chain of contacts through the law-abiding citizenry provides the unacknowledged population surveillance system of the British Police. It is effective because the community as a whole supports law and order and the Police.[6]

The situation in the Republican areas of Northern Ireland was quite different. A substantial majority of the population were at worst actively antagonistic to the imposition of the British law and at best neutral to it. The waverers and many of those who might in the rest of the United Kingdom have been willing to help the Police, if specifically asked, were firmly deterred from doing so by the effective and terrifying system of intimidation operated by the terrorists. Over many of the walls in the Republican areas of Belfast were painted the words 'Touts [vernacular for informers] will be shot'. Indeed many killings and maimings in Northern Ireland have been of citizens who were merely suspected by the terrorists of having helped the Police. So fierce was this intimidation that Catholics on the whole would only speak to a soldier or policeman where no one could see them doing so, that is to say in the privacy of their own home during a search or after they had been arrested and taken to a Police Station. If they were seen speaking to a member of the Security Forces they were sure to be 'visited' by the 'enforcers' that night.[7]

The Royal Ulster Constabulary, because they have been unable to operate in uniform or at large in the Republican areas of Northern Ireland since August 1969, have lost their earlier knowledge of both the troublesome personalities and of who among the Catholic population might be disposed to help them. The bulk of the Army has been in Ulster on short four-month tours. Because of the intensity of patrolling and screening and the system of intelligence records in Belfast, the troops there have had a surprisingly good knowledge of faces and personalities. In Londonderry and South Armagh, on the other hand, this knowledge has been slight, and the result in South Armagh—up to the end of 1975 at least—was a 43 to 1 ratio of British soldiers to terrorists killed.

It is all very well for the Security Forces to be told that a certain man is the gunman who shot someone at a certain time, but if they have no idea of his appearance or where he lives, and no one will tell them, how are they to find him? When this problem is compounded by elaborate aliases, disguises, and the terrorists' practice of sleeping in a different house every second or third night, the chances of a precise arrest of the wanted man become slim. There were frequent examples of badly wanted IRA men passing through Security Force hands several times before their cover stories were broken, and presumably there were many more whose cover was successful.

A typical case was that of a gunman nicknamed 'Beaky'. He had been arrested several times before by my battalion, but he had a complete documentary alias to give him the identity of a youth of similar age who had gone away from the area and was not involved in the Provisional IRA. The parents of this youth had been ordered by the Provisional IRA to identify 'Beaky' as their absent son if asked by the Security Forces to confirm the false name that 'Beaky' would give to them. By chance the real son had come back to visit his parents on the night of 19 August 1973 and gave his correct name when checked by the Army. He was obviously not the person who had been accepted under that name on previous occasions. 'Beaky' was arrested without being told that the Army held the real person whose identity he had adopted, and he continued confidently to give this false name which had served him so well before. The parents were asked to come to the Springfield Road Police Station to identify the youth there who was giving the same name as the son in their house. They were warned of the legal consequences of giving a wrong identification. However they were so frightened of any possibility that the Provisional IRA might think they had failed to carry out their orders that they identified 'Beaky' as their own son, knowing that their real son was at that very moment held by the Army. They were so much more frightened of the Provisional IRA than of the courts that they continued to persist in this double identification until 'Beaky' himself was induced to confess his real name to me and a Police officer in their presence. They then agreed that he was not their son and were duly charged in court. The case of the runaway Member of Parliament John Stonehouse illustrated how easily a false identity can be assumed in Britain.

A system of population surveillance is needed for terrorist-affected areas that will supply the law enforcement agencies, first, with a census of the population giving their addresses, ages and names, and secondly with a means of checking identity by signatures, photographs and fingerprints. Without such a surveillance system the Security Forces can never act with precision. They are presented with a kaleidescopic mass of unknown and undistinguishable people. The total population of my battalion's area was about 70,000 with an itinerant workday addition of some 12,000. The battalion had some 400 soldiers available on the streets, who were there for a four-month tour. Presented with the needle-in-a-haystack problem of finding criminal terrorists in this mass, there was no option but to trawl random selections of people and hope somehow that the terrorists would identify themselves from the others. No system could have been more futile, more ineffective, or better calculated to alienate the mass of the people. Yet the cause was the lack of any precise knowledge of the population in the terrorist-affected areas. The law must recognise this need and authorise the measures necessary.

When operating blind in this way, the Security Forces cannot act with precision and have no alternative but to arrest large numbers of citizens, found in the area of, say, an ambush or a bomb explosion, in the faint hope that somehow they will discover the terrorists among them. The terrorists will, in any case, probably have been the very first to remove themselves. The Northern Ireland (Emergency Provisions) Act 1973 embodies this fallacy by implication at Section 16 (1):

Any member of Her Majesty's forces on duty or any constable may stop and question any person for the purpose of ascertaining that person's identity and movements and what he knows concerning any recent explosion or any other incident endangering life or concerning any person killed or injured in any such explosion or incident.

Did Parliament imagine, when it enacted that paragraph, that the terrorists who had just committed an inter-sectarian murder would wait in the vicinity of the crime to be questioned? The terrorists are of course, likely to have travelled at least five miles away in a car during the ten or fifteen minutes that it takes for someone to tell the Army that there has been a murder and for the Army to move to the spot. However, there are likely to be dozens of possible onlookers moving about the scene of the crime, in the streets or going in and out of houses. To encircle all these with a fair chance of stopping the assassins moving out of the ring, even if they are still in the area, would normally require between 100 and 200 soldiers, and to deploy them coherently in Belfast might take up to an hour from the time of the murder. The chances of catching an assassin at the scene of the crime are therefore small, and it is safe to assume that anyone found near an incident is innocent and has seen nothing; if he had seen anything he would have disappeared to avoid the terrifying possibility of being identified as a witness. The idea therefore that terrorist crimes can be solved by flooding the area with troops after an incident is unrealistic.

The legal obstacles to military and Police surveillance were that there was no provision for the military or Police to make a census or to use the existing census, and no provision to compel citizens to carry identity cards and for the Security Forces to hold copies of them, and their concomitant photographs, signatures and fingerprints. The Security Forces were not permitted access to the population census or to such aids to surveillance as driving licences, or to the social security records. In Northern Ireland every driving licence has a photograph in it and a copy is held in the licensing office, yet all this information held in a Government office was denied to the Security Forces. Most of the terrorists received social security benefits, and certainly the Ministry of Health and Social Security had very comprehensive records in areas, such as the Ballymurphy, where 40 per cent of the males were unemployed. Yet these sources of information were denied to the Security Forces. In 1972 everyone in receipt of social security benefits had to go and collect them from an office in central Belfast during a particular hour on a particular day of the week. It was forbidden for the Security Forces to be told when a 'wanted' man would be going to collect his money, because—as I personally was told—of the 'unpleasantness' that would be caused by an arrest at the Social Security Office. The subsequent deaths of soldiers caused by these men who thus evaded arrest also had a certain 'unpleasantness' about them. By 1973 even this inconvenience had been removed from the gunmen and they were sent their benefits by post, but the Security Forces were not told to what address. The IRA and the Ulster Defence Association were both enthusiastic bank robbers and their funds must have gone somewhere, but the Security Forces were never allowed to peruse bank accounts to try and trace the destination of the proceeds of these robberies. Access to all these records would have given the Security Forces surveillance information to enable them not only to build up a census of the population and to cross-check such records as electoral rolls, but also to cast that vital first light of suspicion on an individual, perhaps by indicating that someone somewhere was receiving letters in two names or that in a particular house someone was receiving social security benefits who was not acknowledged to be living there by the occupier.

The Army in the Republican areas of Belfast, and to a much lesser extent in other terrorist-affected areas, did attempt to build up some general record of the population. They did this because without it they would have been made almost totally blind and ineffective, as indeed they have been in the border areas of Ulster because of the absence of such population control records. This was done, however, '*sub-rosa*' and without open lawful authority. It was done by stretching statutory authorities to an extent that had never been envisaged when these acts were passed, and by assuming that the Army had rights which it possibly did not have. It is essential that this need for a record of the population in a terrorist-affected area is recognised, that adequate authority to make such a census is given, and that clear limits to the Security Forces' powers are set.

Often in the Springfield Road Police Station every Criminal Investigation Branch detective had five murders at one time to cope with on his own responsibility, as well as numerous lesser cases. He could not go out and question anyone in the area. He could only talk to suspects brought in to him by the Army. Some 200 detectives were deployed in England on the search for the notorious murderer known as the 'Black Panther' in 1975. What chance by comparison did the detective in the Springfield Road have of finding his five murderers and proving cases against them without the basic background data of a population record?

(c) The crucial role of inside information in the defeat of terrorism

All terrorist movements depend on being clandestine. In a military sense terrorist warfare is a form of operations devised from the technique of concealment, in the same way as the 'thin red line' was a form of operations derived from the technique of maximising the effect of musketry fire, or as armoured warfare was a form of operations derived from the emergence of the tank.

The tactical strength of the terrorists derives from their being hidden. Once they are exposed, they can be destroyed: the Government forces can then bring to bear on them their superior force, superior ability to concentrate and the power of the legal system. But as long as they are hidden, the initiative lies entirely with the terrorists. Having forced the

Government to spread its strength as much as possible in guarding, the terrorists can strike at will at whatever is unguarded or slackly guarded, or can even strike at the diffused guards themselves. The terrorists depend entirely on being clandestine for their immunity, their tactical superiority, their supplies and their communications. The same element also assures them of the support they receive from the population, partly through the fear of the hidden, all-knowing terrorist organisation's ability to take horrible revenge on 'traitors', and partly on the alienation of the population from the Government due to their rough treatment in the 'dragnet' attempts of blind Security Forces to find terrorists.

It is difficult for those who have not been concerned personally with countering terrorism to understand the complete difference in quality and value between general information from the public and inside information from within the terrorist movement. A terrorist organisation will undoubtedly suffer some damage from information given against it by the general public. This sort of information usually reaches the Security Forces in some such form as 'Last night three strange men carried some boxes into a garage at such-and-such an address'. Such information against them will probably mean no more to the terrorists than losing a few weapons or the odd junior terrorist—and then only if they are unlucky or slack. Damage on this scale represents an acceptable casualty rate to a competent subversive movement, which can make good the losses in men and material without too much difficulty, and repair any gaps that have appeared in its concealment. It may even be able to use such minor casualties to win propaganda points. What will not have been revealed to the Security Forces by this information from the general public is any hard information concerning the terrorists' structure, their commanders' meeting places, their dumps, and above all their intentions. Once their intentions are known to the Security Forces, the terrorists have lost the initiative; the Security Forces can then arrange reception committees for the perpetrators of acts of terrorism. It is only through inside informers that a terrorist organisation can be exposed to this extent, and once so exposed it is helpless until it has discovered and removed the informers. Inside informers to a terrorist movement are like an internal haemorrhage to a human body.

As the history of the Malayan campaign is being more widely revealed, it is becoming ever clearer that the real damage to the Communist terrorists was done not by Army patrolling so much as by the progressive development of informers inside the Communist movement. Richard Clutterbuck writes of the campaign:

There is a popular fallacy that this kind of information will flow into our hands if we simply 'get the majority of the people on our side'. Certainly we must get majority support eventually if the victory is to last, but it plays little part in how we actually win. Caught between armed guerillas and armed policemen or soldiers, the bulk of the people will be on neither side. ... Only a few dedicated Communists or close relatives will voluntarily risk their necks for the guerillas. With the rest, the guerillas must be tough enough to ensure their general acquiescence ... but they will need to coerce only about 10 per cent of them to give active support.

We devised a technique for persuading a handful of their active but unwilling supporters to become our agents and betray the Communists. This, coupled with our exploitation of surrendered guerillas, was how we defeated them; and the mass of the people accepted the end of their ordeal with relief.[8]

He goes on to show how a Communist political commissar, who had defected to the government, destroyed the whole terrorist organisation in a particular area.

The London Metropolitan Police confirmed the vital role of informants in criminal detection in a BBC Television programme broadcast on 6 February 1975. It was said that nine out of ten cases were solved by informers and not by clue hunting, and that if the C.I.D. were to wait for a crime to take place, 'you dash off in hot pursuit not quite sure whom you are pursuing.' A prevalent misunderstanding concerns the role of the informer in criminal detection; his task is usually only to indicate who was involved, after which it is for the detective to find the 'loot' and pin a charge on the suspect. Many of the doubts about the use of informers centre around the question of whether or not their evidence should be admissible in court. However, this question seldom arises in reality. What the informer can do is narrow down the number of suspects from hundreds or thousands to three or four. The detective can then work on those three or four, concentrating his efforts on their movements, fingerprints, contacts and hiding-places. If the informer was right, the detective will probably obtain hard evidence with which to secure a conviction; but without the narrowing of the search made possible by the informer, it would be impossible to concentrate the necessary effort to achieve this hard evidence. Indeed it is highly desirable that an accusation against an individual should be confirmed by evidence other than that of a single informer, because few, if any, informers are completely truthful all the time; they appear to have a congenital urge to deceive the people for whom they work from time to time. The information they give is vital, but whenever possible it should be cross-checked with unconnected informers. A senior policeman on the point of retirement after a lifetime as a detective said to me: 'You must remember that sooner or later every informer will let you down.'

The following extract from the 1974 report of the Commissioner of the Metropolitan Police emphasises more than one aspect of the value of informers, with relevance to the operations of Security Forces:

A person originally arrested and charged with robbing a security guard supplied information which enabled Flying Squad officers to charge more than 100 other persons with various offences of robbery, burglary, attempted murder and conspiracy to pervert the course of justice. Information derived from the same source also made it possible to arrest a number of persons planning to rob a bank in West London before they were able to commit the offence. This operation and other similar cases illustrate clearly the value of the informant in the investigation of crime, as well as emphasising the *benefits which can be gained from concentrating police effort on a specific series of intensive enquiries.*[9]

Any significant damage to EOKA in Cyprus was done through informers, as indeed the EOKA informers similarly damaged the British effort. General Grivas reveals in his memoirs that EOKA had an informer who was a Sergeant in the Cyprus Police Special Branch, who attended and tape-recorded top-level British Security conferences at which the names of British informers in EOKA were given. These were duly executed by EOKA.[10] Grivas states that 'EOKA hides were so varied and so baffling in their design that it was rare indeed for any of them to be revealed except by treachery.'[11]

Another popular fallacy is that searching for munitions without inside information can produce any reasonable return for the effort expended. Without inside information as to the exact whereabouts of terrorist weapons and documents, the Security Forces have little option but to search on the vaguest suspicions—than which nothing is more certain to alienate the population. To search a house thoroughly it is necessary to pull up floorboards, push in wooden panels, prise out fireplaces, sift through debris in the roof, read private letters, look through cupboards and chests-of-drawers containing such things as women's underclothes, and search children's beds. All this usually has to be done between midnight and 6 a.m. to give the searching troops the cover of darkness, as they become too vulnerable to snipers if they stay around one house for two or three hours in daylight. Even so, if a hide has been well prepared, as many were, by plastering and wall-papering over a cavity made in the brickwork, the troops will still not find concealed weapons. A mother who has had soldiers breaking up her home and incidentally terrifying her children at 3 a.m. is unlikely to wish to help the Government. Similarly, information that arms are in a lorry arriving by ferry in Northern Ireland from Britain in a particular week is useless, as it is physically impossible to unload, search, and reload the 2,400 lorries that roll off the ferries each week, quite apart from all the separate containers. It is salutary for example to look at a motor repair yard and workshop and consider how to set about finding an Armalite rifle hidden there and how long the search would take, if none of the people working there either wanted to help or dared to help even if they wanted to do so. It is equally salutary to look at the cars, vans and lorries moving along a busy city street in the rush hour, and imagine how to search all of them effectively, remembering that every commercial vehicle might conceal arms and explosives in its load. How the narcotics trade in New York presents law-enforcement agents with similar problems is vividly described in a book about teenage gangs by the Reverend David Wilkerson:

Couple these profits on heroin with the fact that it is practically impossible to prevent smuggling, and you have the makings of the narcotics trade in New York. It takes a crew of twelve agents the best part of a day to search a single ship for narcotics. There are 12,500 ships arriving from foreign ports each year in New York harbour, and an additional eighteen thousand airplanes. To patrol these thirty thousand carriers, the US Treasury Department, Bureau of Customs is given a pitiful 265 men. The result is that a man not known as a runner can walk into the city with virtually no risk, carrying a million dollars worth of heroin secured in little silken bags attached to his garments.[12]

Clearly the only way for the Police to discover the carriers is from inside information from within the smuggling organisations. The best way to obtain this is by subverting members of these gangs, by one means or another. Inside informers alone can provide the precision necessary to find weapons, explosives and documents, without a large wasted effort and without driving uncommitted citizens into supporting the terrorists because of resentment at the damage and humiliation of searches. No one, except the terrorists, need be offended if the search party knows that weapons are concealed behind a particular wall in a particular room in a particular house.

It therefore emerges that a basic truth of counter terrorist operations is that inside informers and alienation of the general population are in counter-balance. The more inside information the Security Forces possess, the less they need interfere with or even be seen by the mass of citizens.

Informers, however, seldom volunteer; if they did, this would in itself be highly suspicious. They have to be created. The law has always recognised informers, but with a distaste that ignores their vital role in the enforcement of law, although there are increasing signs that the courts are coming to recognise the necessity of such distasteful practices.

In a case in July 1974 involving informers, the court reviewed the previous cases and the law on the subject. The opinion of the Lord Chief Justice, Lord Widgery, was reported as follows:

So far as the propriety of using such methods was concerned it was right to say that, in these days of terrorism, the Police had to be entitled to use the effective weapon of infiltration. In other words it had to be accepted today, if indeed the contrary was ever considered, that it was a perfectly lawful police weapon in appropriate cases.[13]

This welcome recognition of the realities of detection received a setback with Lord Justice Lawton's remarks in the Court of Appeal on 24 March 1975 in the case of *Regina* v. *Turner and Others*. This case concerned the notorious informer Derek Creighton Smalls, who seems to have given a new phrase to the English language in that turning informer is now known in criminal and Police circles as 'doing a Bertie Smalls'. Lord Justice Lawton was reported as follows:

Above all else, the spectacle of the Director of Public Prosecutions recording in writing, at the behest of a criminal like Mr Smalls, his undertaking to give immunity from further prosecutions was one which their Lordships found distasteful. Nothing of a similar kind must ever happen again.

Undertakings of immunity from prosecution might have to be given in the public interest. They should never be given by the police. The Director of Public Prosecutions should give them most sparingly; and in cases involving grave crimes it would be prudent of him to consult the Law Officers before making any promises. In saying what they had, their Lordships should not be taken as doubting the well-established practice of calling accomplices on behalf of the Crown who had been charged in the same indictment as the accused and who had pleaded guilty.

Yet this case concerned, in Lord Justice Lawton's own words, 'a series of raids on banks and other business premises and on security vans carrying money between October 1968 and August 1972, in which £1,257,257 was stolen'.

The courts seem reluctant to recognise the essential connection: that criminal gangs of this nature and terrorist organisations can only be defeated by the development of inside informers and that the law, if it does not wish to be ineffective, must allow for and indeed encourage this. The courts must also recognise that the first requirement for developing informers is the provision of ability to give members of the terrorist organisation immunity from prosecution in return for their defection. Allowing them in open court to turn 'Queen's Evidence' after pleading guilty and being themselves publicly convicted has little relevance to a terrorist campaign, for any terrorist who did this would be signing a warrant for his own death at the hands of his former colleagues. What can happen to those who publicly turn 'Queen's Evidence', even in a criminal matter let alone a terrorist one, can be seen from the following report:

A man who turned Queen's Evidence at his Old Bailey trial was refused leave yesterday to appeal against his eight-year jail sentence—although he may have to serve it in solitary confinement.

Donald Davies, 35, was sent to prison for his part in three armed robberies. Since then he had given evidence for the Crown in further gangland prosecutions.

Lord Justice Lawton said the fact that Davies might have placed himself in dire jeopardy by helping the police and the Crown was a matter for the Parole Board to consider at a future date. His sentence was perfectly proper.[14]

This sort of personal consequence for turning 'Queen's Evidence' is hardly likely to encourage others to do the same. What is needed is the ability within the law to induce a terrorist to defect to the Government's side without his former colleagues knowing that he has done so, in return for an indemnity for his crimes. We should consider briefly the effect on a terrorist organisation of widespread publicity being given to official encouragement of defection in return for an indemnity. Any arrested terrorist will have this 'easy way out' at the back of his mind if the pressures on him seem too strong. Whenever a terrorist is arrested, his colleagues will fear that he will defect and must take steps to protect themselves from the consequences of this with all the disruption that such hurried and unforeseen changes must cause. Whenever a suspect is released his colleagues, if he was a terrorist, will wonder whether he has been released because he has defected, and it will be hard to persuade them to accept him back again into their full confidence. Especial disruption will be caused to the terrorists if the Security Forces release particularly important and uncooperative terrorists quickly and then put the word about that they have been released because of the help they have given. Trust between the terrorists can be broken up in this way. Thus the development of informers within a terrorist organisation has the effect of accelerating and multiplying damage as trust breaks down and energies are turned to collective introspection. This cumulative effect of informers as treachery and defection feeds on itself should not be underestimated.

The next requirement for the development of informers is for the Police, and the military where relevant, to have time in which to question them. Time is needed to check a suspect's story, and time is needed to persuade him to defect. Perhaps the greatest single obstacle to the development of informers in Ulster, let alone to the conviction of terrorists, was this lack of time to question. The details of the laws on interrogating suspects will be examined in a later chapter, but the principal outcome of these was that a suspect could never again be questioned or even be talked to by the Police after he had been charged with an offence, or had had an Interim Custody order, the first step on the road to detention without trial, signed against him. A suspect had to be charged within 48 hours of his arrest, or had to have an Interim Custody Order signed against him within 72 hours of arrest. Because of the pressure on the Criminal Investigation Department, because of the need for administrative action, and for the suspect to be medically examined, be fed and to sleep, this meant that an arrested terrorist was unlucky if he was questioned for more than six hours before being charged. In addition, if the terrorist said he felt unwell, all questioning had to be stopped. Once he had been charged he could never be questioned again—whether he was on remand, on bail or under sentence—unless he agreed to it. The effect of this was twofold. First, there was quite inadequate time to persuade a terrorist of the error of his ways and to induce him to fulfil his civic obligation and legal duty of assisting the forces of law, and therefore a whole array of potential defectors was wasted. The second effect was that there was too little time in the circumstances of a terrorist-affected area for detection. I had dozens of suspects handed back to me by the Criminal Investigation Department of the Royal Ulster Constabulary for me to put them up for detention without trial, with the explanation that the Criminal Investigation Department were sure they were guilty of terrorist crimes, but the 48 hours was running out and they simply had not the time, nor could they mount the necessary effort, to investigate the cases properly and therefore the only solution was for the Army to get the suspects detained. Thus in the circumstances of Northern Ireland, the brief time available for the Police to investigate an offence and to question suspects contributed substantially to the undesirable alternative of detention without trial.

In Northern Ireland no attempt was made after detention or sentence to rehabilitate convicted or detained terrorists or to induce them to follow their lawful duty and assist the Security Forces. The annals of anti-terrorist campaigns such as those in Malaya and Kenya, and the much more recent one in Muscat and Oman, are packed with examples of successful conversions of captured enemy personnel to the Government cause and to their extreme value when subsequently used against their former comrades.[15] The detention centres in Northern Ireland were crammed with men who knew every detail of the methods of operation of the IRA, UDA and Ulster Volunteer Force, and who were regularly updated by relatives' visits. Thus a mine of information and knowledge of the terrorist movements reposed in the hands of the Security Forces in the shape of these convicted terrorists or those committed to detention without trial. This mine doubtless contained not only information but its percentage of defectors. These defectors would have been prepared to return to their lawful allegiance and duty either because their hearts had changed, or alternatively because they had been offered release or some other inducement in return for defection. One of the manifestations of a certain lack of urgency, imagination and enterprise by the Government machine in Northern Ireland has been that up till the time of writing there had been no attempt to rehabilitate detainees or terrorist prisoners. They have simply been put into prisons or detention camps and left to their own devices, with the result that these places became the Universities of Terrorism.

This situation is well documented over the past months and years, but is perhaps most authoritatively illustrated by some quotations from Chapter 5 of the Gardiner Committee report on measures to deal with terrorism in Northern Ireland, published in January 1975. This Chapter includes the following passages:

... We were appalled at certain aspects of the prison situation.

Prisons of the compound type, each compound holding up to 90 prisoners, are thoroughly unsatisfactory from every point of view; their major disadvantage is that there is virtually a total loss of disciplinary control by the prison authorities inside the compounds, and rehabilitation work is impossible.

Each compound ... engages, if it so wishes, in military drills or lectures on military subjects.

The accommodation should be so constructed as to assist the further segregation of detainees; those who are held under interim custody orders, young detainees, those detainees whose involvement in terrorism is weak and detainees who are fully committed, should all be kept apart. At present these distinctions are not made, with the result that all come under the influence of the worst.[16]

Not only does it seem immoral to send people to prison or to detention for them to be forced under the influence and control of those who wish to destroy the state, but at the most practical level it ignores this source of informers and defectors.

If informers are to be developed in an area which is dominated by a terrorist organisation, then the law must provide for everyone to be compulsorily interviewed by the Security Forces in private. Unless this can be done, there is no means by which the Security Forces can identify those who are likely to help them on general grounds or for cash, or those who are involved in the terrorist organisation but who might be induced to defect or to inform. In a militant Republican area in Northern Ireland no one was able to speak to a member of the Security Forces, let alone walk voluntarily into a Police Station, without immediately coming under suspicion by the terrorists and running the risk of getting a 'knee-job' or 'head-job' for his 'treachery'. Therefore if the population is to be spoken to and Government supporters contracted and identified and waverers induced to become active helpers, it is essential for there to be some legal means of compelling people to be interviewed. In order to disguise one friendly citizen, it may be necessary to interview fifty compulsorily so that no one can identify which of them gave the Security Forces a particular piece of information about the terrorists. If an informer is to pass his information to the Security Forces, often the only safe way is to arrest him along with plenty of others so as to conceal his identity. He cannot telephone his information because of terrorist telephone tapping,[17] and the terrorists' habit of destroying all telephones that are not controlled by one of their own members in an area.

The identification of potential informers both within the terrorist ranks and outside them, and the need to protect those who are already working for the Security Forces from terrorist revenge make the legal provision of compulsory interviewing essential. The Army has been driven to arrest widely in Northern Ireland in order to contact people, because otherwise it would have been impossible to develop informers, without whom the Army could never have been effective. The legal authority for doing this under the Northern Ireland (Emergency Powers) Act, 1973, is dubious, particularly in the light of paragraph 50 of the Diplock Report on which this Act was based, which states: 'Our proposal does not involve that questioning prior to re-arrest [by the police from the Army] should be directed to any other purpose than establishing the identity of the person arrested.'[18]

We have already said that informers scarcely ever volunteer, but have to be created, and that they cannot be created, nor can their services even be accepted unless the law makes this practicable and lawful for the law enforcers. If the law does not do this, either there will be a dearth of informers and the terrorists will win, or the Security Forces will in desperation go outside the law in order to develop informers. Once this second alternative has come about and the Security Forces have broken the law, there remain no obvious limits compelling them to stop at any particular stage, and all sorts of horrible practices and abuses can creep in, as was seen in Algeria in the late 1950s.[19]

In Northern Ireland the law only barely permitted the use of informers and put many obstacles in the way of their creation and encouragement. The law must accept that informers are necessary. It must regulate their use and development to ensure that their potentially vital contribution to counter-terrorism is fully exploited. It must also prevent attempts to develop informers in undesirable ways outside the law.

(d) The lack of clear legal guidance to the security forces on when and how they should act to control street disorder

Street disorder is one of the manifestations of civil unrest bordering on insurrection. It is less significant and less dangerous than terrorism, but nevertheless it must be suppressed if the Government is to remain in control. Street disorder ranges from a fight with political overtones outside a pub to a full-scale riot.

In Northern Ireland it mostly took the form of incessant 'aggro' in the Republican areas of Londonderry and Belfast. 'Aggro' in this context meant groups of youths and girls stoning, jostling and abusing troops and Police or their vehicles. If the troops or Police tried to make an arrest, a crowd would gather with amazing speed and try to prevent the troops reaching their quarry. Sometimes the crowd would physically drag an arrested man out of the hands of the troops. Street disorder also meant the fight, not unlike a rugger scrum, that would take place in and outside a pub or a dance hall if the troops tried to arrest a wanted man inside. All the drinkers or dancers would struggle with the troops to cover the escape of the wanted man.

Street disorder of a minor sort was in itself pretty harmless. It was its interaction with terrorism that made it so serious in Northern Ireland. If a dozen youths stoned the Police in England they would be arrested by the Police, but in Northern Ireland the youths were likely to be covered by waiting gunmen who would find the soldiers or Police involved an easy target. Even if nothing so lethal were to happen, a few Police or military attempting an arrest could start the build-up of quite serious rioting by people who turned out on the streets to demonstrate their objection to the arrest. Processions, and demonstrations, whether allowed by law or not, to say nothing of funerals, supplied countless opportunities for street disorder on varying scales of intensity.

In some ways street disorder is the ideal means whereby revolutionaries can win political support to their cause. Young people who have participated in a riot, perhaps through curiosity, drink or love of excitement, become emotionally committed to the cause for which they have rioted. If the Government is to preserve its authority, it must attempt to suppress the street disorders, but the means necessary to do this inevitably weigh on uncommitted people on the fringes of the riot and tend to alienate them. Street disorders provide the terrorists with some of the best propaganda. Television and newspaper photographs only show in narrow focus a few episodes from an affray that may have lasted for hours. They seldom if ever convey any sense of context, of what they display being the result of what has gone before or any hint of what might have been prevented by a particular action of the Security Forces. The actions of the Security Forces in suppressing street disorder tend to be more photogenic than those which have led to them being taken. Four burly soldiers, for example, are shown dragging off one pathetic-looking little man, yet this same man may have been throwing paving stones at them five minutes earlier. Hence the general impression given is of bullying troops and Police grinding down the local population, when, in a broader context, the exact reverse might have been the case. As Lord Justice Scarman pointed out in his Report on the Red Lion Square disorders:

It became clear in the course of my Inquiry that many of those making allegations of police brutality had only seen the forceful conclusion of an incident, and were in no position to judge whether the degree of force used was justified.[20]

Street disorder in Northern Ireland, ranging from minor 'aggro' to major riots, was often started for the propaganda purpose of developing situations that would produce publicity to discredit the Security Forces.[21] All street disorder was conducted by all parties with its propaganda outcome in mind. This was so whether or not it had in fact started for this purpose or with some other aim in mind such as the prevention of an arrest.

The biggest handicaps for the Security Forces in Northern Ireland in dealing with street disorder were not ones of tactics or weapons, but once again turned on the law. There were two main handicaps, one major and one minor. The major handicap was the doctrine of 'reasonable force'—the answer to the rioter's prayer! The minor handicap was the lack of lawful authority for troops to arrest citizens for being disorderly, for obstruction or for assault, until the matter was rectified by Section 12 of the Northern Ireland (Emergency Provisions) Act, 1973.

A soldier has the same rights to use force in the suppression of street disorder as any other citizen, except for a constable who has more rights than the soldier or the citizen. These rights are set out for England and Wales in Section 3 of the Criminal Law Act 1967:

(1) A person may use such force as is reasonable in the circumstances in the prevention of crime, or in effecting or assisting in the lawful arrest of offenders or suspected offenders, or of persons unlawfully at large.

(2) Subsection (1) above shall replace the rules of the common law on the question when force used for a purpose mentioned in the subsection is justified for the purpose.

The equivalent act for Ulster is the Criminal Law Act (Northern Ireland), 1967. Section 3 of this Act only differs slightly from the English Act and runs as follows:

(1) A person may use such force as is reasonable in the circumstances in the prevention of crime, or in effecting or assisting in the lawful arrest of offenders or suspected offenders or of persons unlawfully at large.

(2) Subsection (1) shall replace the rules of the common law as to the matters dealt with by that subsection.

It is not entirely clear whether these statutes have in fact altogether replaced the common law, but fortunately the provisions of the latter are very close to those of the former. On 18 August 1911 the Law Officers gave their opinion on the common law as: 'They [soldiers] are bound to use such force as is reasonably necessary to protect premises over which they are watching, and to prevent serious crime or riot.'

The soldier is therefore required to use 'reasonable' force in the suppression of street disorder. But his problem is to know not what is 'reasonable' to himself, but what will be 'reasonable' to the courts and to public opinion, for it is they who will be the judges of his actions. How does the soldier know what is reasonable? To answer this, reference is usually made to paragraph 23 of the Criminal Law Revision Committee's Report:

No doubt if a question arose on clause (now Section) 3, the court, in considering what was reasonable force, would take into account all the circumstances, including in particular the nature and degree of force used, the seriousness of the evil to be prevented and the possibility of preventing it by other means; but there is no need to specify in the clause the criteria for deciding the question.

Such ambiguities and equivocations are useless as a guide to an eighteen-year-old 'kid' of modest intelligence in uniform in Northern Ireland or anywhere else, faced by a rioting mob. The soldier needs much clearer instructions than these on how much force he may use. 'Reasonable force' can mean quite different things to different people. The idea of a general concept of 'reasonable force' may have sufficed when the group called upon to judge was itself 'reasonably' homogeneous and 'reasonably' predictable. These conditions no longer apply, if in reality they ever did. Indeed in a situation like that in Northern Ireland the soldier can be 'absolutely' rather than 'reasonably' sure that his actions will not be viewed as 'reasonable' by all parties to the dispute and their supporters. He needs to be able to say to the rioters: 'The law is this. If you do so-and-so, then such-and-such consequences will follow.' Not only would this give the soldier some idea of what was expected of him, but it would also make his actions far more predictable to the disorderly than they are at the moment. The absence of predictability produced in the Security Forces in Northern Ireland by the doctrine of 'reasonable' force has led to many violent clashes which neither side intended, simply because the military acted differently from the way the rioters had expected. The doctrine of 'reasonable force' gives the soldier no guidance as to what he should do, but by implication it anticipates that, whatever he does, he will be charged in court and if justified will be acquitted. No one wants to be charged with manslaughter or murder or even assault, and the military, having no idea of what would be considered 'reasonable', tended to permit street disorder in order to avoid this possibility. This absence of guidance was one of the prime reasons behind the frequent inability of troops to put an end to rioting and stone-throwing in Northern Ireland; it was one of the prime reasons for the repeated television pictures portraying British soldiers standing about being showered with bricks while they remained inactive. They should either have been there to suppress disorder, or not been there at all. One of the greater wrongs done to the young soldier in Northern Ireland was this failure to give him adequate guidance on what was expected of him in the suppression of riots and disorders, but to expect him to interpret vague laws and ill-defined concepts at the peril of his life and liberty.

The problem of proving that a riot has taken place is a central difficulty in its suppression. Since the repeal in 1967 of the Riot Act of 1714, it has been a matter of opinion whether a riot is taking place or not. Writing in the *Juridical Review* in 1972, Lord MacDermott, formerly Lord Chief Justice of Northern Ireland, defined a riot as 'a tumultuous meeting of three or more with a common purpose which they proceed to put into execution with force and violence such as to alarm a person of reasonable firmness and courage'. With experience of hundreds of charges for riotous behaviour in Northern Ireland, I found that by far the hardest part in securing the conviction of a rioter was to prove the existence of a riot. In Northern Ireland anyone accused of rioting could produce an array of witnesses to declare that all that had taken place was a peaceful protest demonstration with perhaps a little jostling.

A serious and dangerous riot once took place outside the Springfield Road Police Station in which some four tons of stones were thrown at the Station and its defenders, as members of my battalion discovered when they came to clear them up. One of the leaders of the riot was a particular youth, well known to the Security Forces, who had seen him throwing stones on this occasion, but relied for the prosecution on a clear still photograph of him outside the Police Station holding a stone in his hand. He appeared in court accompanied by several uncles and aunts who swore that he had been on his way to play Ludo at his grandmother's. The youth said that while passing the Springfield Road Police Station on his way, he had seen a stone lying on the ground, and fearing that some of those dreadful youths might throw it at the soldiers, he had picked it up to carry it away from a place where it could be used as a missile. It so happened that the photograph had been at the moment he had picked up the stone for this law-abiding purpose. He was acquitted! Within a month, he had been convicted for his part in a subsequent riot.

In September 1973 the repeated failure of charges of riotous behaviour because of the inability of evidence given by Army non-commissioned ranks to convince the courts that a riot had taken place, led to the Director of Public Prosecutions directing that evidence of a riot should be given by a commissioned officer. This was interpreted in Royal Ulster Constabulary Force Orders as a prohibition on riotous behaviour charges unless a commissioned officer was able to give evidence. The effect of this was to say that a riot could not take place unless a commissioned officer was present—a curious echo of the nineteenth-century joke that the job of an officer was to lend tone to what would otherwise be a vulgar brawl.

The criteria of a riot were established in the case of *Field v. Metropolitan Police Receiver* as:

(1) Number of persons, three at least;

(2) Common purpose;

(3) Execution or inception of the common purpose;

(4) An intent to help one another by force if necessary against any person who may oppose them in the execution of the common purpose;

(5) force or violence not merely used in demolishing, but displayed in such a manner as to alarm at least one person of reasonable firmness and courage.[22]

This is far too vague and too easily disputed to allow the Security Forces to act with confidence against rioters. Particularly in a somewhat diffused situation, it is hard on such an uncertain authority for the individual non-commissioned officer or junior officer, the most likely ranks to have to make critical decisions, to take firm action early enough to prevent disorder from developing. In the Republican areas of Northern Ireland, where the majority are against the Government, it will never be possible to find a general consensus on the justification for military action against a riot. Invariably there will be two diametrically opposed views of the same incident, with each faction backing one side or the other. The impartiality of the media, with their important influence on public opinion, cannot be guaranteed, nor can every media-man be expected to share the official view of the state of disorder. To understand the significance of this it is only necessary to look at Bloody Sunday. There has been remarkably little controversy over what happened on that day. The controversy has centred round whether the extent of the disturbance and its attendant shootings and bombings justified the Army's actions. What is needed is clarity for the military on the question of whether or not a riot is taking place and therefore clarity on both the measures they may take to suppress it and the crime that participators may have been committing.

The problem of arrest in the circumstances of Northern Ireland was dealt with in Chapter 6 of the Diplock Report, where the difficulties of complying with the law on this subject in those circumstances were described as 'preposterous'.[23] Without special statutory authority the soldier has the same powers of arrest as an ordinary citizen. But 'the complexity and obscurity of the law is such that the citizen can seldom be in a position to make even a tentative guess at his rights, either as a person threatened with arrest, or as a private person attempting to effect the arrest of a person he sees committing an offence'.[24] Until July 1973, the law in this confused state was one of the main grounds under which a soldier was directed to make arrests. The soldier's other grounds were the five alternative heads for arrest given him under the Special Powers Regulations 10 and 11 made under the Special Powers Act. Until July 1973 Police or military were not permitted to arrest for assault in a private place—an obvious absurdity. Illegal drinking clubs, much frequented by the terrorists, were private places. If they had been legally licensed, they would have been public places but, being illegal, they were private. If soldiers, or Police for that matter, visited these establishments in search of suspects and the patrons, as was their wont, threw bottles at the troops, the troops had no power to arrest the bottle-throwers. The soldiers' only recourse was to tempt the latter on to the street and incite them to throw further missiles. Since these further assaults would have been in a public place, the soldiers could then carry out arrests.

There was similarly a great need for the military to be able to arrest for the obstruction of a soldier in the execution of his duty. Although no one to my knowledge has yet been charged under Section 193 of the Army Act 1955 in Northern Ireland, this Section makes it an offence for a civilian to obstruct a soldier in the execution of his duty. In Northern Ireland a soldier would perhaps be pursuing a wanted man down the street when half a dozen women would stand in front of him allowing his quarry to escape. What could the soldier do? The chances of the women being charged under Section 193 of the Army Act 1955 were negligible and before July 1973 the soldier had no right to arrest them. He therefore probably had no alternative to watching the wanted man running off down the street. The idea that in the local circumstances the women concerned could be dealt with by way of summons was unrealistic because, except by chance, the soldier could have no idea who they were, where they lived, or whether any identity they might give was accurate or not. They would also, if charged later, produce twenty witnesses to say that they had been somewhere else. Moreover the actual serving of a summons in a place like the Ballymurphy could be a major operation. If by some happy chance a malefactor had been positively identified, it could involve the deployment of a complete rifle company to cover the arrival at the suspect's house of a Royal Ulster Constabulary officer in an armoured car to serve the summons. Such summons-serving as often as not led to prolonged rioting, controlled by the terrorists, against the Security Forces and their bases in the areas where they were served.

Fortunately the situation was saved for the Security Forces in Northern Ireland by the Diplock Committee. As a result of the Committee's report, the Northern Ireland (Emergency Provisions) Act was passed in July 1973, giving wide powers of arrest to a constable under Sections 10 and 11, and under Section 12 (1). To a soldier it said, 'A member of Her Majesty's forces on duty may arrest without warrant, and detain for not more than four hours, a person whom he suspects of committing, having committed or being about to commit an offence.' That section solved the Army's worst problem, but not until the doubt and obscurity of the soldier's position *vis-à-vis* arrest had lasted for too long. Street disorder cannot be suppressed without clear guidance to the military on when and to what extent they can use force, and without their having a general and unequivocal right of arrest.

(e) Powers of a constable for soldiers when they are required to assist the police in policing or to substitute for them

In Standing Committee 'B' of the House of Commons on 19 June 1973 when considering the Northern Ireland (Emergency Powers) Bill, Mr S. C. Silkin, later Attorney-General, said: 'I think one is at liberty to say that if a duty is imposed upon members of Her Majesty's forces to act as though they were constables, then one should expect them to follow the rules that apply to constables.'[25] Mr Silkin was referring to the proposal in the Bill that soldiers should be empowered to arrest on suspicion of any offence without differentiating between the scheduled and non-scheduled offences. It would be hard to quarrel with the principle enunciated here, but he omitted to add the vital corollary: 'If a duty is imposed on Her Majesty's forces to act as though they were constables, then they should be given the legal powers of constables.'

The Royal Ulster Constabulary have not policed the Republican areas of Northern Ireland to any significant extent since August 1969. Unfortunately it was deemed necessary at times to keep up a fiction that they continued to do so. This led to the situation in Crossmaglen and Forkhill in South Armagh. A single policeman was flown in and out of these places by helicopter. He was unable to leave the fortified Police Station defended by a platoon of soldiers. The area outside was governed by the IRA although the Army could, armed to the teeth, move-around it on foot. The Army could not move in the area in any ground vehicle,[26] yet this was described as maintaining the presence of the Royal Ulster Constabulary. The same situation happened in Londonderry, where a single policeman sat in the Bligh's Lane Police Station in the Bogside surrounded by soldiers, but in reality confined to it for lengthy periods. In my battalion's area of West Belfast, it was normal for a rifle company of soldiers to be deployed to cover the movement in the area of a uniformed Royal Ulster Constabulary man. A few brave constables were prepared to accompany Army patrols themselves, frequently disguised as soldiers in military combat suits to avoid being singled out. Anyone whom the Police wished to speak to had to be found by the Army, arrested by them and taken inside a Police Station. The Police were absolutely unable to deploy on the streets to control traffic, check driving and road-tax licences, or stop and question people. In South Armagh, as I myself saw in October 1973, none of the civilian vehicles displayed road-tax licences. The IRA smashed the windscreen of any vehicle displaying such a licence to show that they and not the British governed the area—a view that indeed reflected reality. The absence of Police meant that any policing had to be done by the military, from the pursuit of terrorists to the enforcement of regulations to prevent the spread of foot and mouth disease. Indeed in 1972 Army Commanding Officers in Belfast were ordered to enforce the liquor licensing regulations. Apparently the Licensed Victuallers Association had brought some political pressure on the Government to stop their profits from official bars being eroded by the cheaper liquor sold in 'shebeens' (vernacular for unlicenced bars). There were protests by the military at what was felt to be an unreasonable use of troops, and after a few weeks the matter was dropped. Most soldiers felt that the military should only be used as policemen in enforcing laws directly connected with the insurrection. Nevertheless this underlines the truth that, if the military have been substituted for the Police in an area, then all law enforcement, of whatever nature, has to be done by soldiers. The problem is that soldiers do not have the powers to enforce even the laws affecting terrorism that a constable enjoys.

The Northern Ireland (Emergency Provisions) Act 1973 gave the soldier certain police powers, which are here stated in simplified terms:

(a) Sections 12 and 16. Power to arrest for identification or to question in the street about a recent terrorist act.

(b) Sections 13, 15 and 18. Power to search vehicles, houses and other premises for munitions and kidnapped people but not for documents.

(c) Section 17. Power to enter property and close or divert roads.

(d) Section 21. Power to order an assembly to disperse.

Apart from these powers, the soldier has no more and no less legal authority than the ordinary citizen—a curious reflection indeed that the ordinary citizen and the soldier in the Ballymurphy have exactly the same rights to use a rifle against a gunman. They also have the same obligation in doing so to obey the orders of a military officer or non-commissioned officer. Hence the twenty-three paragraphs of the 'Yellow Card' and its repeated revisions, for it cannot tell the soldier when to shoot and when not to shoot but only give a simplified interpretation of his obscure and complicated position under the common law as adjusted by current policy. This however, is, a diversion, and the concern here is with much less dramatic powers of law enforcement.

The main area in which a soldier attempting to substitute for the Police feels a lack of the policeman's authority is motor vehicle law. Anyone operating against urban guerrillas quickly learns that in principle they do not walk, they drive. Walking is left to the forces of law and order. Indeed the name 'urban guerrilla' is partly a misnomer, for 'urban guerrillas' often operate in the countryside. A more accurate sobriquet would be 'motorised guerrillas'. The effect of this is that they are vulnerable to detection through the vehicles they use. There are a limited number of motor vehicles, all of which have number-plates, to say nothing of engine and chassis numbers. They all have registered owners and histories. It is true that stolen cars are often used by terrorists, but this in itself is a weakness, for anyone in a stolen car or one with false number plates (or, say, 1972 plates on a 1975 car) becomes immediately suspect. There are certain people whose cars are hi-jacked with surprising frequency for terrorist robberies, and a scrutiny of their friends and relations can sometimes produce that vital first clue pointing to a terrorist which can be confirmed or refuted by further inquiries. Driving licences in Northern Ireland have a picture on them and, throughout the United Kingdom they bear the owner's signature. It is true that a terrorist will usually have a false driving licence, but this is not as easy to achieve without arousing suspicion as it seems. Perhaps a false picture does not quite fit the marks of the original removed photograph. Perhaps the individual represented on the licence can be found at home by another patrol despatched by radio to check while the first terrorist is stoutly asserting at some check point many miles away that he is that person.

The problem was that no soldier in Northern Ireland had the right to demand the production, on the spot or later at a Police Station, of any vehicle or driving document. The soldier could search the vehicle but he could not insist on the driver producing his licence, nor could he, if suspicious, compel the certificate of insurance to be produced or the name and address of the owner of the vehicle to be revealed to him. Nor could the soldier issue the driver with an order to produce his driving licence and certificate of insurance at a Police Station within five days, in the way that a policeman can. Only a constable could do these things under the English Road Traffic Act 1972 or in Northern Ireland under the Road Traffic Act (Northern Ireland) 1970. It is, of course, most improbable that a terrorist would comply with such an order to produce his vehicle documents, but this would not matter, and indeed might be the best thing from the Security Forces' point of view. A law-abiding citizen would produce his documents, but anyone failing to do so would, in the circumstances of a terrorist campaign, immediately become a suspect. Even if travelling under a cover name, he would have been seen by a soldier and, if his photograph had been taken at the same time as he was told to produce the documents, his face could be circulated for further inquiries. It would be circulated not only among the Security Forces but also to informers, who would be asked to make discreet inquiries as to who was travelling in a certain car on a certain day under a certain name. Gradually a new terrorist name and personality could emerge, perhaps disclosing a hitherto unknown cell, or perhaps a face could at last be put to a name long known as a terrorist. In such ways as this terrorists are exposed and their concealment ended. Yet this whole fruitful field was largely denied to the military because the power to check vehicle documents and driving licences was vested in a constable under the various Road Traffic Acts, but not in a soldier. It is the irony of so much anti-terrorist debate and legislation that measures which are of peripheral significance in a counter-terrorist campaign such as hanging and detention without trial are proposed and sometimes enacted, while measures that would materially affect the outcome such as empowering a soldier to compel the production of a driving licence go unnoticed.

When the Police have been excluded from certain areas for years on end, then the military who replace them need all the powers of a constable. Any laws in such areas which cannot be enforced by soldiers will simply go unenforced. Thus, for example, if it is decided that soldiers should not have powers to enforce the television licensing regulations, then a decision is in effect being made that the 250,000 Catholics in West Belfast will enjoy permanent free television viewing.

An example of the futility of deploying troops in aid of the civil power without giving them the necessary legal authority to achieve much was provided by the question of Custom clearance certificates on the border between Northern Ireland and the Republic. There were hundreds of uncontrolled crossings across this border. Many of these were not country cart tracks but good-quality, two-lane tarmacadam motor roads, yet these had no Customs post or checkpoint on them, and the border was thus completely open. No British Police or Customs officers have been able to operate in many of the border areas for years, and the only law in these areas, such as it was, was supplied by the Army. Yet the soldier has no authority to demand from the driver of a vehicle he suspected of having crossed the border any certificate or other evidence that he had been through a British Customs post, nor had he any authority to direct such a driver to go to a Customs post or to escort him to one. Nor, curiously, did the Royal Ulster Constabulary have any powers to enforce the border Customs regulations. The enforcement of these was entirely in the hands of the Customs Service Officers under the Customs and Excise Act, 1952.

There are certain powers beyond even the normal ones of a constable, but of a similar nature, that both constables and soldiers need when operating in a terrorist-affected area. The prime one of these is the authority to turn off street lights and to order vehicle drivers to turn off their headlights. To be in a street where gunmen operate in uniform and to be illuminated by street lights or car headlights while the surrounding areas are dark is a truly horrible experience. There were plenty of examples of such shootings in Ulster, but an example from 25 September 1973 is typical. A few days earlier, the Secretary of State for Northern Ireland had ordered the street lights on the Falls Road to be switched on as a goodwill gesture to the Catholics. Inevitably an ambush took place soon after the lights went on at the junction of the Falls Road and Cupar Street. A patrol of my battalion was fired at by four gunmen from positions in the unlit Panton and Leeson Streets. The patrol was quite unable to see where their assailants were with sufficient accuracy to fire back at them with any chance of success. On the night of 8 December 1972 the headlights of a car were switched on in a darkened street. A patrol was caught in their beams, two gunmen opened fire on them from houses on either side of the road but behind the headlights, and five soldiers were wounded. The authority to allow bright lighting in terrorist-affected streets needs to be in the hands of those who have to walk in their glare.

(f) The problem of investigating complaints against soldiers engaged in suppressing civil disorder and of preserving the discipline of the Army in this role

The control and collective accountability of the military when suppressing internal disorder are dealt with elsewhere. There is however a closely-connected question, namely that of the individual answerability of the soldier, or in other words the system used to achieve a disciplined army in these circumstances. In Keir and Lawson's *Cases in Constitutional Law*, it is said that, 'The soldier does not by his enlistment divest himself of the character of a citizen. He is still subject to all the duties and has all the rights of the ordinary citizen, except in so far as they have been expressly altered by statute.'[27]

The Army Act, 1955, is essentially an Act for regulating the relationship between soldier and soldier in peace and war. It concerns itself as little as possible with the relationship of soldier and civilian. Where it does this, it is either because the matter is one in which the civilian is involved with an essentially military matter such as 'procuring and assisting desertion',[28] or because the Army is operating outside the jurisdiction of the ordinary British courts overseas.[29]

Inside the United Kingdom the soldier is liable to be tried by the ordinary civilian courts on any charge for an offence against the laws that apply to all citizens in general. The civil courts cannot try him for military offences against the Army Act. Military courts on the other hand can try him for civil offences under Section 70 of the Act, or military offences which are in effect the same as civil offences, provided that the civil authorities (in Northern Ireland the Director of Public Prosecutions) inform the military that they do not wish to bring charges for these offences in the civil courts.

Under Section 70 (4) of the Army Act, military courts specifically may not try certain offences (treason, murder, manslaughter, treason-felony, rape or genocide) inside the United Kingdom, although they may do so overseas. The principles applied within the United Kingdom are that cases involving soldiers and civilians are normally tried in the civil courts, but that cases involving only soldiers, even if the offences are civil ones, are normally given to the military authorities to try. This works well in, say, an English garrison town like Aldershot or Catterick, is well understood, and gives rise to little trouble. In Nothern Ireland, however, it gives rise to a stream of contradictions. The soldier, seen from his own subjective viewpoint, is at war on active service and subordinate to the close operational control of a coordinated military formation. From the legal point of view, on the contrary, he is seen as one citizen engaged in compelling other and absolutely equal citizens to obey the law. Before the courts there is no distinction between the two sides.

In Northern Ireland many soldiers are charged, although few in fact are convicted, with civil offences ranging from murder to minor assault.[30] This brings three problems in its wake: First, the system for ensuring military discipline can be nullified by the quite different civilian legal system, which tends to weaken the discipline of the Army. Secondly, the soldier can be legally harassed and convicted on the evidence of the very people whose insurrection he is under orders to suppress. And thirdly, the soldier is placed by the processes of military law in a worse position as an individual before the civil law than other citizens; in short, he is deprived of his 'civil rights'.

In the small hours of one morning in October 1973 six rounds were fired from a Thompson sub-machine gun at a patrol of my battalion at the junction of Spinner Street and the Falls Road in Belfast. The patrol was illuminated in the glare of the street lights and could not see the location of the gunman who was somewhere in the darkened area of the Lower Falls.

The patrol fired eight rounds back to frighten the invisible enemy and throw him off his aim, but as they could not see anything to fire at, I considered this to be *prima facie* contrary to 'good order and military discipline', as the guide lines in the 'Yellow Card' directed them always to fire at a definite target, and I charged the soldiers under the Army Act. However eight bullets had disappeared into Belfast, and I had recently received a circular reminding all Commanding Officers that they were not to try cases against soldiers if a civilian interest might be involved unless the civilian Police had supplied a written notification that the soldier would not be charged before the civilian courts. The Police in Belfast were unable to supply such a waiver of civilian jurisdiction, as they could not be sure that some civilian might not emerge weeks later with a complaint that he had sustained damage or injury from these bullets. I was therefore forbidden to try the case under the system of summary military justice which exists for the purpose of enforcing discipline and obedience to orders in the Army. The soldiers concerned got off with a military offence for which a fine or a reprimand might have been appropriate.

There have been a number of cases in which soldiers have been charged before the civilian courts with serious offences such as murder or manslaughter. The near-impossibility of proving such a charge in the conditions of Northern Ireland has led to the soldiers concerned almost inevitably being acquitted by the civilian courts. These cases have taken nine months and more to be tried, during which time the soldier has retained his military rank and in the end got off scot-free without a stain on his character. While in many of these cases the soldier could not have had a serious civil offence proved against him, it was often clear that, whatever else he may or may not have done, he had disobeyed military orders. The reduction in rank of a non-commissioned officer or a period of detention would have been the appropriate military penalty. Yet nothing could be done to take military cognisance of his offence because the matter was in the hands of the civil courts. Therefore, one of the effects of the civil law overriding military law in such a situation in Northern Ireland is that soldiers can rely on their very good chance of acquittal by the civilian courts to disregard military orders which are intended to ensure their proper behaviour towards the civilian population.

There seems to be a parallel between this problem and the objection by the Police in Great Britain to some of the proposals for the independent investigation of complaints against the Police on the grounds that a Chief Constable can only operate effectively if he is responsible for the discipline of his force. The Army engaged in substituting for the Police within the United Kingdom appears to be the only Police Force which is supposed to remain disciplined and effective while responsibility for investigating complaints against it is vested in quite separate authorities.

Any complaint by a civilian against a soldier in Northern Ireland has to be fully investigated by the Police, and their report has to go to the Director of Public Prosecutions.[31] The Police in Northern Ireland have no discretion to reject complaints which are either trivial in the circumstances of Northern Ireland or do not have a reasonable basis of probability. For example, a full Police investigation was carried out in 1973 into an allegation that one of my soldiers had knocked over a beer glass in Beacon's Bar at the junction of the Falls Road and the Springfield Road, while he was searching for a wanted terrorist with the rest of his section. The making of a malicious or frivolous complaint is not, legally, an offence, although it seems that it might be possible, under Section 5 (3) of the Northern Ireland Criminal Law Act, to charge someone who put in a completely unfounded complaint with wasting Police time. However, it appears that no such charge has been preferred. As a result, if soldiers took energetic but legitimate action to seek out terrorists and suppress disorder, the disaffected section of the population promptly countered with a wave of allegations against the soldiers. The effect of this was that the soldiers were discouraged, particularly by the vigour with which a complaint against a soldier was investigated by comparison with the often near-absence of investigation into the death of a soldier or into the flagrant breaches of the law which took place continuously around them. Indeed in the Republican areas of Northern Ireland, and to some extent in the more militant Protestant areas, the only group to which the Police could apply the law without incurring the public odium of some group was the military. The effect on the soldiers' morale and confidence of over-zealous investigation of trivial and unfounded complaints against them cannot be underestimated. While complaints against the military must be investigated, a system is required to filter out those that are frivolous and unreasonable before their investigation becomes tantamount to harassment of the troops.

It seems obvious that, just as soldiers are subject to the civil law in the same way as are other citizens, so they should enjoy the same rights as other citizens when accused of an offence. It is curious that in Northern Ireland they have been put in an exceptionally unfavourable legal position relative to other citizens in two main ways. These are that soldiers were denied the right of silence by being ordered to make statements which could be used as the basis of prosecutions against them, and that they were effectively denied legal advice when suspected of any but the most serious offences.

In Northern Ireland the initial investigation of a complaint against a soldier by a civilian was usually carried out by a member of the Special Investigation Branch of the Military Police. However under Section 28 (1) of the Northern Ireland (Emergency Provisions) Act, 1973, all military policemen were also constables, and in this role the military policeman acted as a constable under the orders of the Royal Ulster Constabulary, who were in charge of the investigation. The soldier being investigated was ordered to make a statement under Section 34 of the Army Act, 1955, which required him to obey a lawful command, on the grounds that such an order complied with the requirement that a lawful command must have a military purpose and that was a military duty for a soldier to report to his military superiors what has happened in an incident in which he has been involved.[32]

In fact this is something of a fiction because a quite separate military report would have been made by the soldier to his immediate superior, which, amalgamated with other factors and information, was passed up the chain of command. Until October 1973 all soldiers were compelled to make statements to the Special Investigation Branch of the Military Police up to the point at which they were cautioned. Since then, as a matter of practice, because of its unfairness, the Military Police have not compelled identified suspects to make statements. However in a case in which a whole group of soldiers were accused of a crime, as many of the soldiers who were in the area at the time as possible would be ordered to make statements as witnesses until from these statements one or more of the group emerged as suspects. These were then permitted not to make further statements. However, by then it was too late, and they would already have made statements. If the offence was a scheduled terrorist offence under Schedule 4 of the Northern Ireland (Emergency Provisions) Act, 1973, then under Section 6 of the same Act these statements became admissible in court, subject only to the provisos that they must not have been induced by torture or inhuman or degrading treatment. Even if the offence was not a scheduled one, the Military Police—acting as special constables under the direction of the regular Royal Ulster Constabulary—had to hand all statements obtained to the Royal Ulster Constabulary, who in turn, without any discretion, had to pass all these to the Director of Public Prosecutions. Thus a soldier was totally denied the right to remain silent and not to convict himself referred to in such ringing tones by the Judges in *Rice* v. *Connolly* and *Dibble* v. *Ingleton*:

... Though every citizen has a moral duty or, if you like, a social duty to assist the police, there is no legal duty to that effect, and indeed the whole basis of the common law is the right of the individual to refuse to answer questions put to him by persons in authority, and to refuse to accompany those in authority to any place, short, of course, of arrest.[33]

All these factors were highlighted in the case of *Regina* v. *Riley and Rimmer* against whom a *nolle prosequi* was entered at the Belfast City Commission on 21 January 1975. Riley and Rimmer were members of a patrol that searched a house in the Ballymurphy on 25 October 1973 accompanied by the occupier who signed a certificate when they left that nothing was missing. They were searched on leaving by their non-commissioned officer. Eight hours later someone who had been away from the house entered a complaint that the soldiers had stolen a diamond ring. All the soldiers were ordered to make statements without being cautioned. From these it emerged that Riflemen Rimmer and Riley had been the two who had accompanied the occupier round the house. They became the suspects and their statements were passed to the Director of Public Prosecutions. These statements formed the whole basis of the prosecution against them and were passed to the Judge as depositions. Unlike any other citizen, they had had no freedom to remain silent and were prosecuted on the basis of the statements they had been ordered to make, without caution, under Section 34 of the Army Act.

A policeman who is under investigation is treated much more leniently than this. A refusal by a policeman to make a statement to an investigator of a complaint against the Police as a witness would be respected, even though this might be required as the 'duty statement' which he can be ordered to make to his superiors under Police regulations. Such 'duty statements' are, moreover, precluded by Police regulations, although not in law, from being used in evidence in court against the policeman who made them. Even if the policeman were disciplined for refusing to make a 'duty statement', this would be under the Police discipline regulations. The maximum penalty under these is dismissal from the Police Force, not imprisonment for years as could be awarded by a court martial to a soldier making a similar refusal. In his book *Police Powers*, L. H. Leigh says of the investigation of complaints against policemen:

It seems right to conclude that a suspected policeman is accorded rights as ample as those accorded to a person charged on indictment, especially now that oral confrontation need not be part of the preliminary enquiry.[34]

The same could not hitherto be said of the investigation into allegations of misconduct by soldiers in Northern Ireland.

What then happened to the protection the soldier could expect to enjoy under the 'Judges' Rules'? The 1964 Judges' Rules, Section (C) of the Preliminary, stated that 'every person at any stage of an investigation should be able to communicate and to consult privately with a solicitor'. The 1918 Judges' Rules, which may be the ones applied in the courts of Northern Ireland, did not mention access to legal advice by persons involved in an investigation, but Royal Ulster Constabulary Force Orders directed that any suspect should be allowed access to his legal adviser,[35] and there is no reason to suppose that the Northern Ireland judges differed on this point or as regarded the right of witnesses to have access to legal advisers from the 1964 Judges' Rules as applied in England. The 1964 Judges' Rules did not state 'every suspect' but 'every person', and the right of access to legal advice therefore applied as much under these rules to witnesses as to suspects. It seems therefore that every soldier involved in an investigation should have had the right to demand and receive qualified legal advice before saying anything to the Special Investigation Branch of the Military Police or to the Royal Ulster Constabulary. In theory the Army supplied this service in the shape of the Army Legal Services, but there were no more than two Army Legal Service officers in Northern Ireland. From time to time there were three and sometimes there was only one, but two was the usual number. There were, however, 15,000–20,000 soldiers and at times many hundreds of complaints. These Army Legal Service officers were on the staff of the General Officer Commanding: they were responsible for broader legal advice to him and to any other officer who needed it in the legalistic atmosphere of Northern Ireland. Moreover these Army Legal Services officers, who were supposed to advise soldiers under investigation, were also responsible for supervising the legal aspects of the Military Police inquiries into complaints against soldiers. Clearly any attempt to give every soldier, who ought to have had it, legal advice from these two officers would immediately have brought the system to a standstill.

The word was sent round in September 1973 that the advice of the Army Legal Services should only be sought in serious cases. But the problem was that no one could know which cases were going to be serious until there had been some sort of preliminary investigation. Sometimes the most dramatic incidents involving civilian deaths did not involve even a single complaint by the public. Equally the most trivial-seeming incident could lead eventually to the conviction of a soldier for something like assault. This situation meant that Regimental officers had to be involved in looking into the cases of all soldiers who were the subject of investigations in order to filter out those few which called for qualified legal advice. The Regimental officer had no legal status in this role of second-class solicitor; he had inadequate legal knowledge, and should anyway have been spending his time and energy in pursuing terrorists rather than in struggling with legal problems. The individual civil rights of soldiers who were involved in investigations of alleged misconduct by the military while engaged in suppressing disorder have been largely denied him up to the time of writing and urgently need to be safeguarded.

A further kind of legal support needed by the military engaged in suppressing civil disorder is financial help to soldiers who are the subject of civil wrongs such as libel. The Ministry of Defence has on rare occasions offered such support to soldiers who have been grossly libelled, but the Ministry of Defence was not prepared to support civil actions by soldiers in the case of unspectacular libels. This is understandable and probably correct, since it does not seem appropriate for a Ministry to pursue a large number of actions of which a proportion are certain to fail. At the same time, it seems wrong that soldiers should have no redress for damage to their reputations. It also seems desirable that the press, politicians and members of the public should be under some pressure to moderate what they say about soldiers to that which is defensible in a libel action. Moreover in the propaganda battle, which plays such an important part in a counter-insurgency campaign, it is normally assumed by the public at large that a statement denigrating a soldier is true if it is not challenged in court.

It is quite unrealistic to think that soldiers normally have the means to support such legal actions out of their own pockets. It therefore seems that some scheme is needed to finance soldiers who have substantial grounds for seeking redress in the courts for libels and other civil wrongs done to them. Perhaps it should be similar to the 'Medical Defence Union' which protects doctors. There is no reason why such a scheme should not be wholly or in part financed by voluntary contributions from soldiers, but it is up to the Ministry of Defence to organise it.

PART II

PROPOSALS FOR IMPROVING THE CONSTITUTIONAL STRUCTURE FOR COUNTERING INSURGENCY

3

PROPOSALS TO RATIONALIZE THE CONSTITUTIONAL STATUS OF THE MILITARY ENGAGED IN COUNTERING INSURGENCY WITHIN THE UNITED KINGDOM

(a) To narrow the gulf between constitutional theory and current practice in the control of the military

The problem that requires solution is that of narrowing the gulf identified earlier between the eighteenth-century law on the control of the military in suppressing civil disorder and the twentieth-century practice; and to do so in such a way that internal security is effective and reflects modern political realities, but in such a way also that the military cannot become an instrument of tyranny, either independently or at the hands of some misguided although constitutionally elected politicians.

On the one hand there is the Scylla of the military complying with the letter of the theoretical constitutional rules, but in fact following an independent policy. Such a situation could arise if the military were to respond on their own initiative to the requirement for them to suppress civil disorder, and if for example they were to disperse by force—possibly lethal force—turbulent strikers collectively breaking the law. On 10 February 1972, during the strike by the National Union of Mineworkers, some 6,000 demonstrators forced the closing of the gates of the Saltley Coke Depot near Birmingham illegally by intimidating the Police.[1] In strict constitutional theory the military had not merely a right, but a clear duty, to suppress such a riotous assembly by force and to restore the situation to one which the Police could control. For the Army to have taken such action would not have reflected the will of the people or of Parliament, but it seems likely that any soldiers who had done so would have had to be acquitted in court of breaking the law and could only have been commended for upholding the constitution. Even if some individual soldiers had been tried for some offences, the processes of the courts are so slow, particularly if appeals have been lodged, that this would have been unlikely to have much effect on the political and constitutional uproar that would have arisen from such an affair. Perhaps 'Bloody Sunday' and the Widgery Tribunal supply parallels, for although Lord Widgery reported with great speed—seventy-eight days after the event—the political consequences of that day seem to have been unaffected by either the outcome of his enquiry or the knowledge that it was being held.

Equally the military might in some similar predicament show more political sensitivity, and only act independently on their own initiative to suppress civil disorder as required by the law if they thought such action had the support of public opinion. Although the consequences of acting on such a basis would probably be less traumatic than a strictly legalistic interpretation of their duty, the long-term consequences might be worse, for the military would have become an independent estate within the realm, with an independent opinion and interest of its own. It is true that currently a Chief Constable is more or less in this position, but no Chief Constable has nation-wide authority to control Police. Each one has a limited territory in which he can exercise his independent authority,[2] unlike the Army which is national in extent and has no rivals in the state. If the military acted strictly in accordance with the theoretical law, they would at least be subject to some limits and be to some extent predictable. If they modified this to an idea of the military only applying the law as far as it was currently acceptable to public opinion, they themselves would be the arbiters of this acceptability. The legal restraints on whom they chose to tolerate and whom to disperse would have been removed. The military would be compelled to choose between the supporters of different political factions, and would thus become, even with the best of intentions, a separate political force themselves. One of the blessings of Britain at the time of writing is that the Army is not, as in so many countries, a separate political faction. The Army is politically important because it is a significant function of the state. There may be, to some extent, an Army lobby that, for example, presses for more armaments or against the amalgamation of the Argyll and Sutherland Highlanders with another regiment, but the support or disapproval of the Army is of no significance in current British politics. The idea that the Army should therefore continue to act as independent crown officers without subjection to the political executive, but at the same time exercise independent judgement and 'political sensitivity' over the extent to which they act to suppress civil disorder is, in the long term, a dangerous one.

The Charybdis consists of making the Army too subservient to Cabinet authority. In view of current doctrines of the sovereignty of Parliament, this may at first sight seem a strange danger to have to guard against. It must be remembered that Parliament does not lose its sovereignty if the military are subject to the law, for Parliament can pass what laws it chooses, but—and this is the point—it can only do so after proper debate and with full public knowledge of what these laws are, and what therefore are the rights and duties of both soldier and civilian. The important distinction is whether the standard of law enforcement is by known laws or by the daily changing whim of the executive. It is subservience of the military to the executive, rather than to Parliament, that is the danger. The Cabinet are human and are politicians and are therefore inevitably highly sensitive to day-to-day political pressures. If they are able to respond to these pressures, they will tend to do so, and the result will be, as it has been in Northern Ireland, law enforcement in terms of the most recent atrocity. In Northern Irish terms this meant that one week the Protestants were 'hammered', while the Catholics had it easy, and the following week the situation was reversed. The military become unpredictable and neither they nor the disorderly citizens know where they stand or what laws will be enforced against them or to what extent. In short, the game no longer has any rules, and the law tends to be enforced against the temporarily unpopular, while the popular have their midsdemeanours ignored. While Parliament as a whole is of course subject to the same pressures as the Cabinet, it seems less volatile than Cabinets, and moreover requires time, debate and publicity before the rules can be changed.

A far worse danger, however, is that of the political executive falling into the hands of tyrants who find in a subservient Army the perfect instrument for their oppression, or at least one that is not prepared to fulfil the constitutional duty that it shares with all citizens of removing tyrants who act outside the law and the constitution. Hitler, after all, came to power in Germany by more or less constitutional processes. The question why the German Army, as crystallized by the German General Staff, did not remove Hitler in, say, late 1942, by which time it was obvious that Germany was unlikely to gain anything from prolonging the war, must continue to fascinate posterity. The reasons are complex and not yet fully explored, but a significant factor in restraining the German Army from such a desirable 'coup' seems, according to the German officers with whom I have discussed it over the years, to have been the feeling among the officers of the time that they had taken an oath to Hitler and that their honour, by which they set great store, prevented them from breaking it. Furthermore, they thought of him as the constitutional head of Germany and believed that it would therefore be wrong to act against him. When a Standing Army was first established in England, it was seen, as far as internal disorder was concerned, as the direct instrument of the executive, at that time the Crown.[3] As a result of the events that led to the 'Glorious Revolution' of 1688 there was fear that a Standing Army might be used by the executive to oppress the people and Parliament. Therefore the first Mutiny Act, which was part of the Constitutional Settlement of 1688, at Section 6 contained the proviso that 'nothing in this act contained shall extend or be construed to exempt any officer or soldier whatsoever from the ordinary process of Law'.[4] As has been truly said of this Section,

This declaration annihilated at once the assumption put forward in all the Articles of War, that the soldier was only amenable to his military superiors and owed no allegiance to, as receiving no benefits from, the civil institutions of his country.[5]

The story of the use of the military for the suppression of civil disorder in the eighteenth century was largely the story of control of the military in this role being taken out of the hands of the executive and put into the hands of the courts. Hence the present theoretical doctrine was evolved by which the troops are in theory subject only to the courts and not to the executive in the suppression of civil disorder.

Democracy can be manipulated, and elected politicians, possibly with the worthiest of motives based on a conviction of their own rectitude, can act like tyrants. Our forefathers were wisely percipient in removing the control of the military engaged in internal peace-keeping from the direct hands of the executive, and it would seem unwise for us to put it back there without sufficient checks and balances. Perhaps a middle course can be found in the way outlined below which reflects the realities of modern communications, provides some check on the unfettered control of the military by the executive, but equally recognises that in a modern democracy the elected Government must have a considerable say in the use of troops within the realm.

The first step seems to be to enact that the military cannot intervene in civil disturbance without the express authority of the executive. This would avoid the unwanted intervention of some over-zealous and legalistic soldier in, say, a demonstration in Grosvenor Square. It would moreover be no more than a return to the position of the early eighteenth century when, up to 1766 at least, the military could not move to aid the civil power without such a warrant from the National Government.[6]

However, once they have intervened on the warrant of the Cabinet, it seems, for the reasons given above, that there must be predictable limits on what the troops will do and will not do. In short they must comply with the law, but the law is fairly broad, and can set the upper and lower limits to the actions of the military. Within these limits the Cabinet must be able to issue directions to the military. It would be quite unrealistic to propose anything else.

(b) To remove the uncertainty from the law during civil disorder by declaring what it is in open court

The foregoing proposals may be little more than an attempt to acknow-ledge formally what is current practice. What is additionally needed is an effective system to see that both the executive and the military do in fact keep within the law. It is possible that a case may come before the courts which calls attention to some malpractice that took place a year or so earlier. In theory a soldier—for example, a Major with fifteen years' service, a pension to come, a mortgage on his house, and a family to support—might refuse to obey a general order that he thought might be illegal and stand trial by court-martial to establish the truth. However, it is unrealistic to think that there is any practical value in relying on this sort of action to ensure, in the circumstances of a counter-terrorist campaign, that the military and the Cabinet remain within the law. It places too great a burden on the individual citizen and opens him to excessive personal financial and career risk, except in a hypothetical case of such obvious illegality that the abuse would be put right anyway through Parliament stimulated by a press outcry. The military have almost no security of tenure in office to sustain them in upholding the law against a superior authority that wishes them to act illegally. The Judge or the Magistrate has considerable security of tenure. The constable cannot be dismissed out of hand. The politician can appeal to the people. The soldier, however, is totally insecure in his appointment. For example, if the Commanding Officer of a battalion refuses to carry out an order that he considers illegal, the Brigade Commander can relieve him of his appointment for half an hour, appoint one of his own staff officers in his place to carry out the order, and, once it has been carried out, re-appoint the original Commanding Officer. This is a further reason why it is especially important for the law to be clearly and publicly stated when the military are involved in internal security.

It has always been possible for a citizen to apply to the courts for an enforceable Prerogative Order, but this is available more in theory than in practice, being hedged about with centuries of precedent, as well as with the problems of interest and of enforcement. A magistrate's court can seek clarification of the law by 'stating a case' to a higher court, but this involves all the disadvantages of an individual prosecution as a means of clarifying the law. A citizen can take up a private prosecution against a soldier or policeman, but such an individual prosecution is uncertain, usually takes a great deal of time, can be expensive, and suffers from the same disadvantages. Moreover, a great many cases nowadays require the approval of the Attorney-General or of the Director of Public Prosecutions before they can be brought to trial, thus in part negating the traditional English view that prosecution is a basic duty of every citizen.[7] For example, all prosecutions under the Northern Ireland (Emergency Powers) Act, 1973, must by Section 26 of the same Act have the approval of the Director of Public Prosecutions. The Crown can refer a point of constitutional law to the Judicial Committee of Privy Council, but such referral is rare and is not generally available to the ordinary citizen. The same applies to the right of the Attorney-General to refer questions on criminal law to the Court of Criminal Appeal. The problem is not one of esoteric points of law, but of practical questions about whether a soldier or policeman can lawfully perform some particular act or not. A private individual can, it is true, seek an injunction to restrain a person or body from some course of conduct, but there are problems here too. The private individual must show that he is seeking an injunction to prevent some act that affects him personally. If the activity that it is wished to stop is a general one and the citizen's desire is to see that the general law is obeyed, then the Attorney-General has to sue on his behalf.[8] The Attorney-General is a politician and has complete discretion as to whether or not he will lend his name to the seeking of an injunction in any particular case. Thus it is easy and tempting for a Government to avoid injunctions being sought that are inconvenient, or for the difficulties, complications and expenses to become too great for any ordinary citizen, policeman or soldier, to go to court in this way. If the law is to be obeyed and is to limit the actions of the military, the Police and the executive to those which are sanctioned by the law in the circumstances of a counter-terrorist campaign, then the courts must advance from their current practice of considering individual cases that have become historic in the terms of a major civil disorder, and provide a system that will ensure this compliance.

What is needed is a system under which the courts will give a declaration on the legality of Police and military operating methods, and on the legality of orders given to soldiers and policemen by their own organisations. The private citizen needs to be able to approach this court and give evidence of what the Security Forces do. There should be provision for legal aid to be given to those who have a *prima facie* case for a reasonable complaint, and the Crown would be required to defend itself. There is equally a need for the individual soldier or policeman to be able to query the legality of his orders before the court. Provision needs to be made for handling orders with a security classification, for the easiest way to cover up a dubious military order or Police Force Order is for Government officials to give it a security grading of 'confidential', and thus prevent the soldier or policeman from ever querying it privately with his own solicitor, let alone raising the matter in open court. It should however be possible to find a sufficiency of Judges and court officials who can be security-cleared to perform this function. It is also necessary for the military and Police collectively or individually to be able to obtain an authoritative declaration from the courts on whether a state of insurrection or active service exists. There is a minor problem in arranging who should present the opposing case, but this again would seem to be the duty of the Crown.

Such a legal procedure seems to exist already, and indeed to be well over a hundred years old. This, the declaratory action, is ever more widely used for the courts to declare the law when it is in doubt for the benefit of public authorities and citizens or private organisations that find themselves in dispute with these public authorities. In his authoritative book on the subject, *Judicial Review of Administrative Action*, Professor S. A. de Smith says:

A public authority uncertain of the scope of powers which it wishes to exercise but which are disputed by another party may be faced with the dilemma of action at the risk of exceeding its powers or inaction at the risk of failing to discharge its responsibilities, unless it is able to obtain the authoritative guidance of a court by bringing a declaratory action. It is equally for the public benefit that an individual whose interests are immediately liable to sustain direct impairment by the conduct of the Administration should be able to obtain in advance a judicial declaration of the legal position.[9]

This seems a most apposite description of the ever-recurring problem in Northern Ireland of neither the disaffected nor the Security Forces knowing with any degree of assurance the state of the law which is supposed to set rules and limits to their confrontations. This is reinforced by Lord Denning's judgment in the Pyx Granite Co. Case: 'If a substantial question exists which one person has a real interest to raise, and the other to oppose, then the court has a discretion to resolve it by a declaration, which it will exercise if there is good reason for doing so.'[10]

To the best of my knowledge, the declaratory action has never been applied to the sort of situations that have been outlined above. But there are good reasons for declaring what the law is in a situation of widespread civil disorder. It may be feared that such a proposal would lead to a stream of soldiers and policemen querying their orders before the courts. If this is the result, then so be it: if the soldier and the policeman are required to act as individual citizens answerable to the law, then it is only just that they should be given the means to find out what the law is that they are supposed to comply with. A declaration by the court is not enforceable, but clearly the organs of Government would be most unlikely to contravene its dictates. If they or the disaffected did so, then it would be possible, as appropriate, to return to the courts for an enforceable order or to prefer criminal charges against those who did so and thus have the law enforced compulsorily rather than voluntarily. The application of the system of declarations to the circumstances of a counter-insurrectionary campaign, would introduce that element of clarity into the law and the consequent predictability of the Security Forces that has been so dangerously absent hitherto.

It may be thought naive to propose such a wide extension of the area in which declaratory judgments may be sought. However, the courts are capable of refusing to hear those applications for declarations that are unnecessary because the law is already clear, or those that are irrelevant or frivolous.[11] The point is that if the law is not clear, the courts should make it so. It may be contended that the higher courts, including the Court of Appeal, seldom do make the law absolutely clear because they wish to retain the flexibility and scope for adjustment that is held to be an advantage of British law. This may be valid in relation to the law concerning, for example, commercial transactions or trespass, but it does not seem sufficiently decisive to meet a situation such as that in Northern Ireland. In an insurgency, lives and liberties—to say nothing of expensive property—are at immediate risk. The penalties for being wrong in law can be most severe not only for the disaffected and for the Security Forces, but also for the broad mass of citizens as third parties whose lives are made miserable by an insurgency that drags on and on. The urgency of such a situation demands a greater degree of certainty and clarity in the law than may be appropriate in other spheres. It is perhaps legitimate to draw a comparison with motoring law, and to reflect that the urgency of death and maiming in road accidents has led to the creation of many 'absolute' offences and an unusual legal clarity in this whole area.

While this need for clarity in the law for the suppression of civil disorder is applicable when the Police are operating on their own, it is especially needed when troops are involved in this role. This is because soldiers are bound to have significantly less legal training than policemen, and, more importantly, to lack the collective experience of a Police Force of operating in an area of uncertain law. Whereas the young policeman will probably have been guided by his superior officers in what he should and should not do during his first two probationary years of service, the soldier can be pushed straight into an uncertain legal position in its acutest form without experience, advice or a mentor, and indeed nothing to go by but written instructions.

In a letter to the *Criminal Law Review* of March 1975 the former

Assistant Director of Army Legal Services at Army Headquarters, Northern Ireland, from 1972 to 1974, wrote:

Whereas in Britain the mere issue of firearms to the police is still occasion enough to produce newspaper headlines, in Northern Ireland members of the security forces have for more than five years now been conducting military and police operations against terrorists with legal support—in terms of a simple and unambiguous statement of their right and/or duty to use force—it would be over-generous to describe as scant. Whilst the lawyers have engaged in academic debate on the relationship between section 3 of the Criminal Law Act 1967 and self-defence, or on the effect a mistaken belief in the right to use force might have on criminal responsibility, or on the merits of the Australian Initiative, the soldiers and policemen in Northern Ireland have daily faced the Evil Choice [whether to shoot or not] in constant risk of the lives of themselves, their comrades and the long-suffering Ulster public.[12]

The system of declaratory actions should therefore be extended so that a clear declaration on the law is readily available to all who want one with good reason when a state of civil disorder exists.

(c) To clarify the personal accountability of the soldier to the law

The fundamental problem is that the soldier when operating to suppress civil disorder is acting as part of a military force subject to military orders. Indeed, were it not for his status as a soldier he would not be there at all, but he is accountable to the civil courts under the terms of the legal fiction that sees him in these circumstances as simply a private citizen who happens to be passing the scene of disorder.

The resulting clash between the spheres of accountability of the soldier to the civil and military law respectively often places the individual soldier in a personally impossible legal position, as occurred to the driver of an armoured personnel carrier who, on 17 September 1973, was ordered by a Corporal sitting beside him and commanding the vehicle, to drive it across the junction between the Kashmir Road and Clonard Gardens in Belfast as fast as possible in pursuit of a gunman, but who was later prosecuted in the civil court on a charge of dangerous driving for complying with this order. It is unimportant whether he was acquitted or not and whether the defence of 'necessity' was accepted or not. The point is that the driver of an armoured car in the middle of a battle was charged with 'dangerous driving'. A similar problem often arose with traffic lights and 'halt' signs. Military vehicles that stopped at these provided predictable 'sitting-duck' targets for the terrorists. Fortunately new regulations, have been proposed to cover Police vehicles, fire engines and ambulances in such situations, stimulated presumably by the anomalous position shown up by the cases of *Buckoke* v *GLC* in 1971,[13] in which it was ruled that the driver of a fire engine on the way to a fire could 'shoot the lights' provided he took care. The decision was however said to be the driver's alone, and he could not be ordered by his superiors to break any traffic regulations for any purpose.

This clash of military and civil law arises not from stupidity but from the near-impossibility of reconciling certain requirements for the accountability of the soldier when operating inside the United Kingdom. The requirement is for a system that will discipline the soldier in the ordinary military sense of that word, while recognising the realities and difficulties of anti-guerrilla operations. At the same time it must give the citizen proper redress for any complaints he may have against a soldier, and so deny the military a position as an independent power above the law. For Northern Ireland at the time of writing the latter requirement is met, but not the former. The soldier, the private citizen and the terrorist are all treated in exactly the same way. Indeed it is strange that when a soldier is tried for an offence scheduled under the Northern Ireland (Emergency Provisions) Act, 1973, he is dealt with under an act developed out of the Diplock 'Report of the Commission to consider legal procedures to deal with terrorist activities in Northern Ireland'.[14]

To quote again from the letter to the *Criminal Law Review* by the former Assistant Director of Army Legal Services in Northern Ireland,

It is hard to avoid the conclusion that the failure of the law to distinguish adequately and clearly between the use of force on the one hand by those seeking, at the State's direction, to restore and maintain peace in the land as part of their professional duty, and armed by the State with lethal weapons for that very purpose, and on the other hand by those acting in purely private capacities who, if the decided cases are a reliable guide, are frequently contributors to, if not the authors of, their own misfortunes, is a serious and intolerable defect.

It is no good answer that the jury (or, in Northern Ireland at present, the judge sitting alone) will be sure to interpret "reasonable" reasonably, and acquit where acquittal is merited, nor that the sentence in the event of conviction will be sure to reflect a course of conduct judged to be tinged only faintly by unreasonableness. The use of the prosecution process merely to test in public whether a constitutional duty has been performed is an alarming misuse of that process. The effect of a series of such prosecutions on those left to make the Evil Choice in similar situations in the future would be incalculable.[15]

There are two popular fallacies concerning this question that need to be refuted. The first is that military law is a type of law outside the control of Parliament and the democratic process. The basis for military law is the Army Act, 1955, as amended by the Armed Forces Acts of 1969 and 1971, all passed by Parliament. Parliament is always at liberty if it chooses to amend these Acts and so alter the way in which military discipline is enforced. The Courts Martial Appeal Court, consisting of civilian Judges of the Court of Appeal and of the Queen's Bench Division and their equivalents in Scotland and Northern Ireland, hears appeals from the decisions of courts-martial, which can indeed go to the House of Lords on points of law of fundamental public importance. While the superior civilian courts are reluctant to interfere in decisions of courts-martial that concern purely military matters, they are prepared to redress grievances when fundamental common law rights are concerned—such as immunity of person or liberty.[16] Military law, therefore, is as much part of the ordinary national law as any other part, and its wrong administration can, normally, be set right.

The other fallacy is that the soldier somehow enjoys a 'soft option' by being subjected to military rather than to civil law. The facts are contrary to this in the circumstances of an anti-terrorist campaign. On so many occasions it is impossible to prove, due to conflict of evidence or the absence or reluctance of witnesses, that a civilian offence such as manslaughter has been committed by a soldier, whereas it would be comparatively easy to prove some 'absolute' military offence such as disobedience to standing orders governing the use of weapons. When juries were still trying scheduled offences in Northern Ireland, it was usually possible through the Northern Irish challenging system to procure a jury of the religious persuasion that would approve of whatever act the soldier was charged with. It was therefore rare for a soldier ever to be convicted by a jury, due to its sympathy for him, whatever the evidence against him, and there were one or two notorious cases of acquittals of soldiers on this basis. A court-martial, it may reasonably be supposed, would have shown less sympathy for a soldier who had flagrantly disobeyed his orders and misconducted himself.

Military summary justice is much quicker and sharper than its civilian equivalent, and again there is no reason to suppose that military Commanding Officers would be less severe towards their soldiers than civilian magistrates. There is on the other hand every reason to believe that the military Commanding Officer would better understand and be able to assess more accurately the pressures bearing on the soldier in such operations. The great merit of dealing with all soldiers by military law alone is that the soldier would be accountable for his actions in the terms of the instructions given to him. He would not, as at present, be called to account in terms of the legal fiction that these military orders were of no importance, in spite of their being the means by which the state directed his conduct which eventually put him in court.

The law books tend to see the solution to this contradiction of accountability of the soldier in terms of an Act of Indemnity for his actions while suppressing a rebellion. For example Keir and Lawson say that while 'in practice the matter is always dealt with by Parliament, and as a matter at once technical and political it is probably best so arranged', the question as to what would happen if Parliament failed to pass an Act of Indemnity is left open.[17] At one time Acts of Indemnity were the normal course (for example the 1801 Act)[18] to cover acts that the military had committed while suppressing rebellion in Ireland from March 1799 onwards. On the other hand it seems unrealistic in the current political climate to imagine that Parliament would now pass an Act of Indemnity to cover actions of the military in suppressing the rebellion that has been in progress in Northern Ireland since 1969. It is equally unlikely that Parliament would ever enact that the military should only be subject to military law when operating as a formed military force in support of the civil power, however logical this might seem to be. Such a logical way of disciplining the military runs counter to the current fashion for seeing the legitimate Security Forces of the democratic state as of no more than equal status to those who wish to overthrow the law and constitution of the nation. Lord Paget, speaking in the House of Lords in 1975, remarked on this referee concept of the role of the state when civil disorder prevails. It is a concept which sees the task of the state as being to ensure that there is a 'fair' contest between the Security Forces and the insurgents, and from time to time to trim the handicaps imposed on each side to ensure that neither is ever in a position to overwhelm the other. He said: 'The role of a succession of Her Majesty's Governments has been that when faced with terrorism they have regarded themselves as a kind of referee to keep the ring between the terrorists and their own Forces, leaning a little to the side of the terrorists, ...'[19]

It seems, therefore, that the military will be obliged to continue operating under the current illogical system without even the benefit of Acts of Indemnity to lend a touch of realism to the realities of defending the state against armed internal attack. That it is possible at all for the military to carry out their state-appointed task in face of this handicap rests mainly on their generally good chance of an acquittal under the ordinary criminal law.[20] There are however certain things that should be done to improve the situation.

The situation whereby the slow processes of the civil law prevent military discipline from being enforced to the benefit of all except ill-conducted soldiers should be ameliorated. This could be done by enacting that the civil authorities would lose the right to try cases with which the military are competent to deal under the Army Act, 1955, unless the Director of Public Prosecutions had charged the soldier concerned in the civil courts within one month of the military authorities notifying him that they intended to try the case.

The soldier when confronted by the civil law should enjoy exactly the same protection as the ordinary citizen to whom the law purports to equate him. This could be achieved by the following measures. All statements which a soldier is ordered to make to his military superiors as part of his military duty should be privileged, in the sense that they could neither be used as evidence in court nor shown to the Director of Public Prosecutions, nor used by him in deciding whether to prosecute or not except with the express consent of the soldier concerned. Such a provision is made under Sections 135 and 137 of the Army Act, 1955 so that soldiers can be compelled to give evidence at Boards of Inquiry and at Regimental Inquiries. The purpose of this is to enable the complete truth to be elicited at these inquiries and the errors discovered put right, while at the same time the soldiers concerned are not compelled to incriminate themselves. According, for example, to Paragraph 5 of Section 135,

Evidence given before a board of inquiry shall not be admissible against any person in proceedings before a court-martial, commanding officer or appropriate superior authority, other than proceedings ... for an offence against section seventy of this Act where the corresponding civil offence is perjury.

Similar embargoes on the use of evidence are sometimes made for public enquiries, as for example in paragraph 4 of the Cameron Report on Disturbances in Northern Ireland:

In order that expressions of opinion and statements of fact should be made as freely and frankly as possible, and without fear of penal consequences to witnesses or others, the Attorney General, on behalf of the Government of Northern Ireland, gave the assurance that (1) No statement made to the Commission of Enquiry whether orally or in writing will be used as the basis of a prosecution of any person or body of persons. (2) No such statement will be used in any criminal proceedings.[21]

Similar provisions should be made to give an immunity as far as criminal proceedings are concerned to statements which soldiers are ordered to make, as part of their military duty, to inform their superiors of the state of operations.

Lord Goddard, Lord Chief Justice, in the case of *Regina* v. *Harris-Rivett* in 1956[22] ruled that the Judges' Rules need not be applied in the investigation by soldiers of alleged offences by other soldiers, which removes yet another protection from the soldier who is concerned in the investigation of a complaint by a civilian of misconduct by the military. However the Defence Council has voluntarily directed that the Judges' Rules should be applied in the Army. It would seem best that they should enforce their directive.[23] The soldier should be realistically informed of his legal rights. These should be available printed on a card which the soldier would be required to read before answering any of the questions of an investigator. To inform soldiers being investigated specifically of their rights would indeed seem to be no more than a belated compliance with the 'Administrative Directions on Interrogation and the Taking of Statements' accompanying the 'Judges Rules':

Persons in custody should not only be informed orally of the rights and facilities available to them, but in addition notices describing them should be displayed at convenient and conspicuous places at police stations and the attention of persons in custody should be drawn to these notices.[24]

A soldier who is ordered to attend an interview with an investigator in a military location from which he is not allowed to depart is effectively 'in custody', compared with a civilian who can refuse to go to a Police Station unless he is arrested.

The soldier under investigation should also be specifically asked by one of his superior military officers whether he wishes to exercise any of these rights. The special relationship and responsibility of military superiors to their subordinates when operationally deployed should be formally acknowledged: it should be recognised that Army officers have a status which both entitles and obliges them to advise any of their subordinates concerned with an investigation of the best course for those subordinates. A sufficiency of qualified legal support should be available for it to be normal for soldiers subjected to an investigation to receive qualified legal advice before responding to the investigators. The concurrent dual status of the Military Police as both soldiers and civil Police should be ended as far as relations between them and soldiers are concerned. Enlisting Military Police as special constables does not produce problems of their status in relation to civilians because they have no special status *vis-à-vis* civilians as soldiers, excepting certain general aspects in Ulster. The problem from the double status of Military Police arises in their relations with soldiers because of their current use of both military and civilian law, each to reinforce the other and to avoid the protections that each system provides for itself. For example, there is provision under the Army Act, 1955,[25] for a Commanding Officer to dismiss any case which he considers should not be proceeded with. This provides a safety net to prevent the use of statements unfairly extorted from a soldier by the Military Police. In Northern Ireland, however, the Military Police investigator, having used his military authority to extract the statement, then has to act as if he were a civilian policeman, by-passing the military Commanding Officer and handing the statement to the civil Police authorities for the Director of Public Prosecutions. This statement can then be produced at the soldier's trial, or at least in the depositions. It should therefore at least be enacted that a Military Police investigator may act towards a particular investigation either as a soldier or as a policeman but not as both.

It is further necessary to restore to the Police their traditional discretion only to investigate and pursue complaints which appear to them to have a reasonable basis of probability. The orders they have had in Northern Ireland since September 1973 to investigate fully all complaints against the military whether reasonable or not seem to be *ultra vires* and should be withdrawn. In England and Wales under Section 49 of the Police Act, 1964, a Chief Constable has authority to reject unfounded complaints against the Police himself without referring them to the Director of Public Prosecutions. In Northern Ireland under Section 13 (5) of the Police Act (Northern Ireland), 1970, the Chief Constable of the Royal Ulster Constabulary has similar authority to reject unfounded complaints against the Police. It would seem appropriate that a similar power should exist for complaints against the military, when troops are directed to act as policemen. Administrative direction should not be used to order the Police to act unreasonably. Such an order to be valid would have to be contained in a statute. This would help to prevent the Irish practice of harassing the military by a spate of complaints, knowing that they would result in time-consuming and disconcerting investigation. To the satisfaction of the terrorists, these divert soldiers from pursuing them and tend to induce soldiers not to act with vigour and energy in the hunting of terrorists for fear of the subsequent investigations. The soldiers believe that at least a proportion of these investigations, whether well founded or not, will end in their own prosecution in order to display the 'impartiality' of the civil authorities in that a substantial proportion of complaints resulted in prosecutions. A specific offence of malicious complaint against the Security Forces when engaged in supressing disorder should also be enacted, to discourage the rebellious from this easy and legal means of reducing the effectiveness of both the Police and the military.[26]

It is a fallacy to think that soldiers and policemen should enjoy exactly the same degree of protection from complaints against them as every other citizen. They are the agents appointed by other citizens to undertake the task of law enforcement on their behalf; therefore soldiers and policemen, compared with other citizens, become exceptionally vulnerable to harassment by complaint. Hence they need especial protection against this form of attack by the disaffected. Perhaps the precedent should be followed that was set by Sections 141 (1) and (2) of the Mental Health Act, 1959. These give a type of 'personal indemnity' to people, including Police, for actions done in pursuance of the Act, unless there is bad faith or want of reasonable care. No civil or criminal proceedings may be brought against any such person without leave of the High Court. Moreover, such leave will not be granted unless there is substantial ground for the contention that there is bad faith or want of reasonable care. While the old-fashioned blanket Act of Indemnity, to take effect after the end of insurgency, no longer seems suitable to solve this problem, such a running system of personal indemnity as has been proposed above might give the Police and the military the legal protection that they need to be effective in such a violent situation as that in Northern Ireland. It would at the very least sift out the frivolous and malicious complaints designed merely to harass the Security Forces, and leave resources free for the full and speedy investigation and trial of the genuine and serious complaints.

The ultimate aim is not to remove the accountability of the military, but to prevent a situation like that in London during the Gordon Riots in June 1780. Large parts of London were burned while the substantial military forces available stood by paralysed, not by physical fear but by fear of the personal legal consequences if they intervened unlawfully. In other words, just so much legal harassment of the military can be tolerated, but if it is not restrained within bounds, this can by itself destroy the effectiveness of the Security Forces.

(d) To increase the legal advice available to soldiers involved in policing

In a legalistic environment such as that of Northern Ireland, the military require more legal support than they have had so far for the first years of the emergency. If enough independent legal advice were available to them, then it would probably be rare for them to need to query their orders in court. For they would be able to have their doubts answered outside court, as indeed the vast majority of legal questions are dealt with in civilian life by clients seeing a solicitor.

The inadequacy of the legal advice available to military commanders can be illustrated by my own experiences over the question of 'Vigilantes', namely groups of citizens of both religious persuasions who patrolled the streets of their own communities. Their ostensible motive of protecting their fellows from bombers and murderers was frequently genuine, and since the Security Forces were plainly too thinly spread to give vulnerable streets this protection, it would have been unjust to prevent them from providing their own security patrols. However, these 'Vigilante' groups would sooner or later be penetrated by terrorists who would 'take them over' and use them either as look-outs to cover acts of terror or to enforce their rule by intimidation and 'voluntary' cash collections. It has been estimated that the intimidation racket in the Shankill was worth £3 million a year to its bosses.[17]

The 'Vigilantes' were therefore sometimes good and sometimes bad. They repeatedly asked for Army permission to patrol and to stop and search strangers, not altogether unreasonable requests in an ambience of bombing and intersectarian murders. I and other officers used to conduct endless arguments with them about their legal rights, which turned on such doctrines as the right of self-defence—a doctrine imperfectly understood, to say the least, by all parties to the discussions. These matters used to be discussed at higher level Army conferences, and all sorts of rules of conduct for 'Vigilantes'—laying down when they would and when they would not be tolerated and what they might and might not do—were promulgated by the Army. It was not until some months after I had left Northern Ireland that I heard of Section 7 (1) of the Public Order (Amendment) Act (Northern Ireland), 1970, which concerns itself with associations of persons who try to usurp the functions of the Royal Ulster Constabulary and is relevant to what 'Vigilantes' may and may not do. How much better for adequate legal advice to have been available at an appropriate level to expound the law on this and other matters to the military. Indeed it can be thought that the more 'grey' the area of law, the more legal support is required. The law governing the operations of the military in the suppression of civil disorder is one of the 'greyest' of the 'grey' legal areas. Two Army Legal Services officers for 15,000 to 20,000 soldiers was plainly inadequate in numerical terms, but it is also important that soldiers should have access to legal advisers who are not part of the military hierarchy. The Army Legal Service officers are on the staff of the General Officer Commanding and are responsible among other things for implementing his wishes; they cannot at the same time be expected to advise that his orders are illegal, especially since they may have been involved in drafting those orders. This aspect was referred to by Justice Black in the United States Supreme Court in 1957:

Courts-martial are typically *ad hoc* bodies appointed by a military officer from amongst his subordinates. They have always been subject to varying degrees of 'command influence'. In essence, these tribunals are simply executive tribunals whose personnel are in the executive chain of command. Frequently, the members of the court-martial must look to the appointing officer for promotions, advantageous assignments and efficiency ratings—in short, for their future progress in the service. ... They cannot have the independence of jurors drawn from the general public or civilian judges.[28]

There is therefore a much increased need for independent legal advice to be available to the military, so that the most desirable end of all is attained, namely the Army complying with the law because it has its own internal system to help it do so.

Two or three Army Legal Services officers can in reality do no more than advise the General Officer Commanding and his staff. The Metropolitan Police have for example an establishment of fifty solicitors and there are plans for this number to be increased. A comparable scale for the Army in Northern Ireland would be about thirty solicitors. It may be thought that the Metropolitan Police require a higher scale than the military in Northern Ireland because of the wider range of crimes with which they deal. However this is partly offset by the inexperience of the military in policing and their lack of legal training compared with the collective knowledge of a long-established Police Force. It comes to the same proposition that occurs in other contexts: that, if the military are expected to substitute effectively for the Police, they must be given roughly the same means as those enjoyed by a Police force carrying out comparable duties. This applies to the legal support needed by the military as much as to other aspects of Police work that they may undertake. In Northern Ireland the legal department of the Royal Ulster Constabulary was only established in March 1973, and did not function fully until 1974. It was completely occupied in advising the R.U.C. and had no capacity to spare to help the military.

One of the main advantages of giving the military, when deployed in the suppression of civil disorder, qualified legal support on the same sort of scale as a Police force is that these solicitors can 'be around' for general discussion. Their prime duty of course would be to give specific advice to the military on specific questions, but beyond this they would be available to accompany the troops from time to time on operations to witness their legal problems and errors at first hand. They would 'be around' in officers' and sergeants' messes and at interrogations and for 'chats' with commanders. The diffusion of awareness of the law that would thus spread within the military would probably do more than any other single measure to make the military abide by the law in practice and not just in theory, down to the very lowest levels.

(e) To end the common law concept of martial law

It seems that the time has come when the particular common law doctrine of martial law existing as a state of fact deriving from the inability of the civil courts to function should be ended by statute. This doctrine seems to be a device developed centuries ago to ensure that some sort of justice, be it only the will of the Commander-in-Chief, would exist where the civil courts could not operate. It is, however, hedged around with doubts and obscurities, and its use by declaration in South West Ireland between 1920 and 1922 seems to have been ineffective. In this latter case the device of martial law was used to replace the normal civil courts in the areas where they had been made inoperative by disaffection and intimidation. When a similar possibility had to be faced in the United Kingdom in 1940 under the threat of invasion, emergency civilian courts were authorised to operate in the country in case the normal system of justice should break down as a result of enemy action.[29]

In Ulster the inability of the ordinary system of justice to cope with the combination of insurrection and terrorist intimidation of witnesses led to the introduction of detention without trial. At first this was by order of the executive. Then there was a period of semi-judicial process as recommended by the Diplock Committee, ended by the Northern Ireland (Emergency Provisions) (Amendment) Act of August 1975, when straight detention by order of the Secretary of State was reverted to. The great merit of these systems of detention without trial from the point of view of the military was that they were operated by civilian lawyers or by Ministers of the Crown and not by Army officers, with all the drawbacks of a court-martial of civilians. Indeed it is worthy of note that a German civilian, who had allegedly shot a Russian sentry in the British sector of Berlin, was tried in November 1970 by a military court established by the British Commander-in-Chief in his status as 'conqueror' or 'occupier' of Berlin. This court was nevertheless staffed by civilian officials, the magistrate was Sir Frank Milton from Bow Street, and the trial was before Judge Block, who had recently retired from the Old Bailey. This underlines the reluctance of the military to try civilians before Army officers even when legally correct, if they can avoid it.

The idea that the common law concept of martial law gives the military a free hand to do what they please in suppressing an insurrection does not bear examination; the military can be, and have been, called to account after suppressing an insurrection for their actions in the process of doing so. In the case of *Higgins* v. *Willis* in 1921, Chief Justice Molony, giving judgment, said,

Yesterday in delivering the judgment of the Court in *Rex (Ronayne and Mulcahy)* v. *Strickland*, ([1921] 2IR–333), I laid it down that we had no jurisdiction, *durante bello*, to inquire into or pass judgement on the conduct of the Commander of the Forces in repressing rebellion, and I further stated that when the war was over the acts of the military during the war, unless protected by an Act of Indemnity, could be challenged before a jury, and that in that event even the King's Command would not be an answer if the jury were satisfied that the acts complained of were not justified by the circumstances then existing, and the necessities of the case.[30]

Martial law does not therefore protect the military from the consequences of unreasonable acts committed by them while suppressing a rebellion. The civilian-operated systems for detention without trial in Northern Ireland, in areas where the ordinary courts cannot operate, seem a great improvement on *ad hoc* military courts; hence the case for martial law, either by declaration or under the obscure and ancient common law doctrines, seems to have been removed. It would seem sensible to put an end by statute once and for all to martial law just in case some injudicious attempt should ever be made to revive it, and to leave to Parliament the enactment of whatever legislation is needed at the time to supply the best type of civilian justice that can be operated in an area affected by terrorism and insurrection.

4

PROPOSALS FOR A SYSTEM OF CIVILIAN CONTROL TO MANAGE AND COORDINATE THE WHOLE OF SOCIETY IN ONE CAMPAIGN TO END DISORDER AND TERRORISM

We have tried to show above the need for coordinated government to combat insurrection and terrorism. Insurrection and terrorism are based on a multiplicity of interacting and connected causes; their origins are seldom simple, and they must be combatted in the same dimension, i.e. across the whole spectrum of the activities of society. It is dangerously simplistic to see terrorism and insurrection as an economic problem, or a political problem, or a security problem; they are almost certainly all of these. Just as the problem is one of the whole system of society, so the Government must meet it on the basis of a coordinated response by the whole system of government.

The last time that such a situation arose in an acute form in the United Kingdom was during the Second World War, when the whole nation and not merely the armed services had to be geared to one end, the winning of the war. This involved not only civil defence in its narrowest terms, but the coordination of the whole social and economic effort of the nation. The system that evolved for meeting this need was based on the Regional Commissioners, whose story has been told in the Official History of the Second World War.[1] In a typically British way, the authority and coordinating function of the Regional Commissioners was never exactly laid down and continued to grow dramatically in scope throughout the war. Their role, which varied from dealing with the colour problems that arose when American servicemen came to Britain to housing those made homeless by air raids, is, however, well illustrated by some extracts from the Official History of Civil Defence:

There were two considerable gaps, it had been clear, in the structure needed for war—first, means to coordinate the miscellaneous functions of the various Departments involved; secondly, absence of a civil 'chain of command' or machinery for the Government to exercise its authority over passive defence throughout the country.[2]

Another most important example of the Regional Commissioner's coordinating functions could be found in the preparations against invasion and for D-day. Without the Commissioners, helped as they were by the attachment of military and police liaison officers at their headquarters, co-operation between military and civilian authorities would have been infinitely more uncertain than it was.[3]

... The Home Security and Regional (Civil) War Rooms provided an excellent intelligence network and centre for interdepartmental liaison in day and night operation throughout the war; ... .[4]

108

The official history, *Problems of Social Policy*, tells how, from the first intensive air raids on London, the homeless were coped with. Except for its quicker tempo and its ultimate solution, the story has notable similarities to the attempts of Civil Government in Northern Ireland to cope with the consequences of insurrection there since 1969. When the heavy air raids started in 1940, the extent of the homelessness they would cause had been catastrophically underestimated in contrast to the overestimates of human casualties. There were ninety-six separate local authorities in the London Civil Defence Region, each with some part of the responsibility for housing the homeless. At first they simply could not cope, and each night's raids saw yet more homeless thrown on the streets. In one place there would be a surplus of accommodation and in other crowds of homeless, but there seemed to be no way of putting the two together. By mid-October 1940, 250,000 Londoners had been made homeless and the ninety-six authorities had rehoused only 7,000. The stories of the homeless wandering from one Government agency to another and simply being passed on to some other office bear a close resemblance to the same stories told of those made homeless by intimidation in the Northern Ireland Community Relations Commission research paper 'Intimidation in Housing' published in February 1974.[5] Yet in London, unlike Northern Ireland, the whole problem was effectually solved by the end of November 1940. It was solved by the appointment on 26 September 1940 of a Special Commissioner to solve the problems of homelessness in London. He was given wide powers and told to ask for yet more authority if he needed it. This expedient solved what had seemed to be almost insoluble by injecting the simple principle of coordinated management of the whole system in terms of its objective—the housing of the homeless. Moreover this Special Commissioner could compel the idle and incompetent among the local authorities to play their part, however marginal, in solving the problem. However, lack of a desire to do something was not the basis of the problem; this lay in the absence of a coordinating authority able to give orders that would be carried out. The problem reached dramatic proportions since in 1940–1 one in six of London's population was made homeless by bombing. Yet once the system of coordinated management of the whole problem of the homeless had been established under the Special Commissioner, these were virtually all accommodated by the night after they had been bombed out.[6] It was the lack of this effective overall civil management which made it so difficult for Northern Ireland to meet its comparatively small problem of damage and homelessness at the hands of the terrorists. The French have, perhaps, more experience than the British of civil disturbance, and they have a highly developed system for coordinating not only military and civil action, but all the departments of Civil Government. The authority of the civil Regional Prefect in relation to defence, including defence against civil disorder, has been described as follows:

The Prefect of the Region in fact has the majority of the heads of services whose responsibility extends over the Region and sometimes over the Zone, not only under his authority but within his immediate sphere of influence because of their residence in the regional capital and often also because of their departmental functions.[7]

The French system for coordinating civil and military action is itself highly developed and fully coordinated. The boundaries of the civil and military authorities coincide. Joint civil and military exercises are held in peacetime to practise the techniques of dealing with internal disorder. Legislation has been prepared in advance for four situations. In the two least severe of these, including the '*état d'urgence*', the civil authority in the shape of the Prefect has authority to direct the actions of the military as well as those of the Police and of the civil departments. However, if an '*état de siège*' is declared, the military take over authority for the whole Government machine and give orders to the Prefects.[8]

The British colonial system always had the great advantage for a successful counter-insurgency campaign of a coordinating authority for overall Police, military and civil departmental action at all levels in the shape of the Governor, the District Commissioner and the District Officer. While the District Officer did not necessarily have complete authority over every action of the various civil and military services, he was a significant official with overall authority and direct access to the top. He therefore had very considerable ability to weld all the efforts of the Government into a machine directed to one end, the defeat of the insurrection. In Malaya the successful campaign was achieved after the Government had decided to combine the posts of the highest civil authority, the High Commissioner, and of the highest military authority, the Director of Operations, and to give the new appointee overriding powers in every part of the Government of the country.[9] That the first appointee was a soldier was incidental. The point was that one man could order both the civil and military authorities what to do and so ensure that they worked together and that the efforts of the one reinforced rather than negated the efforts of the other.

If then an overall coordinating authority is needed in Britain, how is it to be supplied, and who is to man it? The situation at the top in Northern Ireland, before the ending of the Stormont Parliament in March 1972, was chaotic. Up to that point there were the Northern Ireland Government, the Ministry of Defence, the Home Office and the Foreign Office, each with ill-defined interests and responsibilities in Northern Ireland. At least the ending of Stormont brought with it the appointment of a single political head in the shape of the Secretary of State for Northern Ireland supported by his own Northern Ireland Office civil servants drawn from Whitehall. From that time onwards coordination of the affairs of Northern Ireland has been fairly good at the top, although even at that level the physical separation of the military at Lisburn from the civil departments at Stormont and the Police at Knock has sometimes led to three different campaigns being waged. The evidence for this was the frequency with which Army Commanding Officers in Belfast were told, after being surprised by some new Government action or announcement, that the Army had been unable to give them any forewarning as no political or civil official had in turn forewarned the military. A more effectively coordinated campaign might have been conducted if the 'operations' branches of the Army and Police had functioned from Stormont itself. If it had done nothing else, this close proximity to the military and Police report centres might have educated the British politicians and civil servants at Stormont to the true level of violence in the province or the way the extremist organisations enforced their rule, the stark viciousness of which they seemed not to have comprehended.

It was below this top level that coordination of the Government effort· against the terrorists and rebels petered out, and the Secretary of State 'legislated in a vacuum'. In very general terms, the only organisation that could implement his policy in the Republican areas was the Army. Moreover the Army, as has been shown, was sucked into the highly political area of projecting to the public, via the media, the Government's side of a disputed incident and sometimes Government policy. The arguments for keeping the Army out of the areas of politics and propaganda as far as possible apply with almost equal force to the Police. The job of the Police is to prevent and detect crime; it is not, at least in the United Kingdom, to administer or coordinate Government activities. A plausible case could perhaps be made for putting the military under Police control during civil disorder, but this would only touch the fringe of the problem when coordinating the whole effort of Government to counter insurrection and terrorism. It would immediately be necessary to put a whole array of other services under Police control, such as the fire and ambulance services, public transport, local government officers, electricity supply, establishments such as airports, and some private enterprises such as building and repair contractors. The Police are not trained or equipped, nor are they appropriate for the fulfilment of this role. What is therefore needed in an area affected by insurrection and terrorism is a civilian chain of authority to represent the National Government down to the local level, to be the focus for the support of all the other services and departments of Government and a central source to which they could look for direction and coordination. For the basis of such a system it is necessary to look no further than that established in embryo for the Regional Commissioners in the Second World War. This chain of civilian command should be organised by area, not by function. An insurrection is a malaise affecting every part of a community, not just one aspect of it such as health, and the Government has to counter it across the whole face of the community which is affected.

It is probably easiest to envisage such a system in concrete terms, although the principle could be adopted with great flexibility to fit varying areas and situations. A specific system is therefore suggested that would fit Northern Ireland. A Regional Commissioner would become the executive head of all military, Police and civil departments in the province. His immediate subordinates, subject of course to the limits that the law allows, would be the General Officer Commanding the troops, the Chief Constable, the Head of Intelligence, the Head of Information, and the Head of the Northern Ireland Civil Service.

In the context of a counter-insurgency campaign, the ordinary peacetime Departments of the Northern Ireland Civil Service constitute one 'bloc' in the Government machine relative in importance to the military, Police, information and intelligence 'blocs'. While they have a vital part to play in the overall Government campaign to end the insurgency, they still retain their interest in matters of a longer perspective than those that concern the other 'blocs'. In order therefore to allow them to pursue these other interests, but at the same time to be knitted into the whole restoration of order campaign, they should be grouped under one Head Civil Servant with authority to give orders to any of them on matters concerning the security effort.

In each of Belfast, Londonderry and the country areas of the province there would be a Sub-Commissioner with, as his chief subordinates, the head of the next level down of each of the military, Police, intelligence, information and civil services. The boundaries of each of these services would have to be made to coincide so that there would be no question of one man having his responsibility divided between two chiefs. At the next lower level the same system should be repeated again. At this level, which would be roughly that of the present Police division or battalion area, the Chief Executive should be a civilian District Commissioner with the heads of the same services at the local level as his immediate subordinates. Whether a similar 'command module' would be needed below this level for the Army company or Police sub-divisional area is disputable. It would probably be best to repeat the system again under a civilian District Officer with only an Army officer, a policeman and an information officer as his immediate subordinates.

The Head of Information and the information officers would be a new civil branch established for the purpose of representing the Government to the public through the media, of relieving the Police and Army of their current undesirable involvement in the field of public opinion manipulation, and to ensure that in even the most local and limited security operations the factor of public opinion was taken fully into account when plans were being drawn up. This information service would be a recognition of the obvious but hitherto largely ignored truth, that a counter-terrorist campaign cannot be won and insurrection suppressed unless the Government also wins the propaganda battle, that this propaganda battle has to be fought at every level and not just at the top, and that propaganda is the business not of the military or of the Police, but of the Civil Government.

The Regional Commissioners and their junior equivalents would be civilian appointments. The thirteen commissioners in the Second World War were three past holders of high political office, a former Permanent Secretary to the Treasury and another retired civil servant, a retired admiral, a retired general, a past Director of the International Labour Office, the head of a Cambridge college and four industrialists.[10] The point is that the origin of the Regional Commissioner or of the Junior Commissioners would be irrelevant. They would be in civilian appointments. It would be perfectly possible to have a military man or a policeman in one of these posts, if he were the best man for the job, but for that period he would be seconded to the civil service, would not wear uniform, and would not be expected to control and deploy the military or the Police in his area, but only to give directions to the incumbent heads of these services, who would be his subordinates. The cry sometimes heard for bringing a 'General Templer' into Northern Ireland[11] should not be for a General, but for a single managing director of the Government machine.

The authority of the Commissioner at each level over his supporting service heads would be in the classic relation of the 'line' manager to the 'staff' manager or, in military terms, of the 'commander' to his 'heads of arms and services'. That is to say, the Commissioner could give orders to these subordinates which they would be obliged to obey, but they would have the right of appeal to the next higher level of their own service, who would only be able to have the order withdrawn if he could persuade a higher level of Commissioner to order the Junior Commissioner to do so. The merit of this system is that it would prevent separate services pursuing separate policies and interests. A dangerous way—from the management point of view—to set about organising a counter-terrorist campaign has been demonstrated by the Government 'incident centres' announced by the then Northern Ireland Secretary, Merlyn Rees, on 11 February 1975 to supervise the ceasefire with the Provisional IRA. It would have been better if they had been located in the joint Army and Police stations, because they could have helped to coordinate political negotiations with the Provisional IRA into Security Force action.[12] As it was, they provided yet another separate chain of command operating in isolation from the other branches of Government and therefore inevitably coming into conflict with them for reasons of pure misunderstanding if no other. It is impossible in Northern Ireland to separate political negotiations from the activities of the Police and the military or from economic affairs in this way, because all these activities interact too immediately and too trenchantly for any Government action in one sphere not to have an instant affect in the other spheres. For example, the same street affray that might lead to the breakdown of the ceasefire could be handled quite differently by the military on the one hand and the civil incident centres on the other if they operated from separate locations. Equally, these two branches of the same Government might have quite different information on who was causing the disturbance and on its aims and therefore quite different views on how it should be dealt with. Yet the citizens would see them both as organs of the same Government and see duplicity in their differences of approach, or else simply exploit these to their own advantage. This is why there has to be one coordinated and co-located system of Government management of these situations and not several separate ones. Only thus can a single agreed coherent Government policy be evolved which is therefore comprehensive to the people at whom it is directed.

In the late summer of 1973 one battalion commander in Belfast was so infuriated by learning repeatedly through the clandestine informers whom he handled inside the terrorist organisations of secret negotiations with these organisations and proposals to them from the Northern Ireland Office that were kept hidden from him through official channels, that he set up in his own battalion a 'political intelligence' cell in a separate office with the task of discovering current British Government policy.

The Regional Commissioner would of course be responsible to a Minister—in the case of Northern Ireland, the Secretary of State. Any other responsibility would be unthinkable in a democracy. It might then be asked in what way this would differ from the present system. It would differ less, it is true, at the top level of this civilian chain of command than at the lower levels. Nevertheless, even at the top level the significant effect would be that the Secretary of State would lose his management function for coordinating and controlling the services involved in suppressing disorder. The management responsibility would rest on the shoulders of the Regional Commissioner, leaving the Secretary of State free for political activity.

With the intensity of the troubles in Northern Ireland, no one man can satisfactorily combine responsibility for day-to-day management of the campaign and for running long-term negotiations and policy-making. Indeed it is very seldom that policy-making posts such as 'Chairman' or 'Commander' can be successfully combined with executive posts such as 'Managing Director' or 'Chief of Staff'. In a counter-insurgency campaign it is desirable that they should be separated if they are both to be well performed. This arrangement would get over the lacuna at the top in Northern Ireland during Ministers' frequent absences from the province to attend Parliament or the Cabinet in London. Even at battalion level, the need for executive decisions to wait several days till Ministers returned from London was discernible. An example of the gap created by the absences of Ministers from Northern Ireland was provided by the case of the terrorist who was alleged to have killed a corporal in a North Country regiment in the Ballymurphy. Shortly after this murder, the informer network produced the name of the responsible terrorist; the latter was 'on the run' for three months before being arrested, knowing he was a wanted man. Despite every effort, the Police Criminal Investigation Department was unable to find sufficient evidence on which to base a charge against him in court. His case had already been submitted to a Minister in advance of his arrest in order to obtain prior confirmation that, if arrested, there was sufficient evidence for an Interim Custody Order to be signed against him. The Minister had agreed that, if the Security Forces succeeded in arresting this man, he would sign an order to detain him. However, after the arrest, and in spite of his assurance, the Minister changed his mind in view of the prevailing state of 'low profile' and refused to sign the order. About six hours before the terrorist was due to be released, some very strong additional evidence came to light. This was rushed to the Minister's office at Stormont by an Army officer, who received the reply that it was indeed very damning and would almost certainly tip the scales in favour of an Interim Custody Order, but that unfortunately the Minister concerned with the application had gone to England. The Minister's Under-Secretary contacted the Minister in England, who replied that he would not reverse his decision to release the terrorist until he had seen the new evidence himself. This happened on a Friday afternoon and the Minister only returned to Belfast on the Monday. The terrorist was therefore released that evening. On reading the additional evidence the Minister agreed that he would have signed an Interim Custody Order against the terrorist before his release if he had seen it in time. The terrorist was thus 'on the run' again, pursuing his activities for a further six weeks until he was re-arrested when an Interim Custody Order was signed against him without further demur. This release of the known murderer of a soldier took place because the Minister concerned was in England rather than in Northern Ireland. It seemed an inefficient way to conduct a counter-insurgency campaign and most disheartening to the men whose lives had been at risk in making such an arrest.

At the lower echelons the proposed systems would permit the 'thread of government' to extend right through the province. It would bring all the forces of Government and many of those of the community at large into one coordinated, uniformly directed effort to end terrorism and insurrection. It would put an end to the problem of the Government 'legislating in a void'. It would bring good government down to the level where the efforts made could really be seen and appreciated by the people who had personally themselves to choose between the Government and the rebels.

Junior ministers have hitherto been given functional responsibilities in Northern Ireland. They seemed to play only a small part in affairs there because, in the context of terrorism, responsibility for education or housing had little impact, when the real problems in these fields were not teaching but religious segregation, and not construction but intimidation and squatting. It seems probable that the junior ministers would be better deployed as the immediate political superiors of the Sub-Commissioners. Thus there would be a junior minister for Belfast, a junior minister for Londonderry, and a junior minister for the country areas. This might dilute the pure stream of the civilian executive chain of command from Regional Commissioner to Sub-Commissioner, but it would have the advantage of bringing political involvement, control and awareness right down to the level of operations. It would also enable a junior minister to acquaint himself fully with the complex and interacting problems of a city such as Belfast, and to arrange and answer for their solution as a whole rather than piece-meal. It would also help to end the feeling that politicians and Government are remote and different from ordinary people, which pervades the citizens of such places as the Ballymurphy.

The relationship between the Civilian Commissioners and the elected representatives of Local Government would present problems. In Northern Ireland these would not be too severe since the MacRory reforms vested all the more substantial powers of local administration in Stormont. In the end, however, democracy requires local communities to have their own local government and elected councillors to manage local concerns. This relationship would have to be flexible. If a community were in open insurrection and insisted on electing prominent rebels as its councillors, then almost all powers would need to be in the hands of the Com-missioners, and the councillors would simply be a channel for voicing the views of the community. As things improved, more and more powers could be returned by the Secretary of State to the local councils, until eventually they would operate as in time of peace, with only strictly security matters reserved to the Commissioners. By this stage the insurrection would be nearing its end.

It could be that the warrant from the Central Government directing the military to intervene in civil disorder should also nominate for each military level down to the battalion precisely who is the civil authority the troops are to support. If no such authority exists, then the commander of the troops would himself have to be appointed as the civil authority for the area in question. It might concentrate the mind of Government wonderfully on not neglecting to establish an appropriate machinery of Civil Government if they had to admit any such failure publicly by appointing a military commander as the civil authority because there was no one else.

PART III

PROPOSALS FOR IMPROVING THE LAWS THAT GOVERN THE OPERATIONS OF THE MILITARY AND TO SOME EXTENT OF THE POLICE SO THAT THEY CAN BE EFFECTIVE IN ENDING INSURGENCY

5

A PROPOSAL FOR DORMANT EMERGENCY LEGISLATION FOR COMBATTING DISORDER AND TERRORISM THAT CAN BE INVOKED WHEN THE NEED ARISES

The difficulty in countering terrorism and insurrection caused by over-concentration on court procedure and sentencing, as compared with underconcern with detection and enforcement of the laws, is compounded by another factor, namely that most of this legislation is prompted by some recent crisis and is therefore passed in a great hurry. Thus we have the legislation of the last atrocity to accompany the politics of the last atrocity. This is illustrated by the speed with which the Prevention of Terrorism (Temporary Provisions) Act was passed on 29 November 1974 as a result of bombing in Birmingham. A further illustration was the need to phase out the Special Powers Act in Ulster and substitute for it the Northern Ireland (Emergency Powers) Act 1973. This had to be done because the Special Powers Act, which had only changed marginally since 1922, was found to be quite unsuitable in that it offered exaggerated powers which were not needed on the one hand and yet ignored those that were needed on the other. An example of the first kind was Section 2 (4) of the Special Powers Act:

If any person does any act of such a nature as to be calculated to be prejudicial to the preservation of the peace or maintenance of order in Northern Ireland and not specifically provided for in the regulations, he shall be deemed guilty of an offence against the regulations.

It is possible to think that merely to be a Roman Catholic in Northern Ireland would have been an offence under that section.

Fabian Tract 416 of November 1972 quotes Lord MacDermott, former Lord Chief Justice of Northern Ireland:

... Instead of meeting the problems I have mentioned piecemeal, it would be better and more effective to enact an emergency code for the United Kingdom which would be applicable, as events warranted, to the whole or any part thereof and be operative only in times of crisis. The enactment of such a code would facilitate advance preparations and the implementation of our international obligations; and by its very existence it might go far to discourage subversion.

The *Tract* goes on to recommend that such a statute be made at leisure, which could be implemented in an emergency. This might at least give a chance for Parliament to inform itself from those who have first-hand experience of the problem of what is really needed to combat terrorism and insurrection. At the time of writing Parliament seems to be left to base its debates on the latest press articles and from constituents' letters leaving the unfortunate Members to debate anew the irrelevant and fruitless topics of capital punishment or proscription of subversive organisations. There is already similar standby legislation available to be implemented in a crisis in the shape of the Emergency Powers Act 1920, as amended by the Emergency Powers Act 1964, which provides *inter alia* for the use of troops if the supply and distribution of food, water, fuel or light are likely to be interfered with. It would seem logical to have a similar act to be held in abeyance for use if insurrection or terrorism were to break out.

Perhaps it has hitherto been considered unwise to air these problems too openly because suggestions of a potential Army 'coup' might have followed. Perhaps the need has not been faced because of genuine belief that "it could not happen here", and that it is "better to let sleeping dogs lie". If an article in the *Sunday Times* of 13 July 1974 is correct, there has been since 1972 a Cabinet Committee considering how best to respond to threats to public safety, and arranging for inter-departmental coordination to deal with these. This, however, is not enough if the fundamental constitutional and legal provisions are inadequate; these can only be remedied by new legislation. It would perhaps be wiser to recognise that it just could happen here—after all, something like it repeatedly happens when troops are deployed at London Airport—and to pass the necessary laws with the calm deliberation possible in quieter times. Moreover, it would seem a pity to repeat the situation which prevailed between 1969 and July 1973 in Northern Ireland when the Army had to operate there under constitutional and legal conditions that went a long way towards making it ineffective. To pass such legislation in time of calm might also prevent the wild oscillation of legislation that, at one pole, makes it almost impossible for disorder to be suppressed and, at the other, offers measures of a dangerous and unnecessary severity.

6

METHODS OF POPULATION SURVEILLANCE

(a) Recognising, recording, photographing and fingerprinting a population affected by insurgency

The case for population surveillance in a terrorist-affected area has been made above. Without a knowledge of who is who, what they look like and there they live, the Security Forces are blind. The fundamental tool for defeating terrorism and insurrection is therefore a population census that is usable by the Police and Army, which they can build up and maintain on a basis of specific legal authority.

The first requirement for such a census is that the Police and Army should be given the legal right to interview citizens for this specific purpose. A man cannot be detained or taken to a Police station for questioning unless he is arrested.[1] If he is arrested, he must be suspected of some offence. At the time of writing, therefore, there was no compulsion on a citizen to attend an interview to identify himself. Anyone seen entering a Police station in the disaffected parts of Northern Ireland was likely to be questioned by the terrorists when he left as to why he was there. The terrorists maintained sentries to watch the Police stations and note comings and goings. If the terrorists discovered that the citizen had gone there voluntarily, he would probably be 'knee-capped', i.e. have his knee caps shot off with a pistol, to warn him and others never again to show such co-operation with the Security Forces. The extent of 'knee-capping' and other such terrorist punishments was reported as follows in the *Daily Telegraph* of 5 September 1975,

Known punishment shootings by extremist organisations since the ceasefire in Northern Ireland on February 10, have passed 100—74 by Republicans, 26 by Loyalists. There must, however, have been far more than those recorded.

These punishments, meted out by men to their own communities, include 42 shootings in the kneecap, 40 in the legs, five in the thigh, four in arms and elbows, three through the abdomen and six through other parts. ...

The terrorists had even refined the punishment of knee-capping to three degrees of pain; that is, the 'humane' way of shooting through the thigh muscle, the middle way of shooting sideways through the knee, and the full treatment of shooting through the knee from back to front to give maximum pain and inflict maximum damage.

The Army was therefore compelled to arrest people in the Republican areas simply in order to talk to them. This was done under Section 12 of the Northern Ireland (Emergency Provisions) Act, 1973, which authorised the military to arrest without warrant for four hours. The arrested person was then questioned as to his identity under Section 16 of the Act. However, according to Section 12 (1),

A member of Her Majesty's forces on duty may arrest without warrant, and detain for not more than four hours, a person whom he suspects of committing, having committed or being about to commit any offence.

The vast majority of those arrested by the Army in Northern Ireland were arrested without being suspected of anything except in the most general sense, because there was no other way whereby the Army could find out who were the people living in the terrorist-affected areas, what they looked like or where they lived. The system of military 'headchecking' in terrorist-affected areas had a similar basis. A 'headcheck' was when soldiers entered a house to find out who lived there and what they looked like. The authority for entering the house was either that the occupier had agreed to the soldiers coming in when asked for permission on the doorstep, or that a search had been authorised under Section 13 (2) of the Northern Ireland (Emergency Provisions) Act 1973, but it never took place except in the most cursory fashion. Once inside, the soldiers asked the householder to complete a questionnaire on who lived in the house and a few other points. Sometimes the householder refused to answer these questions and there was no legal way of compelling him to do so. More usually the householder was quite happy to answer these questions as long as he or she could do so in private without being overheard by anyone other than the military, for fear that the listener might inform the terrorists that the householder had co-operated with the Security Forces. As long as the interview had been in private, the citizen living in the terrorist-affected area could always assert boldly to the 'terrorist police' that he had said nothing. The words 'terrorist police' are used because this is in effect the role of certain sections of a terrorist organisation. Indeed I recall one aggrieved householder in the Ballymurphy in the autumn of 1973 complaining, when questioned by the Royal Ulster Constabulary about an attempted murder in the area where he lived, that he had already said all he knew to the Official IRA Criminal Investigation Department investigating the crime, and did not see why he should have the tedium of saying it again to yet another bunch of inquiring detectives!

The requirement therefore is for statutory authority for the Police or Army to conduct a census and in doing so to be able to compel all citizens to attend an interview of, say, no more than two hours in either a Police station, a military base or a private house. Moreover, this interviewing must be done without anyone except the interviewee and members of the Security Forces being present to prevent intimidation by the terrorists. To ensure that there shall be no infringement of the civil liberties of the citizen compelled to come to such an interview, he should be given a card with his rights set out at the start of it, as well as being allowed to take legal advice before being questioned. This identification interview should be sharply differentiated in law and public presentation from arrest on suspicion of being a criminal or terrorist, although there should be a penalty, to be imposed by the courts, on anyone failing to attend without good reason. To avoid the problem of over-frequent re-interviewing, it would probably be best if the Security Forces were allowed to compel attendance at such an interview only once every six months.

What should citizens be compelled to say at such an interview? The right to remain silent in order not to incriminate oneself is such a fundamental element of British liberty that it should not be overridden if possible. It would therefore seem wisest if the only things a citizen could be compelled to say at such an interview were his name, address, occupation and date and place of birth. That is, he should be compelled to identify himself but no more, and if so minded he could sit through the remainder of the interview in silence.

What then would be the objects of such an interview? They would first be the simple ones of finding out who lived in the terrorist-affected area, where they lived and what they looked like. Additionally, however, other purposes would be served. It would give a push to citizens who had a general intention of helping the Security Forces but had never done so because of laziness, and those who had remained quiet because no occasion had arisen when it became of immediate urgency for them personally to exert themselves and give information to the Security Forces. There must be a mass of information denied to the Security Forces by this factor, particularly when the dangers and effort required of a citizen in, say, the Ballymurphy to impart a piece of clandestine information to the Security Forces are considered. This view is reinforced by the significant proportion of information that came through the Confidential Telephone in Northern Ireland which in the end turned out, for example, to have come from women slighted in love who wished to be revenged on an unfaithful terrorist lover. They had the information but it needed such an incentive to induce them to impart it. One returns to the basic thesis that intelligence on criminals and terrorists seldom just emerges, but has to be developed and created.

These compulsory interviews would also enable the Security Forces, with a certain degree of error, to categorise the population into 'pro-government', 'neutral' and 'anti-government'. In security operations, as in most human activities, it is important to know who are your friends and who are your enemies. This information would be valuable not only from the point of view of security operations, but also as an indication to the Government of what policies would be acceptable or unacceptable. Such information was very difficult for Ministers to acquire for themselves, on which to form their own judgments; they had streams of people trying to persuade them of particular views, but in the circumstances of Northern Ireland it was desirable for Ministers to see and listen for themselves in the troubled areas and so be able to differentiate truth from special pleadings. How difficult it was for Ministers to obtain first-hand impressions of the feelings of the people is shown by the fact that in the eight months which I spent in the Springfield Road Police Station, one Under-Secretary visited the area for some two hours, another opened a local factory and a third visited a local hospital. These were the only visits that Ministers felt able to make to the area during that period. However, guidance on the political views of the people could be obtained from the results of the compulsory identification interviews suggested. Such accurate information might help Ministers to reject some of the "fantasy" solutions that so easily gain credence when the true picture is obscure.

The citizens who would be likely to give information in the future—who could be asked, albeit surreptitiously, about incidents and terrorists in the areas where they lived or worked—would be those falling into the 'pro-government' category on interview. These would be the people likely to meet their legal obligation to assist the forces of the Crown in the suppression of insurrection and crime. There is however no means whatever of identifying these law-abiding citizens in a terrorist- and rebel-intimidated society unless they can be interviewed privately and asked in such a way that suspicion is not thrown on them. Hence the need to enact authority for the Police—and for the Army, where the latter are substituting for the Police in a terrorist-dominated area—to have the right to compel all citizens to attend security surveillance census interviews. Once the principle is accepted that the Security Forces in an insurrectionary situation must be able to compel members of the population to identify themselves, then there is every reason for extending this identification to physical features. The physical features concerned are photographs, signatures, a few lines of handwriting and fingerprints.

In order to know what a named person looks like, for the purpose either of finding him or checking someone's claim to be him, the obvious course is to look at his photograph. If troops are unfamiliar with a terrorist-affected area, the Police have been excluded from it for years and its population is unhelpful to the Government, then a photograph is the only way that a person's appearance can be ascertained. This sometimes seems to be forgotten by legislators who expect the Security Forces to know by instinct the face that belongs to a name they have been given. Widespread photography of the population of the Republican areas of Belfast was carried out from 1971 onwards. There appears to have been no specific legal authorisation for this, although equally there appears to be no law to prevent a person being photographed without his consent, unless he is physically assaulted in the process.[2] The Northern Ireland (Emergency Provisions) Act, 1973, specifically authorised the photographing of a person arrested as a suspected terrorist without his consent. This statutory authority for compulsory photography presumably envisaged a comparatively small number of cases involving specific suspects, and did not include those arrested with a view to being charged in the courts. In fact it gave sufficient reserve powers for the Army to continue with its policy of photographing as many as possible of the population; the great majority gave their consent, knowing that if they did not, forcible execution might be authorised. It is also quite difficult for people to prevent themselves being 'snapped' in unguarded moments if the military photographer is patient. This enabled the Army to build up a photographic surveillance record of a substantial proportion of the people in the Catholic areas of Belfast. In England photographs of acquitted persons are destroyed,[3] and at times this was the case in Northern Ireland with photographs of rioters and other alleged malefactors who had been acquitted, but at other times all photographs were retained for intelligence and population identification. Photography *ad lib* in the street was forbidden, although it appears to be lawful. This prohibition seems to have been based on doubts as to the legality of photographing a crowd outside a pub simply so as to have their faces on record so that names could be fitted to them later.

One problem that occurs when a witness identifies a suspect from photographs is that the former may be suspected of having a preconception of whom he will identify at a subsequent physical identity parade. But this is not a great hindrance, because what is important is to have the first eliminating indication of who were involved in an incident and to which terrorist group they belong. Once this has been indicated, it is often possible to achieve a conviction on quite different evidence without the name of the original witness coming out in public or a physical identification parade being demanded of him. It is the first trace linking a name or a face to a crime that really counts in detection.

Photographs that show the shape of the individual's ear are useful because it is thought impossible to alter the ear shape which, like fingerprints, is a distinctive feature that almost always differs between individuals. Handwriting and the way of signing the name are further means of identification and in particular for attributing particular subversive documents to their originators. For example, my battalion was able to incarcerate an explosives officer in the Provisional IRA by these means. This particular man was a "respectable" student at Queen's University, Belfast. The battalion one day searched the flat of a girl who was a known supporter of the IRA and found some of his university essays there. Shortly afterwards, in a quite different place, instructions on the manufacture of bombs were found. The handwriting of these instructions was the same as that of the essays. Documents which may include orders to terrorists and communications between them can be used to find and connect the terrorist leaders, who remain hidden in the background and direct operations. In Northern Ireland, as in Cyprus, the terrorists relied on a courier communication system based mainly on women. The IRA had an inordinate fear of telephone tapping by the Government, and therefore tended to prefer the use of written messages. My battalion, like most, found a variety of subversive documents, and given specimens of all citizens' handwriting, it should have been easy to trace their originators.

According to the Diplock Report, it is one of the 'Effects of Intimidation' that

... the only kind of case in which a conviction of a terrorist can be obtained by the ordinary processes of criminal law is one in which there is sufficient evidence from one or more of three sources: (1) oral evidence by soldiers or policemen, whose protection can be more readily ensured; (2) physical evidence, such as fingerprints, and (3) an admissible confession by the accused.[4]

The Gardiner Committee reported that it was given details of 482 instances of civilian witnesses to murder and other terrorist offences being too frightened to make any statement or go to court.[5] The beauty of a clear fingerprint is that it is absolute evidence. It cannot be denied, although it may be possible to make some legitimate claim why it appeared on the

Armalite rifle or the bomb. (Despite some recent suggestions to the
contrary, fingerprints cannot be "lifted" from one object to another.)

The authority for the Police to take fingerprints in peacetime is
uncertain. Leigh, in *Police Powers*, points out that in this connection even
the laws of England and Scotland do not appear to be identical.
Accordingly, 'it is difficult to expect the Police to conform to a rule of
strict legality when the legal rules are of doubtful content or simply
misunderstood.' However, Section 40 [of the Magistrate's Courts Act 1952
as amended by Section 33 of the Criminal Justice Act 1967] provides that
where any person not less than 14 years of age who has been taken into
custody or summoned is charged with an offence before a magistrate's
court, the court may, on the application of a police officer not below the
rank of inspector, order that his fingerprints or palm prints shall be taken
by a constable.[6]

There is in addition an array of confusing judgements on the matter of
fingerprints, some tending in one direction and some in the other. But one
point is clear, namely that if the accused is acquitted or discharged, his
fingerprints and all copies or records of them must be destroyed. This
provision does not apply to photographs, but in practice photographs of
acquitted persons are also destroyed.[7]

It is therefore clear that, in the absence of special legislation, the
Security Forces should not use photographs, and may not use fingerprints,
to build up surveillance information on the population that would enable
them to pounce with precision on terrorists. This seems an inappropriate
rule with which to handicap the military and Police in the context of a
terrorist campaign.

The legal position on fingerprinting in Northern Ireland is substantially
the same as in England under Section 70 of the Magistrates' Courts Act
(Northern Ireland) 1964, whereby:

70.—(1) Where any person who has been taken into lawful custody is charged with
an offence a magistrates' court may, on the application of a member of the Royal
Ulster Constabulary not below the rank of sergeant, order that the fingerprints of
that person shall be taken by a constable.

(4) Where the fingerprints of any person have been taken in pursuance of an
order made under this section, then if that person is acquitted or discharged under
section 45, or if the charge against him is dismissed, struck out or withdrawn, the
fingerprints and all copies and records thereof shall be destroyed.

The upshot of this is that the Police have no right to obtain a suspect's
fingerprints until after he has been charged. Once he has been charged,
however, he cannot be questioned, so that if fingerprints are found on a
weapon, a suspect must be charged and a warrant to fingerprint him
obtained. If the prints do not match, no further questions can be put to the
suspect, who probably has to be released. The Police may be almost certain
that the fingerprints belong to one of ten men, but they can hardly charge
ten people for one crime hoping that the prints of one of them will match
the prints on the weapon. If the prints do match those on the weapon, the
Police have no right to question the suspect as to how they got there or to
use this damning evidence to needle him into revealing more about his

accomplices. Moreover, there is high authority for the proposition that an arrest should not normally be made until the Police have substantially investigated the matter.[8] Yet fingerprints play a vital part in terrorist or criminal detection. The result of this situation, in my own experience in Northern Ireland, was that until the position was improved by the Northern Ireland (Emergency Provisions) Act of July 1973, fingerprints were not used to combat terrorists in that province. There were plenty of weapons and bomb-making materials bearing fingerprints and plenty of suspects, many detained in Long Kesh without trial, but the two were never brought together. Failure of the law to permit this realistic means of detection was a substantial reason why detention without trial had to be continued. If widespread fingerprinting had been allowed, it would in many cases have been possible either to convict in the ordinary criminal courts a man detained without trial who was suspected of terrorist offences, or to eliminate and therefore release him.

Section 10 of the Northern Ireland (Emergency Provisions) Act of July 1973 says:

(1) Any constable may arrest without warrant any person whom he suspects of being a terrorist.

(4) Where a person is arrested under this section, an officer of the Royal Ulster Constabulary not below the rank of Chief Inspector may order him to be photographed and to have his fingerprints and palm prints taken by a constable, and a constable may use such reasonable force as may be necessary for that purpose.

Thus in order to be compulsorily photographed and finger-printed without being charged and a warrant granted by a magistrate's court, a citizen had to be arrested under Section 10 of the Northern Ireland (Emergency Provisions) Act, 1973, with a view to detention without trial as a suspected terrorist. If he was originally arrested under Section 11 of the Act with a view to being charged before the ordinary courts for an offence linked to terrorism, then the normal rules applied and the citizen had to go before a magistrate's court before he could be compulsorily fingerprinted, after which he could not be questioned. Not only did this continue to inhibit the use of fingerprints to detect and convict terrorists in spite of intimidation, but the difference between the two sections of the Act opened up a technical defence to the terrorist—that he was arrested under one section but treated in this respect as if he had been arrested under the other. This is the sort of booby-trap in the law for the suppression of terrorism that hampers the Security Forces and in the long run contributes to the necessity of detention without trial.

The effect of Section 10 of the Northern Ireland (Emergency Provisions) Act, 1973, was to reduce the number of people objecting to the Army photographing them. It also led to a slight increase in the use of fingerprinting to try and discover the perpetrators of particular crimes where there was a limited circle of suspects, but it did not in any way lead to the development of a record of the fingerprints of even substantial numbers of the community.

Quite apart from the physical features that could be permanently recorded thereby, such surveillance interviews would have the great advantage that some member of the Security Forces would personally have seen all the individuals in the terrorist-affected areas. Photographs are a help to identification, but disguise is easy by wearing wigs, growing moustaches, and so on. However someone who has physically seen a person at close quarters can often penetrate the most elaborate disguise: this penetration derives from aspects of personality that can never be recorded in writing or photographed, e.g. demeanour, carriage of the shoulders, timbre of the voice, look in the eyes. This personal knowledge of an individual by the Police or Army would make it exceedingly hard for a terrorist to move about in disguise or to maintain an alias if it was seriously challenged.

If an insurrection backed by the intimidatory apparatus of a terrorist organisation arises, the Police and military can only operate effectively and with precision if they are permitted to acquire the basic data of the identity of the population with which they are concerned. This census should therefore include the fingerprints, photographs and signatures of everyone in a rebel-affected area. The law-abiding can come to no harm through the Security Forces possessing this information; indeed they are less likely to be bothered by repeated identity checks. It is only those who break the law who will be disadvantaged by the improved possibility of the Security Forces identifying them. Why should anyone other than the rebels object to this? Insurrection and terrorism are not a sporting event in which the law should act as a referee to handicap the law-enforcement agencies to make the contest a 'fair' one which neither side can win. The law must make it as easy as possible for its own enforcement agencies to carry out their task within the general notion of limiting the resulting erosions of citizens' liberty to those that are necessary, effective and humane.

(b) Identity cards

The next step in this matter of identifying the population is the introduction of identity cards. At present in Northern Ireland, let alone in the rest of Britain, the only means of checking someone's identity is to ask him. Sadly 'X', wanted for murder, does not answer 'X' when asked his name by a policeman or soldier. If the soldier's or policeman's suspicion is aroused, which often happens because he is speaking to a new and unknown face in a district which he has come to know well, he has no option but to arrest the citizen on suspicion of being a terrorist, take him to a Police station and go through the elaborate, time-consuming and irritating process of checking the citizen's identity by visiting his home and questioning his neighbours. With a system of identity cards showing photograph, fingerprints and signature, the Security Forces would then be able to look at the suspect's card and know that the person questioned was, at least in probability, who he claimed to be.

There are three principal objections to identity cards: that they constitute an unacceptable infringement of liberty, that they can be forged or stolen, and that there is no way to counter mass refusal to carry them. The first notion is curious in relation to the general effect on life and liberty of a terrorist campaign. There have in recent years been proposals in the British press that identity cards should be issued to, variously, football fans to keep hooligans away from matches, building workers to help stamp out the 'lump' method of income tax evasion, and commercial lorry drivers to check thefts at the docks. Some of the British trade unions operate an identity card system: for example, when the driver of a private contractor's lorry arrives to deliver or collect goods at a strange commercial yard which is closely controlled by the Transport and General Workers' Union, he will be asked to show his union card. If he cannot produce one, he will be turned away from the premises by the shop stewards. Moreover, if he does produce a union card but the shop stewards have any suspicion that he is not the person to whom the card was issued by the Union, the number of the card and the identity of its proper holder will be checked with the transport contractor concerned through the Union's district office. The reason why the Union operates this identity card system is obvious. If it did not, it would have no chance of enforcing the Closed Shop principle in as dispersed and diffused a profession as lorry-driving, where the local Union officials cannot possibly know by sight everyone with whom they come in contact whom they believe should be in their Union. These reasons that have compelled the Transport and General Workers' Union to operate an identity card system are the same in essence as those which necessitate a parallel system for the Security Forces to cope successfully with terrorists.

In many countries identity cards are compulsory—for example, in Italy, West Germany, Argentina and Israel. In France, although not compulsory, they are widely carried to enable people to prove their identity as quickly and easily as possible.[9] The question of introducing identity cards in Britain was raised several times in the House of Commons debate on the Prevention of Terrorism (Temporary Provisions) Bill in November 1974. Roy Jenkins, the Home Secretary, seemed to base his reasons for not proposing this step immediately on practical grounds of efficacy and cost rather than because they infringed liberty excessively.[10]

The Gardiner Report of January 1975 felt that the question of identity cards in Northern Ireland should not be foreclosed on the same administrative ground as applied to the whole of Britain with its population of 55 million, the Northern Ireland population being only 1½ million. The conclusive argument is one of precedent. In the Second World War, identity cards were regarded as a small but necessary infringement of liberty. Terrorist-backed insurrection is a form of war, probably the typical modern form. Therefore, if they help to defeat this evil, identity cards should be accepted as a small but necessary price leading to a much greater good.

It is of course true that identity cards can be forged or stolen. A card issued in a sealed, laminated folder would be difficult to forge, but attempts to do so would be made and some would succeed. But a forgery is seldom perfect and the slightest sign of erasure or alteration would arouse the suspicion of the checker, who could then refer the holder of the card for deeper investigation. Moreover a complete personality is very difficult to substitute completely, as there are so many different points of contact with verifiable facts which have to be right if the forged identity is to stand up to scrutiny. In my own experience, the holders of false documents frequently attract that first vital attention to themselves, which singles them out from the innocent mass, by such indications as looking too old for the age stated on the document, too well dressed to live at the address given, or having calloused hands unlikely to belong to someone whose occupation was stated as 'clerk'. Of course many holders of forged identity cards would pass unnoticed through many checks, but nevertheless this would be a powerful weapon in the struggle for the Security Forces to act with precision against those who have a good reason to hide their identities. The same considerations apply to stolen cards. These would be listed, and it could be made an offence not to report the loss of a card. Discrepancies would be sure to appear between the false and real identities attached to a card. Alterations would probably show tiny scratches or glue marks. It is sometimes argued that important terrorists would make their initial applications for identity cards in false names. This they would certainly do, but it would not be too important. Once their fingerprints and photographs had been taken, they would be tied to that particular false identity, and it would be almost as difficult for them to revert to their proper identity as to change to another false one. Moreover, their original false identity would be the one in which their name would begin to emerge through the whispers of the informer network. This name would have a face to it, and the fact that the name was false would be of only marginal importance in finding the wanted man. Additionally, if information were received, perhaps from someone who had known the terrorist at school or in childhood, that a particular person had registered under a false name, this would indicate strongly that the particular person merited investigation in depth.

The most trenchant argument against identity cards is that there is no way of countering a mass refusal to carry them, enforced by terrorist intimidation. Something of his kind would certainly happen in the Republican areas of Northern Ireland if identity cards were introduced there. The answer to this was found in Malaya. As Richard Clutterbuck wrote in *The Long, Long War:*

The most important measure called for the entire population over twelve years old to register at the police stations, where copies of their photographs and thumbprints were made. One copy was placed on an identity card to be carried by the registrant; another was retained at the police station. Many unsuspected Communists, reluctant to have their photographs and thumbprints recorded on police files, first drew suspicion on themselves by failing to report for registration. More important, registration hampered all Communist movement and activity, despite efforts to disrupt the system by terror, wholesale destruction of identity cards, and forgery.

The police then set up cordons at early morning and screened every inhabitant in a village. Action could be taken against anyone who should not have been there, and those inexplicably absent were thereafter subjected to surveillance. An identity card system will only work if the holder has an incentive to look after his own card. In Malaya, the card was needed to obtain the basic necessities of life. 'People soon realized that life with identity cards was easier than life without them.' Outside the villages, the need for an identity document prevented guerrillas in disguise and their secret couriers from moving about freely on the rubber estates and the roads.

Anyone found by a police check to be outside his normal neighbourhood without a convincing explanation would attract special attention in the future, and it was from shreds of evidence such as these that intelligence was built up and agents recruited to betray the Communists. The system had its greatest effect inside the villages, however, because it became almost impossible for guerrrillas to live among the people. It truly separated the guerrillas from the people. This is the prime requisite in defeating a guerrilla insurgency; it gives the people protection and forces the guerrillas to make prearranged contacts with their supporters. Such contacts provide the most fruitful field for the intelligence that kills.[12]

The way to ensure that people carry identity cards, even if they are totally opposed to the Government, is to make it impossible for them to obtain any Government services and many private ones without producing it. For example, the purchase of a railway ticket or the drawing of supplementary benefits should be made dependent on the production of an identity card. The use of National Insurance cards to identify people was suggested in the House of Commons on 28 November 1974.[13] In Singapore, for example, it is almost impossible to get any official licence, permit, or benefit without going in person to a Government office and producing an identity card. The system in Northern Ireland whereby state benefits are paid by post should be ended. The drawing of all such handouts and as many other contacts with the state as possible should have to be carried out in person at a Government office with the individual's identity card being scrutinised by a soldier or policeman. Such scrutiny is after all less humiliating and less of an infringement of personal liberty than the embarrassing personal searches that have taken place for years in Northern Ireland. All post office services, for example, should be made dependent on the production of an identity card. Life would therefore become extremely difficult and expensive for anyone without such a card. In order, moreover, to encourage citizens to safeguard their identity cards, the process of replacing lost ones should be made slow, demanding and difficult, taking at least six weeks, during which time the errant citizen would be denied, except in dire emergency, all Government services.

Many private concerns such as hotels and bars could be drawn into such a scheme. In Northern Ireland at present, customers are searched on entry to nearly all places of public entertainment or drinking and many shops, under arrangements of the management. It would be no great matter, and in the interests of their own security, for these places to deny entrance to anyone without an identity card.

A particular problem that arises with identity cards in Northern Ireland is that a person's religion would be detectable immediately and reliably from the name and address on his identity card, since Catholics have different forenames from Protestants—e.g. 'Kevin' as opposed to 'Ian' and 'Liam' as opposed to 'William'—and since the polarisation into Catholic and Protestant streets and areas is so clear-cut. This is not as serious as it sounds since instincts concerning the religious divide are so well developed that Ulstermen in general know anyway a person's religion by looking at him and have certain confirmation of this within a minute or two of speaking to him. Even outsiders, such as myself, developed with astonishing speed the ability to distinguish Protestants and Catholics with fair accuracy by their appearance. Surnames are less revealing of a person's religion. The answer therefore seems to be that the cards should not carry addresses or forenames but only initials. The firemen in Belfast, who are of both religions, use both a Protestant and a Catholic Christian name by which their mates would call them according to the religion of the area in which they were fighting a fire.

(c) Overall intelligence data system

The next step in developing an effective system of population surveillance would be to link all these identities and identity cards into a computerized intelligence system. The 'Luddite' attitude of some to the use of computers for intelligence is illustrated by an exchange which took place in the House of Commons, here reported in *The Times* of 6 December 1974:

There were angry exchanges in the Commons ... as Mr Rees [Secretary of State for Northern Ireland] was challenged over the accuracy of an article in *The Times* yesterday stating that the Army had secretly begun an intensive intelligence operation in Northern Ireland, using a computer to record personal information about nearly half the population of the province. [Mr Rees] said that ... although there was a computer which was used for vehicle checking and vehicles crossing the border there was no computer for intelligence purposes. ... [this] Mr Rees said was a matter for him and the matter had not been put to him.
    Mr Leslie Huckfield, Labour MP for Nuneaton, said that he had done some researches into *The Times* report and had concluded that the computers were ready in Northern Ireland, the punch cards and the machinery were ready and that over the next two months it was intended to use precisely the system described in *The Times*. There would be disastrous political consequences if Mr Rees went ahead with the kind of computer system described. ... It would mean that the Secretary of State would have at his disposal the whole of the 'big brother' apparatus to back up the emergency measures for the province. ...

The same newspaper reported on 13 December 1974 the introduction into service of the Home Office's Police national computer system 'to give local police forces throughout the country immediate access to selected criminal records'. The system included an index of New Scotland Yard's fingerprint file, and the files were to be based on name, sex, colour of skin, height and date of birth. If this was acceptable in the rest of Britain, why not also in Northern Ireland, where the Police were overwhelmed by a terrorist-backed insurrection, and were only able to function at all with the support and frequent substitution for them of the Army?
    The Army in Northern Ireland had been pressing for the use of computers for intelligence at least since 1971, but until the introduction in 1975 of a strictly limited system for checking vehicle numbers at border crossing points, have been forbidden to use them. This has led to military clerks sorting inefficiently and slowly by hand and eye through masses of

intelligence cards to extract information and subversive connections, that could be printed out by a computer in a few seconds. The population surveillance records are the heart of a terrorist-defeating system, exactly as criminal records are the heart of any Police crime detection and prevention system. The French authorities, for example, have a full family dossier on each individual along with all other details. If the intention is to defeat terrorism, the records of the population must be as modern and efficient as possible. To prohibit computers for this purpose is like equipping the Security Forces with bows and arrows. Yet a British electronics firm, Muirheads, had at that time produced a movement monitoring system through which an immigration control officer could transmit a traveller's photograph and fingerprints to a central registry and receive within five minutes confirmation as to whether they belonged to the right person. The West German authorities had bought and installed this British product on a massive scale.[14]

The final step in achieving a system of population surveillance that will make possible the eradication of terrorism and the suppression of insurrection is to link private and other Government department information into the Security Forces' intelligence data system. In Northern Ireland the military and Police were not allowed access to information in other Government departments, let alone in civilian institutions, that would have helped them in their struggle against terrorism. For example, neither the Police nor the military were allowed copies of the photographs of every registered driver in the province that were held in the driving licence office, nor were the Security Forces allowed access to the information on the population obtainable from the social security and national insurance records. This prohibition appears to have been founded on the erroneous belief that this information was in some way privileged and that it was somehow illegal for it to be used by the Security Forces. In principle, however, unless information has been given to a public department or private organisation such as a Bank in confidence, as for example under the periodical population census, there is no rule of law to prohibit its disclosure to the Police or to the Army. Moreover, the civil servants holding this information have a common law duty to help the Police with their investigations. There are, furthermore, many special statutory provisions giving the Police or other public authorities, such as the Inland Revenue, access to private confidential information such as Bank accounts. There is no doctrine of Crown Privilege between Government departments. Crown Privilege concerns the disclosure of official documents in open court and not their transfer between one Government office and another.

Some legal guidance may be drawn from the cases on Crown Privilege. For example in the case of *Conway* v. *Rimmer* in 1968 Lord Reid said:

There may be special reasons for withholding some kinds of routine documents, but I think that the proper test to be applied is to ask, in the language of Lord Simon in Duncan's case, whether the withholding of a document because it belongs to a particular class is really 'necessary for the proper functioning of the public service'.[15]

It therefore seems that the only valid grounds on which this prohibition could have been made in Ulster was that it was in the public interest;

presumably administrative orders were issued to this effect. But if this reason was invoked, it was a grievously wrong one. It is also probable that the Police in Ulster could have obtained these documents by using the procedure set out in the Official Secrets Act of 1920, Section 6 (1), according to which the Police, if satisfied that there is reasonable ground for suspecting that an offence has been committed and for believing that a particular person is able to furnish information as to that offence or suspected offence, may apply to the Home Secretary for authority, which he can give, to require the production of that information.

Access to privately held information is less straightforward if the holder wishes to preserve its confidentiality. For example, a Judge would be most unlikely to make an order for disclosure of privately held confidential documents under the Banker's Books (Evidence) Act, 1879, unless there were reasonable suspicion that the incriminating evidence was there. It is unlikely that an order would be made for a general enquiry to see whether some offence has been committed. The principle to be followed, from the case of *Annesley* v. *Earl of Anglesea* of 1743,[16] was enunciated by Lord Denning in 1970:[17]

... No private obligation can dispense with a universal one which lies on every member of society to discover every design which may be formed, contrary to the laws of the society, to destroy the public welfare.

Hence there is powerful support for the view that significant public good overrides private confidentiality. Access to all official and many private records such as Bank accounts would greatly help the Security Forces to achieve accurate basic data on the population affected by insurrection. Discrepancies revealed by a comparison of different types of record would indicate personalities that stood out from the mass of the population. Deeper investigation of these identities would follow, and, although many discrepancies would be explained, the first indication of clandestine rebel personalities would be likely to emerge from discrepancies that could not be explained. It seems therefore that any knowledge of the population held by Government and private organisations in a terrorist-affected area that is wanted by the Security Forces should be made available to them. If this principle is not sufficiently clear from the present state of the law, then it should be positively enacted.

If, therefore, the Police and military are to act with precision against terrorists whose basic art is concealment, their first requirement is access to all the data needed to build up an accurate knowledge of every individual in the population with which they are dealing. This information will not only help to indicate subversive individuals, but can also greatly enhance the probability that the Security Forces will detect the perpetrators of a crime and prove a case against them in court in spite of all the difficulties presented by an antagonistic population and terrorist intimidation. The greater the possibility of the Security Forces detecting and convicting terrorists and rebels in the ordinary courts, the less the need for such devices as detention without trial. These two are in counter-balance.

7

PROPOSALS FOR ENCOURAGING INFORMATION FROM WITHIN THE TERRORIST RANKS AND FOR THE INFILTRATION OF THEIR ORGANISATIONS

(a) How defectors are developed

While a security census of the population in a rebellious area is the basis of all effective and precise Security Force action within that population as a whole, the only weapon that can destroy a subversive organisation in the end is information given to the Government from within the terrorist ranks. The supreme importance of inside information compared with other types of information about the terrorists has already been pointed out, as well as the general disfavour shown by British law to the use of this the most effective weapon for destroying terrorists, or indeed highly organised criminals.

Inside informers seldom appear of their own volition. They have to be consciously created, usually from among members of the terrorist organisation who have been arrested. The rank of the informer in the subversive organisation is of less significance than might be supposed. A relatively junior member of a terrorist organisation who defects can do enormous damage to his former colleagues because the orders and information given even to the bottom layer in an operational terrorist unit usually give as much guidance on its activities as the Security Forces need. Indeed, the mistake is often made of ignoring the contact intelligence that can be gained from quite junior defectors in the anxiety to secure as an informer one of the top half-dozen men in the organisation. Again, curiously, the policy information given by someone at the top of a terrorist organisation, though sometimes fascinating from an academic view point, can often be of little use in achieving the operational destruction of the organisation, because the top members of a terrorist organisation are probably concerned on the whole with the more or less open political manoeuvrings of the organisation.

Another fallacy is the belief that interrogation is a separate art, a kind of skilled mystery. What in fact is required for successful interrogation, ending in useful information and possibly a defection, is an intimate knowledge of the milieu in which the suspect moves. It is this intimate knowledge of the geography of where the suspect says he lives, of the whereabouts of the friends he says he talks to, of the little quirks of terrorist organisations, such as the special way of pronouncing *fianna* in the

133

IRA Youth Organisation, that rings a warning bell in the questioner's mind when some tiny shred of inconsistency appears. Thus, if the terrorist being questioned is their Chief of Staff, he should be questioned by someone high in the Security Forces' intelligence staff, but if the suspect is a lowly volunteer or private in the IRA, he is probably best questioned by the army corporal or sergeant in whose area he lives; in other words, a successful interrogation is most likely if a suspect is questioned by his Security Force opposite number. The Criminal Investigation Department in London recognises this, and a detective who specialises in the East End is not normally asked to question suspects from Mayfair.

It is almost impossible for a questioner to interrogate successfully unless he can build a psychological link, a sort of empathy, between himself and the suspect. Indeed, it is agreed by all experienced and successful detectives that the first requirement for obtaining information is to win the suspect's confidence, not to frighten him. A frightened man will often admit anything, even to crimes he cannot possibly have committed. Questioner and suspect may be opponents but, rather like soldiers at the Front in the First World War, they can develop a strong mutual bond directed against those outside their personal conflict. This bond—their shared experiences, and knowledge and the mutual respect of opponents—can be played on really quite easily by a sympathetic questioner to free the suspect's tongue. Persuading a terrorist to defect is akin to the wooing of a woman—with persuasive and even glib arguments on one side and, on the other initial resistance and vacillation between the urge to consent and the urge to refuse, and if all goes well, the development of confidence. Indeed, the interrogator is seeking to achieve a seduction rather than either a rape or a rebuff.

Centralised interrogation was not successful in Northern Ireland, and almost all the useful and usable information which I received in my operational tour came from low-level questioning by people who lived and worked in the same milieu as the suspect. The fallacy of centralised interrogation may have had some effect in leading to the assaults on suspects under arrest recorded by the Compton Committee which reported in November 1971 on the so-called 'interrogation in depth' techniques used that autumn by the Security Forces.[1] The trouble is that a specialist interrogator can often see no way except violence to overcome a suspect's silence. He knows so little, however well briefed he may be, of a strange suspect from an unfamiliar area that he can be sorely tempted to hit him in order at least to start some sort of dialogue. The interrogator who shares the life of the suspect, albeit on the other side, does not have the same difficulty. It is relatively easy to induce a suspect to talk about people and places they both know. The failure of centralised specialist interrogation, and the success of questioning by operational members of the Security Forces, both Police and military, from the same milieu as the suspect, has been one of the lessons of Northern Ireland.

This leads to consideration of who make successful questioners. The best type of man is one with intelligence, patience, quick wit, charm, and above all a natural sympathy which enables him to see things from the point of view of the person being questioned. Such people come in any rank or age group. Indeed most people, who are neither incorrigibly impatient, bullies, brutes nor plain dim-witted, can interrogate successfully. It is not an esoteric skill but largely an exercise in the good manners that 'win friends and influence people'. One successful interrogator was a private soldier who can, with respect, only be described as a young 'tearaway' from East London: he used to be put to guard younger members of the IRA who had been arrested since they were sometimes prepared to say things to a boy of their own age that they would never have said to an older man. On one occasion a young member of the IRA had resisted all blandishments from older, more formal interrogators to talk, and had kept his mouth shut; he was then put on a chair to await his release guarded by this bored-looking young soldier. Clearly the relief felt by this terrorist at having successfully resisted his questioning compelled him to talk with someone. He opened conversation with his guard by asking 'What's it like in your army?' He and the young soldier then got into conversation about what it was like in their respective armies. After an hour or two, the terrorist volunteered six foolscap pages of personal confession and detailed information on the activities of his colleagues, as a result of which it was possible to make a number of arrests on charges of murder and attempted murder. It is much more common than might be supposed for arrested terrorists to defect and turn informer.[2]

I was concerned in my battalion area with about 100 informers over the whole period, who had been at least fringe members of one subversive organisation or another, and some of whom remained in these organisations and attained quite high rank. Why do these terrorists turn informer, and how are they persuaded to defect? Very few offer themselves, although this appears to have happened in the case of Kenneth Lennon, the murdered police informer, because the Starritt Report shows that he approached the Police and offered to sell information about the IRA, on the fringes of which he operated.[3] Such breaks are rare and potential informers and defectors have to be carefully identified from among the mass of suspects scrutinised by the Security Forces and then carefully encouraged and developed into working Government agents. M. R. D. Foot discusses this question in the official history of the Special Operations Executive in France in the Second World War:

Some of the interrogators who dealt with captured [allied] agents in Paris were intelligent and sensitive men who had mastered the basic rules of interrogation: never admit to ignorance, and frighten your victim, but not too much.... They made a little information which had come into their hands about SOE go a long way, and with its help secured some damaging admissions. What motives induced so many captive agents to unburden themselves as fully as they did under interrogation? The shock of arrest seems in many cases to have induced a sort of relief; having treasured for months the secret of their clandestine activity, some people seemed to have been unable to resist the comfort of admitting and discussing it.... Another element besides relief might encourage some captured agents to talk; this was conceit. Some people could not bear to have it suggested to them that their position had been at all a subordinate one; and in order to explain to their captors how important they had been, they revealed a great deal that would have been better left unsaid.[4]

The strangest informant who came my way was an officer in the

Provisional IRA of some seniority who suffered from overweening ambition as well as a certain artlessness. He had wanted his immediate superior's job, but had been passed over by the superior headquarters of the IRA, which appointed an outsider over his head. So he informed on the newcomer, who was immediately arrested. Almost incredibly the same happened again, but on the third occasion our informer was finally appointed to the coveted post; so we arrested him. His indignant complaint in the Springfield Road Police Station that he had never been allowed to 'have a go' lives in the memory.

There seem to be five reasons why suspects are induced to think that it is in their own interests to inform and defect: because they are tortured, because they are induced to do so by cash, because they are blackmailed into it as the lesser of two evils, because they lose their nerve, and because they are genuinely converted from their terrorist beliefs to supporting the Government cause.

A definition of torture and the dividing lines between reasonable restraint, ill-treatment and brutality will not be attemped here. However, torture and brutality surely involve deliberate physical assault in order to inflict pain, as opposed to physical force used to make an arrest or to overpower an escapee, and a degree of physical discomfort, confinement and fear significantly greater than one would accept as appropriate in a normal civilian prison for non-subversive criminals. To say that a suspect must have no fear, no pressure, no periods of solitary confinement, and indeed no restraint, is absurd. Suspects need not be handled so delicately, but it is important that they should be treated as prisoners with rights and not as outlaws. Moreover, the limits of what may be done to them must be clearly published and available for the prisoner, his legal advisers, the guards, and the interrogators to see. It must be possible for prisoners to make complaints. Solzhenitsyn's *Gulag Archipelago* reveals that the Soviet penal system was not bad in theory, but that the practice was so appalling at least partly because no one was ever allowed to see what the penal regulations and prisoners' rights were, and there was no one to hear and investigate complaints.

These safeguards against brutality have existed for years under the British legal system. Yet in counter-terrorist campaigns there are undoubtedly repeated instances of petty brutality to suspects. In May 1975, an ex-Provisional IRA Officer, Martin Meehan, who had allegedly been beaten up after his arrest by the Army, was awarded £800 damages. The Attorney-General stated in Parliament on 17 April 1973 that there were at that time 150 civil claims for ill-treatment by the Security Forces in Northern Ireland and that thirty-nine cases had been settled by the plaintiffs accepting payment.[5] There have been a number of other compensation awards in settlement of civil actions to people in Northern Ireland who complained of brutal treatment when they were arrested by the Security Forces. There are unfortunately always a number of policemen and soldiers stupid enough to see the solution to their information problems in striking suspects, justifying their actions with the idea that the suspect comes to no real harm and that lives may be saved by the information he gives as a result of being beaten.

It is extremely tempting—and not unknown—for a tired, frightened, frustrated investigator, whose comrades have perhaps recently been killed or wounded, to 'thump' a suspect. For example, on the 19 September 1975 a Detective Constable in the Royal Ulster Constabulary was given a suspended prison sentence of 18 months for assaulting a suspect. The Judge believed that it was a case of a Police officer succumbing to temptation; he had not acted out of revenge. He was a determined investigator who, failing to obtain the admission he sought, succumbed to the temptation to use strong-arm methods.[6] How can these incidents be prevented? The ordinary processes of complaint and criminal charge are ineffective at present, basically because these beatings usually take place when there are few witnesses on either side, and those few are almost always totally committed to one side or the other. The court case therefore ends with a flat opposition of evidence and the impossibility of proving a charge, while no one besides the witnesses ever comes to know exactly what happened. It must not be forgotten how easy it is for a suspect to harass the Security Forces with false accusations of beating up. The beating up of suspects could be prevented if in principle any member of the Police or Army considered suitable by his superiors, irrespective of his rank, age or appointment, were allowed to carry out the interrogation of suspects, but only in certain rooms in certain Police stations and Army bases designated for such questioning. Rigid arrangements for medical inspection before and after interviewing could be made. Any interrogation outside these rooms would automatically be a breach of military or Police orders, for which disciplinary action could be taken under the appropriate service codes. These rooms should be monitored by a quite independent group of policemen taken from other forces or even other nations, living separately from the rest of the Security Forces. This group should have an unrestricted and immediate right to enter the interrogation rooms unannounced at any hour of the day or night. The possibility that a Detective Sergeant from such an alien group might at any moment walk through the door would mightily help an interrogator to resist the temptation to use his fists on a recalcitrant suspect. Petty beating-up of suspects will be prevented not by independent investigation of complaints, which is no more likely than present investigations to find out the truth, but by the possibility of independent eye-witness accounts of what really happened.

It has been suggested that tape recordings or videotape films of all interrogations should be taken, as these would establish beyond doubt what had happened. Although this might be so, such an arrangement would be disastrous from the questioner's point of view. The thread of confidence which links a criminal or terrorist informer to his questioner is so delicate and so personal that the knowledge that their discussion was being recorded would undoubtedly dry up most informers, with resulting benefits to criminal and terrorist organisations. This thread of confidence is built up by the interrogator convincing the suspect that, for any one of a whole range of reasons, it is in his personal interest to inform on his colleagues. This is usually such a fragile link, that the slightest counter-pressure can lead to its being broken.

It would be ingenuous to suggest that torture, or the threat or mild practice of 'beating-up' do not produce information. It is a regrettable fact that they do produce information[7] at the cost of relatively little intellectual and nervous effort by the interrogators; it is the lack of personal mental exertion in 'beating-up' suspects that makes it the favourite resort of the dim-witted interrogator. This method usually produces information quickly without extended periods for questioning. In a sense 'beating-up' and 'time to question' are in counter-balance. The greater the time for questioning, the less the need or temptation to resort to brutality. However, the advantages of information gained through brutality are, like the advantages that derive from most crime, short-term, restricted and quickly and overwhelmingly outweighed by the disadvantages. The whole concept of obtaining information from suspects by torture or some milder form of the same process should be rejected for both subjective and objective reasons.

A subjective reason for rejecting torture is the damage which it causes to the moral confidence of the Security Forces; to be effective, energetic and yet self-disciplined, policemen and soldiers in a counter-terrorist campaign need to feel morally correct. If they are acting wrongly, they inevitably begin to wonder why they are there at all. Another subjective reason is that once the slightest hint of torture has been permitted, there is no logical reason for stopping anywhere. In his Minority report to the Parker Report of March 1972, Lord Gardiner wrote:

I, like many of our witnesses, have searched for, but been unable to find, either in logic or in morals, any limit to the degree of ill-treatment to be legalised. The only logical limit to the degree of ill-treatment to be legalised would appear to be whatever degree of ill-treatment proves to be necessary to get the information out of him, which would include, if necessary, extreme torture.[8]

Objectively, torture misses the main object of interrogating suspects. This is seldom to get a particular piece of information, which at best would only help to an arms find or an arrest, but to develop willing informers in the terrorist ranks, who will tell the Security Forces their plans, month by month, with total voluntary commitment to giving the best information they can. It is inside information of this kind that destroys terrorist organisations, rather than the single piece that makes them lose in a single encounter, and no man who has been tortured will provide this. Moreover, the willing informer will provide the vital service to the Security Forces of answering the questions they never knew they needed to ask. The suspect who is tortured will eventually answer what is asked of him, but he has no need to volunteer the devastating pieces of intelligence that have been totally concealed from the Police and Army.

Brutal interrogation is the surest way to harden the resolve of terrorists by giving them a moral justification for their own crimes. It is also a propaganda gift to the terrorists, swinging popular support behind them better than almost anything else particularly among their own communities. The concept of the 'fair' fight is almost universal, and the support of public opinion will be denied to Security Forces that are thought to torture helpless prisoners.[9]

The best arguments for rejecting torture are implicit in Lord Gardiner's report, in its reference to Allied practice in the Second World War:

The evidence we heard from the main interrogation centres during the war, where so much vital information was obtained, was that the prisoners and suspects were treated with kindness and courtesy and ... as is now well known, it was accompanied by interrogation, the cross-referencing of information and the use of microphones and 'stool pigeons' in cells. We were told that there were occasions when information was wanted, and was obtained in a matter of hours, relating particularly to the course of U-boat packs or the path to be taken on the next air raid and that, even after the Germans knew of the methods and warned their men about microphones in cells and the use of 'stool pigeons', the methods were still effective owing to the overwhelming desire to talk to another human being whatever the circumstances.

Lord Gardiner went on to conclude that 'substantially as much information might ... have been obtained by those methods' in Northern Ireland.

Lest the legality of the use of 'stool pigeons' and other tricks of interrogation should be doubted, the words of Lord MacDermott, Lord Chief Justice of Northern Ireland, in the case of *Regina* v. *Murphy* in 1965, should be recalled:

'Detection by deception is a form of police procedure to be directed and used sparingly and with circumspection; but as a method it is as old as the constable in plain clothes and, regrettable though the fact may be, the day has not yet come when it would be safe to say that law and order could always be enforced and the public safety protected without occasional resort to it....'[10]

Lord Gardiner's minority report quotes the evidence of a group of medical specialists on interrogation procedures 'designed to impair cerebral functions so that freedom of choice disappears', as likely to damage the subject's mental health, in proportion to their effectiveness.[11] The purpose of interrogation of a terrorist suspect is not to 'impair choice', but to win his confidence and so persuade him to choose the Government side. In practice, instead of 'hooding' and 'posture on the wall', the right approach would be to put the suspect in a single cell—not 'solitary confinement' which implies deprivation of normal contact at meals and recreation—and leave as the only reading material in it persuasive literature on why the authorities should be helped and the advantages of so doing. Let the suspect's own doubts work in his own mind helped by nothing more than persuasive logic. The pressures of being a suspect in themselves are usually enough to set a man's mind working on his doubts and fears. The importance of this factor is crystallized in Sir Geoffrey Jackson's book *People's Prison.* 'No account, description or representation [of interrogation]', he says, 'can communicate the depth of weariness and nervous and physical exhaustion with which so strange an experience leaves its participant.' He calls this a sense 'almost of inward haemorrhage'.[12]

The real pressure of interrogation comes from inside the suspect's own head, from his own fears, doubts, guilt, and need to discuss his problems. In a certain way, external physical pressure seems to assuage and relieve these internal pressures. It is the internal pressures that the interrogator should exploit by allowing—and doubtless encouraging—the suspect to work himself into a state where of his own free will he wants to help the Security Forces. What is needed in Northern Ireland to achieve this end more often than at present is time, time to persuade and to let the suspect opt on his own to help the authorities.

Having ruled out absolutely any kind of ill treatment or torture as an acceptable form of interrogation, and suggested an alternative approach, one is led on to the next principal reason why suspects 'sing' and perhaps turn informer—namely, loss of nerve. The way this usually happens is that a suspect is in reality a terrorist and has a cover story which he has learned by heart and for which he has supporting documentation and witnesses. This is gone over again and again in interrogation, and perhaps some small inconsistency appears, perhaps the story changes a little, or more probably some physical fact on being checked is found to be wrong and to invalidate a significant part of the story. The suspect is then confronted with a demonstrable impossibility or discrepancy in his story. He is compelled to invent an alternative lie to explain the inconsistency, but his new story is likely to reveal even more obvious lies. The suspect then has to lie again and again, until eventually he can stand it no longer and, with the obvious relief that is one of the stranger aspects of even the most incriminating confession, admits defeat and tells all. What is needed to achieve this breakdown by loss of nerve is time to question the suspect, time to check on every detail of his story, and time to re-question him over and over again.

The simplest and most mundane reason for turning informer is for cash. The readiness to pay cash awards to informers was a significant feature of British operations against Communist terrorists in Malaya. One Communist was paid $M400,000, the equivalent of £50,000, for organising the defection of twenty-eight hard-core unit commanders together with another 132 terrorists. A defector received nearly $M80,000 for persuading his former colleagues to surrender.[13] Ten years' salary was the going rate to a Communist for betraying a district committee member.[14] It is interesting to compare this with the £20 a month paid in 1973 to Kenneth Joseph Lennon for informing to the Special Branch at Scotland Yard on the IRA.[15] The first requisite for buying information is therefore sufficient cash. The second is the ability to give the informer an indemnity for the crimes he has committed in the terrorist organisation and perhaps for the crimes he will have to commit. No one will become an informer if he may still be prosecuted for what he did before defecting or what he may have to do to preserve his credibility with the terrorist organisation. There was no system in Northern Ireland for indemnifying a defector in this way.

The next reason for conversion is blackmail, that is saying to a captured terrorist 'Help us or else'. For example, a terrorist might be arrested *in flagrante delicto* with a bomb or some other lethal weapon in his hands. He would know that a long prison sentence was a near-certainty if he were charged in court. The prospect for a young man or woman of emerging in middle age from prison, having missed the 'best years of their lives', is scarcely welcome. The Security Forces could then offer the terrorist indemnity from prosecution in return for his help. Once the terrorist had helped the Security Forces, he would be totally and irrevocably committed to them for fear that they might leak what he had done to his terrorist colleagues who would be sure to kill him, probably by a slow method, for his treachery. In Malaya a defected woman Communist terrorist was photographed between two smiling policemen to ensure her continued loyalty. She was told that if she did not co-operate, 50,000 leaflets with that photograph would be scattered in her jungle area.[16] It was forbidden in Northern Ireland to secure the defection of a terrorist by these means, partly on grounds of distaste, and partly because there was no machinery for granting a terrorist an indemnity from prosecution in return for his help. Why should he help the Government forces, if they were unable to promise him anything in return except a 'fair trial' at which any hint of his defection would secure his subsequent murder? The moral objections to such a course seemed excessive in the context of a terrorist campaign in which, by November 1974, 20,387 shooting incidents, 4,133 bomb explosions and 1,086 violent deaths had been recorded.

It can be argued that there is no moral difference between physically torturing a suspect into confession and pressuring him in this way. But the difference is that an innocent man can be tortured but not blackmailed, except in the case of an elaborate 'frame-up' for which the perpetrators would themselves be liable to severe punishment. An innocent man can go on saying he has done nothing and knows nothing, but the thumbscrew is tightened until he admits to something in order to stop the pain. Any man who is offered indemnity for his crimes in return for defection can always answer 'Charge me in court, and I will be acquitted', thus releasing the pressure on him. Of course this sort of bargain with criminals and terrorists is distasteful, but it is equally so to incarcerate a human being for twenty years even after a fair trial. If the Security Forces would gain an appreciable advantage in such a context by letting a terrorist buy his immunity from prosecution and his liberty in the dangerous currency of passing inside information, then it seems unreasonable to prevent him from doing so.

The final reason for defection by terrorists is genuine conversion. Although unusual, it does happen and I have myself witnessed such a conversion of a member of the Provisional IRA who was arrested by the Security Forces although previously unknown to them. During his initial four-hour screening interview with the military, he revealed just a glimmering of moral doubt about the casualties and damage that his organisation was causing, and of intellectual doubt as to whether they would really help the Catholic people of Northern Ireland, however purposeful and dramatic its policy may have seemed in the first flush of youthful ardour. At the end of his four-hour interview he was released from arrest, but remained voluntarily for three days engaging in political and moral discussions. At the end of this time he was convinced, or more accurately had convinced himself, that the policy of the Provisional IRA was morally wrong and would do more harm than good to the Catholic people of Northern Ireland. It then transpired that he held a much more significant and knowledgeable position in the Provisional IRA than we had ever dreamed of. By this time he had become a totally committed, totally enthusiastic supporter of the Government cause, and as such told all he knew, holding nothing back.

To avoid any possibility of this person being identified it can only be said that he was the direct cause of the Provisional IRA being smashed in a particular area of Northern Ireland, and that they did not recover from this blow for years in the sense that, while they were able to replenish their numbers and munitions during the cyclical 'ceasefire' or 'low profile' periods, they were unable after this defection to break the Security Forces' intimate knowledge of their activities. This meant that when the 'ceasefires' or 'low profile' periods ended, these particular terrorists did not enjoy clandestine cover and it was possible yet again to mop up the new organisation. All this was achieved from a genuine turning away by a citizen from the terrorist cause to the Government one. Not a single punch or even shout was involved, let alone physical ill-treatment or severe conditions, and, as far as one is able to judge, the Provisional IRA never suspected this particular defection. Fortunately this defector, although involved in bombings, had not personally killed or attempted to kill anyone. He was not prosecuted for his previous offences while a terrorist, but it was never possible to grant him a cast-iron indemnity from prosecution that would ensure that he could never be prosecuted if his name were to emerge as the result of other inquiries. He was prepared to defect in spite of this risk, but how much more honest it would have been to give him a definite guarantee of immunity from prosecution in return for his remarkable assistance to the forces of law and order. It should also be noted that time was needed to bring him to the point of conversion. Fortunately in his case only three days, but then he was already half-way to defection when his questioning began. Terrorists simply cannot be persuaded to take this sort of step, involving not only great personal danger but a deep moral upheaval, in a four-hour interview or while being hurriedly investigated with a view to prosecution. Time is needed and, in most cases, plenty of time.

This was not an isolated case in Northern Ireland, and the possibilities of achieving this sort of defection are well exemplified in books on the Malayan emergency and the Mau Mau campaign in Kenya. Richard Clutterbuck describes the comparative ease with which defections were achieved from among the Communist guerrillas in Malaya who found that 'they were spending the best years of their lives in a miserable existence to aid a cause that was doomed to failure'.

Once the guerrilla began to lose heart, his hatred of Communism would grow. The Party had misled him and brought him hardship and danger to no purpose. It was wasting his life; worse it had made a fool of him.

   While the disillusioned guerrilla awaited his opportunity to surrender, his hatred centred on the Party's representatives, particularly his own MCP [Malayan Communist Party] branch leader and the men who supported him. He knew that if these men suspected his true thoughts for a moment they would kill him. It seemed quite logical to him to kill them instead.[17]

All terrorist movements contain members who are thinking on these lines. They are probably apparently active and enthusiastic terrorists, because an effect of the brutal severity of terrorist internal discipline is to prevent a man from ever expressing his real doubts. They are the 'Achilles heel' of any terrorist movement and, if it is seriously desired to defeat terrorism, the law and the operating methods approved by the Government and the courts must make it possible, and as easy as possible for the military and Police to identify and to convert these potential defectors. For this three pre-conditons are needed: the right to interview, plenty of time to question, and the ability to grant to a defector a firm indemnity against prosecution.

(b) Proposals for overcoming the legal obstacles to persuading terrorists to defect; insufficient time to question; the granting of indemnities

Having established what are the prime requirements for creating informers and defectors from among the terrorist ranks, it is necessary to examine the obstacles and what needs to be done to overcome them.

The fundamental difficulty over time to question arises because in general a suspect cannot be questioned after being charged and he has to be charged very soon after arrest. This may not matter too much in Britain where it is possible to talk to suspects without arresting them, but in the circumstances of insurrection in Northern Ireland, terrorist suspects could only be spoken to by the Security Forces once they had been arrested. This may be a just protection when the only subject on which a suspect is to be questioned is a particular crime which he may have committed. However, in the circumstances of Northern Ireland the interrogator may not be especially interested about the particular offence of which the arrested person is suspected, but may be much more concerned with what he knows of other crimes and the terrorist organisation in general, as well as the possibility of inducing him to defect. An additional difficulty is caused by the significant differences in this area between English and Northern Irish law.

The Police and military are not helped by the general confusion of the law. As Leigh says, 'despite innumerable decisions and much legal writing on the topic, the legal content of police powers concerning the interrogation of suspects remains obscure.'[18] In England the critical item of legislation appears to be section 38 (4) of the Magistrates' Courts Act 1952, namely 'Where a person is taken into custody for an offence without a warrant and is retained in custody he shall be brought before a Magistrate's Court as soon as practicable.' While this is clearly meant to imply bringing the suspect before a Magistrate to be charged the next morning, it is flexibly interpreted in England. For example, the Price sisters were arrested at about 1100 on 8 March 1973, but were not charged until 14 March. Others, for example Robert Millhench, seemed to 'assist the Police with their enquiries' for a remarkable time with remarkable complaisance.[19] The Home Secretary, Roy Jenkins, admitted in a television programme in December 1974 that the Police were always in danger when holding suspects (for example, the Price sisters) for a long time, of being thought to have acted improperly. They had to bend the rules. The Police therefore attached great importance to specific powers given under Act of Parliament to hold terrorist suspects for longer than normal. However, the situation is much less relaxed in Northern Ireland—as witness Section 132 of the Northern Ireland Magistrates' Courts Act 1964:

Where a person arrested without warrant is not, within twenty-four hours of his arrest, released from custody, the member of the Royal Ulster Constabulary in charge of the constabulary station where such person is in custody, shall bring him or have him brought before a Magistrate's Court as soon as practicable thereafter being, in any event, not later than forty-eight hours after his arrest.

The Judges' Rules give guidance to the Police on how they should question suspects, when they should caution them, and so on. The 'Judges' Rules' are now different in Northern Ireland and in England.[20] However, because there are no legal reference books for Northern Ireland, it seems impossible to find out with precision what rules are applied in that province.

The English Judges Rules 1964—and in this they do not appear to differ from the Judges Rules as applied in Northern Ireland—state:

I. When a police officer is trying to discover whether, or by whom, an offence has been committed, he is entitled to question any person, whether suspected or not, from whom he thinks that useful information may be obtained. This is so whether or not the person in question has been taken into custody, so long as he has not been charged with the offence or informed that he may be prosecuted for it.
III(*b*). It is only in exceptional cases that questions relating to the offence should be put to the accused person after he has been charged or informed that he may be prosecuted.

The effect of all this was to give the Police and Army in Northern Ireland an absolute limit of forty-eight hours in which to question anyone who was to be charged with an offence. Thereafter he was never questioned again, either before or after sentence on any matter whatever without his consent, nor would any attempt to rehabilitate him ever be made. It seems that in strict law a suspect could have been questioned after being charged on any matter not connected with that particular offence. This, it appears, was not done in Northern Ireland.

Under Section 10 of the Northern Ireland (Emergency Provisions) Act, 1973, it became possible to hold a suspect for questioning for seventy-two hours before an Interim Custody Order was signed on him, if he had been arrested as a suspected terrorist with a view to detention. If the arrest had been made under Section 11 of the Northern Ireland (Emergency Provisions) Act, 1973, with a view to charging the suspected terrorist with a specific offence, then he had to be charged within forty-eight hours of arrest, thus putting an embargo on further questioning.

Schedule 1 to the Northern Ireland (Emergency Provisions) Act, 1973, paragraph 37 (3) states that 'subject to any directions of the Secretary of State, a person detained ... shall be treated as nearly as may be as if he were a prisoner detained in a prison on remand....' The effect of this was that once a suspect had had an Interim Custody Order signed against him, he could never again be spoken to by the Security Forces, just like the suspect who had been charged.

It took only one night of bombing in Birmingham to put right, at least to some extent, this situation that made it so exceedingly difficult to detect and convict terrorists in Northern Ireland. The Prevention of Terrorism (Temporary Provisions) Act 1974 was passed on 29 November 1974. Subsection 2 of section 7 of this Act authorises the Police to detain a suspected terrorist for forty-eight hours and the Secretary of State to extend this period in any particular case up to seven days. Leigh says of this section that the power to arrest is predicated upon reasonable suspicion, and is not a power to arrest for the purposes of interrogation.[21] Seven days is an improvement, but in the terms of a counter-terrorist campaign, it is still short and is hedged around with the question of whether the Police can arrest for interrogation, and the requirement for the personal approval of the Home Secretary, a Minister in the Home Office or another Secretary of State to authorise a longer period.[22]

Under the French and West German investigative legal systems, there is no habeas corpus or presumption of innocence as in Britain. In France the police may hold a suspect for seven days without access to a lawyer and even for several months or years without being charged, while a prosecution investigation proceeds. In West Germany investigatory detention is allowed for up to six months after a cursory appearance before a 'detention judge'. The Baader-Meinhof leaders were only charged two years after being arrested. Under Swedish law it appears that in some circumstances the police may detain suspects for long periods before they are formally placed in custody.

However desirable these examples may appear from the point of view of dealing with terrorist subversion, investigatory periods of such length seem excessive to anyone brought up in the common law tradition. It is worth looking at the compromise reached in the Netherlands, a notably liberal society, between the inconveniently short investigatory periods allowed by British law and the oppressively long ones allowed by much of continental law. The Dutch allow a total possible period of detention for investigation of 106 days and 6 hours. At each stage after the initial period of 'Police detention' the Police must return to a superior judge or court and make a case for the authorisation of yet more detention, not dissimilar to the British system of returning to court for further remands in custody. The difference is that questioning is permitted during this period in the Dutch case, but not in the British one. The Dutch system works as follows (the Articles quoted refer to the Dutch penal code):

1. 'Police detention':
(a) initially of 6 hours (excluding 'night hours' viz 12 midnight until 0900)—Article 61.
(b) re offences punishable with custodial sentences, 'prolonged police detention' for 48 hours (Article 57), renewable for a further 48 hours (Article 58).

2. 'Pre-trial judicial custody':
(a) ordered by Rechter–Commisaris, 6 days renewable for a further period of 6 days (Articles 63–64).
(b) in cases of crimes punishable with 4 years or more and certain other special offences the district Court can order up to three periods of 30 days detention, making a maximum of 90 days in all (Article 66).

3. This makes the total period; 6 hours + 4 days + 12 days + 90 days = 106 days 6 hours.

If there is to be a serious attempt to detect and convict suspected terrorists and to develop informers and defectors among them, then a period of investigatory detention of the order permitted by the Dutch penal code must be authorised when terrorism and insurrection is rife to replace the inadequate periods currently allowed by British law. Moreover continued questioning of suspected terrorists must be allowed after they have been charged, sentenced or ordered to be detained, in order to use the rich source of information and defection they offer. The correct safeguard should be that nothing a man says after he has been charged should be admissible against him in court or usable by the Director of Public Prosecutions to formulate a Crown case against him in respect of the offence with which he has been charged or warned for prosecution. The other side of this coin is that no pressure of any sort other than questioning, verbal persuasion and the offering of an indemnity or cash for defection or information should be allowed, and questioning should be limited to restricted continuous periods, e.g. eight hours a day in periods of not more than four hours each with one day in seven free from interrogation. This would help to avert the kind of confusion into which a man can fall if he is rigorously questioned more or less non-stop for even as brief a period as forty-eight hours. The object is not to destroy a suspect's power to make rational choices, but to persuade him to make a rational choice in favour of the Government and his lawful duty as a citizen.

The idea that adequate time to question suspects before trial is needed in a terrorist situation leads on to the question of interrogating them after detention or sentence with a view to rehabilitating them as law-abiding citizens or of securing their services for the Government as informers or defectors. There is no law against attempting to persuade a convict or indeed a detainee to mend his ways and return to his lawful duty as a citizen of helping the forces of law and order. Indeed the idea of correcting the causes that put a man in prison and of returning him to society as a law abiding citizen is a fundamental and much encouraged concept in any civilised penal system. There should thus be rehabilitation of sentenced or detained terrorists. They can be rewarded for their defection from terrorism either by simple release if in detention or by early release on parole if sentenced.

Parallel with the need for time to investigate and rehabilitate is the need to be able to grant a defector or informer indemnity for his crimes while a terrorist. In short it must be legally possible to let a terrorist 'do a Bertie Smalls'. The discretion of the Police not to prosecute is somewhat vague and obscure. However during my operational time in Northern Ireland, I and the Police were repeatedly told by our superiors that any attempt to offer a terrorist a bargain of freedom from prosecution in return for help would be a criminal offence on the part of the policeman or soldier offering it. It was therefore administratively forbidden, although exactly what the offence would be was never specified. It might have been the offences of 'Assisting Offenders' under Section 4 of the Criminal Law Act (Northern Ireland) 1967 or 'Concealing an Offence' under Section 5 of the same Act. The offence of blackmail used to be mentioned and accusations of this in the local Irish press were frequent.

Smith and Hogan in their book *Criminal Law* point out that Section 5 (1) of the Criminal Law Act 1967 makes it an offence to compound an arrestable offence in return for any 'consideration', which 'presumably bears much the same meaning as in the law of contract and extends to money, goods, services, or any act or forbearance'.[23] Perhaps it was this that led to the position that, if a complaint were made that any officer or soldier had offered any inducement to a suspected terrorist to help them, this was immediately made the subject of a rigorous Police enquiry against the officer or soldier concerned. In one case in Northern Ireland, two suspects were questioned unsuccessfully by the Police for some time, but later an Army officer convinced one of them—untruthfully—that his colleague had told everything to the Police. He also convinced the suspect that he could get him easier treatment by the authorities if he co-operated. In the hope of this advantage, the suspect promptly told the officer the whereabouts of a car containing 700 lb. of explosive, which was thereupon recovered by the Security Forces. The suspect also gave a wealth of other valuable information about his terrorist organisation and colleagues. The officer who achieved that blow against the terrorists and prevented the 700 lb. of explosive from going off was subsequently investigated for blackmail. This was on the complaint of the suspect, an acknowledged bomber, because the officer had offered him an inducement to confess. In the face of such a handicap it was sometimes hard for the military to believe that the courts or the Government in Northern Ireland seriously wanted them to overcome the terrorists. The inevitable conclusion was drawn by some that the best policy was to do as little as possible against the terrorists, since energetic anti-terrorist action only brought trouble on to the head of anyone who attempted it, and hope to survive until the time came to go home. In effect the Police and military were never able to offer an indemnity to a terrorist who wished to defect to the Government or to return to normal life, and there was no ascertainable means of achieving such a thing. The Police and Army were also totally inhibited from offering even the smallest inducement to a terrorist to help them.

It does, however, seem from the 'Bertie Smalls' case that British law sometimes permits information and defection to be bought by an indemnity from prosecution. It is an interesting question why, if such a system of offering indemnity for information existed, it was not widely used in Northern Ireland. This seems to have been a case of not using to the full the means for suppressing such a grave state of disorder which were actually allowed by the law.

Here we must consider the problem of *agents provocateurs*. The ideal situation from the Security Forces' point of view is to have someone working for them who actually operates within the terrorist ranks. If he is to survive, he must clearly play his part in terrorist activities, which will, almost inevitably, involve him in committing further crimes, or at least being an accomplice to them. Lord Widgery recognised this when in a Court of Appeal judgment in 1974:

'Common sense indicated that, if a police officer or anybody else infiltrated a suspect society, he had to show a certain amount of enthusiasm for what the society was doing if he was to maintain his cover for more than five minutes....

'Of course, the intruder, the person who found himself placed in the organization, had to endeavour to tread the somewhat difficult line between showing the necessary enthusiasm to keep his cover and actually becoming an *agent provocateur*, meaning thereby someone who actually caused offences to be committed which otherwise would not be committed at all.'[24]

A leading case on informers and *agents provocateurs* is that of *Regina* v. *Birtles* on 19 May 1969. Lord Chief Justice Parker gave judgement in this case:

'... It is vitally important to ensure so far as possible that the informer does not create an offence, that is to say, incite others to commit an offence which those others would not otherwise have committed. It is one thing for the police to make use of information concerning an offence that is already laid on. In such a case the police are clearly entitled, indeed it is their duty, to mitigate the consequences of the proposed offence, for example, to protect the proposed victim, and to that end it may be perfectly proper for them to encourage the informer to take part in the offence or indeed for a police officer himself to do so. But it is quite another thing, and something of which this Court thoroughly disapproves, to use an informer to encourage another to commit an offence or indeed an offence of a more serious character, which he would not otherwise commit, still more so if the police themselves take part in carrying it out.'[25]

Hence, penetration of subversive organisations is allowed, but the infiltrator must behave reasonably and contribute the minimum necessary to retain his cover to the activities of the terrorists.

The success of the Security Forces in the Malayan campaign was largely due to the readiness there to grant indemnities to terrorists for their crimes. Richard Clutterbuck quotes the following passages from a surrender leaflet showered into the jungle in August 1957:

3. You will NOT be prosecuted for any offence connected with the emergency which you have committed under Communist direction before this date.

5. As regards the remainder, they will be repatriated to China (with their families if they so wish) and will not be made the subject of any investigation but will be given fair treatment while awaiting repatriation.[26]

Since such indemnities were so highly successful in Malaya, it is a pity that the Government has eschewed such a devastating anti-terrorist weapon in Northern Ireland by its policy regarding the use of indemnities there. There is of course great danger in offering an infiltrator indemnity for what he may do in the future rather than what he has done in the past. It would be so easy for someone with such an indemnity behind him to overstep the intended mark through either malice or misunderstanding, and defectors and informers as a breed tend to be inherently unreliable. The best that can be done for the defector who returns to infiltrate the terrorist organisation is to give him an assurance that his problem of retaining his cover is understood and that if he behaves reasonably and as moderately as possible he will be granted further indemnities—as it were, in arrear.

Immunity from further prosecution in return for co-operation can be granted by the Director of Public Prosecutions, as was done in the 'Bertie

Smalls' case. However Lord Justice Lawton, giving the judgement of the Court of Appeal in this case, cast strictures on the Director of Public Prosecutions and recommended that in grave cases he should consult the Attorney-General before doing so.[25] It is indeed important to keep the Director of Public Prosecutions as far as possible from appearing as merely another Government official or as a senior director of Police investigations and therefore as subject to political direction and institutional pressures. It is of course never possible for him to be wholly independent because, like the Law Officers, he bridges the gap between politics and justice and must take such factors as 'the public interest' into account when deciding whether or not to prosecute.[28] It was accusations of sectarian bias on the part of the Royal Ulster Constabulary, the Crown Solicitors and the Northern Ireland Attorney-General that led to the establishment of a Director of Public Prosecutions in Northern Ireland in 1972 to provide an independent and impartial person to decide on prosecutions.[29]

Lord Justice Lawton went on in the same case to approve of the practice known as 'Queen's Evidence' by which accomplices who have already been convicted could give evidence against their former colleagues in crime.[36] However, this practice is not suitable for the circumstances of a counter-terrorist campaign, because it involves publicising the identity of the informer, and not only is he personally put in danger, but he is prevented from helping the Security Forces in the future. This problem of personal publicity should not be confused with the need to publicise the existence of a system for granting indemnities. The existence of such a system should be made as widely known as possible through notices in the press, on television and in Police stations, to cause as much mistrust in the terrorist ranks as possible, and to ensure that every terrorist has this 'easy way out' in the back of his mind if he is arrested.

It has been suggested that only the courts should be empowered to grant such indemnities in order to prevent bias in their use, with friends of the Government being let off and those without official approval being prosecuted. This suggestion is not without some merit, but it has the overwhelming drawback of pulling the Judges into an executive rather than a judicial role. Their impartiality would become tainted and their freedom to pronounce on the lawfulness of any particular indemnity would be curtailed. It could bring them into disrepute in the same way that the quasi-judicial Diplock procedures for detention without trial were felt by the Gardiner Committee to have besmirched the ordinary processes of law in Northern Ireland.[30] For reasons similar to that which led in August 1975 to detention without trial being once again made a pure executive act for the restoration of order,[31] the granting of indemnities, should be (and be seen to be) an act purely of the executive carried out in order to suppress terrorism.

It seems therefore that the proper basis for granting such indemnities should be the Royal Pardon. When a Royal Pardon is granted, the commission of an illegal act is recognised, but the perpetrator thereof is relieved of the consequences of his crime. Its great merit is that it may be granted before conviction; this would nullify the problem of the publicity arising from someone turning 'Queen's Evidence' in open court. A Royal

Pardon has the further advantage that it can be conditional, i.e. the pardon can be withdrawn and the original charge or sentence reinstated if the informer or defector does not fulfil whatever conditions have been set. Hence, pressure can be put on an indemnified informer to 'deliver the goods' if there is any suspicion that he has lost his enthusiasm for defection once the pardon has been granted.[32]

How then should these pardons be granted? In theory they are granted by the Crown and therefore in practice by Ministers in the person of the Home Secretary. However, the Home Secretary has many other things to do and the granting of these indemnities should be a widespread and continuing practice if the terrorist organisations are to be broken up. Moreover, it may be that the Home Secretary is not the Minister responsible for conducting the coordinated Government campaign against insurgency, as is the case in Northern Ireland at present—the disadvantages of divided responsibility have been outlined above. It would therefore seem that it should be enacted that the power to grant Royal Pardons, if terrorism is rife, could be delegated to a Special Commissioner appointed for this purpose. He would be answerable to the Minister responsible for the overall conduct of the campaign to restore order, and the way he carries out his granting of pardons should be subject to judicial review.

(c) Military or police interrogation

Should soldiers have the same powers of interrogation as policemen? From the strict legal point of view, there is essentially no difference between one category and the other. There is in principle no legal objection to one citizen, whether soldier or policeman, asking questions of another. The law mainly concerns itself with the obligations of the person questioned to answer truthfully and to stay and listen; that, in essence, is to be under arrest. However, the desirability of soldiers conducting interrogations should be considered. The answer to this lies, as with the extent to which soldiers should operate in plain clothes, in the degree to which the military are substituting for the Police in a particular campaign. The vital need for the questioner to be steeped in the milieu of the suspect if questioning is to be successful has already been demonstrated. If, therefore, troops are operating where the Police cannot go, or if they operate without policemen, then they must be able to conduct interrogations themselves. For the Army to bring suspects into a Police station to be questioned by policemen who do not operate on the ground will inevitably lead to many failures of interrogaton from the mutual incomprehension and lack of sympathy between questioner and questioned.

The close inter-relation between Police work on the ground and questioning must also be appreciated. The failure to understand this is one of the reasons that has led to the error of centralised interrogation and specialist questioners divorced from operations on the ground. Successful questioning and, indeed, successful comprehension of a security situation are not so much matters of reading reports, intelligence summaries and interrogation records, but of the 'feel' that can only come from close personal involvement. Hence if the activities of the Police and the Army are truly integrated both on the ground and in their bases, then it is of little importance whether questioning is done by Police or by soldiers. If, however, there is physical separation or mutual disregard and suspicion between the two forces, then the military must be able to question suspects on their own. If the Army, in such circumstances, is powerless to do this, it will be unable to acquire the intelligence, the 'feel' or the involvement necessary for success against terrorists, and the military will have little effect in ending disorder.

Questioning by the military in Northern Ireland was given a particular twist by the reluctance and often refusal of citizens wishing to help the Government to speak to the Royal Ulster Constabulary. This refusal was usually made by Catholics on the grounds, however misguided, that they would not speak to the members of the instrument of Protestant oppression. It was made by Protestants on the grounds that there were associates of the protestant para-military groups in the Royal Ulster Constabulary who would give to those organisations the names of anyone from their own community who gave information against them. This would lead to the informant being murdered or beaten up in one of the secret rooms where these things were done, which enjoyed the macabre sobriquet of 'romper rooms'. Indeed one Protestant, who had seen a Catholic gunman shoot a soldier, refused to speak to anyone but to me personally and, after persuasion, to a policeman attached to the Royal Ulster Constabulary from a force in Great Britain, on the grounds that he could only be sure with officials from outside the province that his name would not be 'dropped' to assassins on one side or the other.

Uniformed policing, detective work on the ground, criminal intelligence and the questioning of suspects are activities so closely inter-related that, if the fight against terrorism is to succeed, no artificial separation between them must be allowed to arise by limiting the carrying out of questioning to policemen rather than soldiers—which would tend to develop precisely such separation.

To sum up, the key to smashing a terrorist organisation is the development of inside informers and the infiltration of their ranks. The law must make this possible and easy by a recognised and well-publicised system. The fundamentals of this system are the right to interview, plenty of time to interrogate and persuade, and the ability to indemnify defectors for their crimes committed while in the terrorist ranks.

8

ADDITIONAL POLICE POWERS FOR THE MILITARY TO MAKE THEM EFFECTIVE AGAINST INSURGENTS

(a) Minor police powers needed by the military

A soldier can do nothing useful to combat terrorism, suppress insurrection and assist or substitute for the Police unless he is given the necessary legal powers to do so. Merely to deploy soldiers and hope that their presence on the street will somehow achieve better law enforcement is a fallacy. The Army is extremely jealous of its constitutional subordination to the law, and will therefore do nothing that it is not lawfully authorised to do. It is quite wrong, and very dangerous, to imply that the troops ought to 'bend the law' a little and 'be tough', and that therefore it is not necessary to authorise exceptional powers for them because a blind eye will be turned to any excesses by 'our gallant lads'. The Army does not want to be involved in this sort of thing and will remain as inactive as the law requires it to be, as it did two hundred years ago in the Gordon Riots. Hence, if the soldier is required to substitute for a policeman, he must be given the powers to make this substitution effective. The other result is that where the Army is substituting for the Police, the only laws which will be enforced are the ones that the military are authorised to enforce. Thus if the military do not have the authority to enforce the traffic laws, speeding and dangerous driving will go unchecked. There is of course no suggestion that the military should have any Police powers or be involved in policing at all until the situation is such that they have been deployed to assist in the suppression of civil disorder and terrorism. It is only after this point has been reached that Police powers for the military should be invoked.

The other aspect is that the military need more clarity in their powers than the Police, or at least than the Police in normal times. The military come in to suppress disorder, often abandoning their other duties quite suddenly. Their officers will have had some cursory training in the law, but even this will be mostly in military law, while the legal knowledge among the junior ranks is probably confined to what can be gleaned from detective serials on television. Most important, the military do not possess the years of collective experience of operating the law that resides in a Police force. The military will have to take their guidance mainly from written instructions. Moreover the military are accustomed to clear and definite orders, of the 'you will do this, but you may not do that' type. It is

152

therefore both fair to the soldier and most likely to evoke the best possible result from him if the parts of the law which regulate his conduct in the suppression of civil disorder are made clear for him at least, giving him specific powers to do specific things.

The question of police powers for the military was fully developed in both the Diplock Report of December 1972[1] and the Gardiner Report of January 1975, which at Chapter 4 specifically considered these matters and how the enactments resulting from the Diplock recommendations had worked in practice.[2] It can be deduced from these two reports that troops can be of no assistance to the Police except in the use of lethal weapons, unless they enjoy some powers additional to those of the normal citizen to stop and question, to arrest and detain, and to search and seize. The confusion and obscurity of his common law right of arrest are such as to make it extremely inadvisable for a soldier ever to try to exercise this power or to obey a military order to use it. The soldier must therefore have statutory authority to arrest but, unless this is simple and clear, it can leave him no better placed.

But even at common law (as modified by the Criminal Law Act 1967) there are differences in detail between the powers of the police officer and those of the ordinary citizen to arrest without warrant which make the exercise of the power by the latter hazardous both in law and in fact. ... As a result security guards, stores' detectives and stewards at public functions [one may add soldiers] when they purport to exercise their lawful powers run very considerable risks at law for failure to arrest lawfully, and in the right circumstances may be liable not only to an action for damages for assault and battery, and/or false imprisonment, but also to criminal prosecution as well.[3]

To get round the technical legal problems of a soldier making an arrest, the Diplock Commission recommended and Parliament enacted under Section 12 of the Northern Ireland (Emergency Provisions) Act 1973 what amounts to a blanket power for a simple 'soldier's arrest', with authority to take the suspect to a military base where he could be identified and the question of what he had done sorted out.

However great a derogation of prized liberties this may seem, it is pointless to deploy troops in support of the Police unless they are given some such simple and general power of arrest. For example there can be no purpose in deploying soldiers as sentries to keep intruders away from an electricity power station and not giving them such a power of arrest, for without it they can only look on passively as the intruders go about their business. It is true that the combination of the Criminal Law Act, 1967, and the Official Secrets Acts—probably unintentionally—strengthens the rights of any citizen to arrest intruders into certain specified military locations. However, these rights are circumscribed by provisions as to the intentions of the intruder and confer no special rights on a soldier greater than those of a civilian. The case has already been made for a general right by the military and the Police anywhere to arrest for assault or a breach of the peace in an insurrectionary situation. It is simply not possible in circumstances such as those of the last few years in Belfast to quell petty disorder without such a power. The situation is always too inflammable for lesser remedies and the only satisfactory solution is to arrest the participants and take them to a Police Station where they can, separately, cool off. Nine times out of ten, it is not necessary to charge them and a caution will usually suffice. However, the legal authority to take the disorderly away from the scene of disorder is vital.

The need for authority for troops deployed in aid of the civil power to 'stop and question' is also clear, a view supported by both the Diplock and Gardiner Reports. The same may be said of powers to search and seize, where soldiers suffer such petty obstacles as the denial of authority to search for documents. In a terrorist situation, the military must have the authority to search for material connected with the terrorist campaign without restriction outside dwelling-houses, and on the authority of a commissioned officer within dwelling-houses. It must always be remembered that if it is made exceptionally difficult for the Security Forces to obtain authority to search a particular class of location, that is the place which, with complete logic, the terrorists will chose to hide their material.

To combat terrorism, soldiers also badly need the power to act like constables as regards vehicle documents and directing traffic. It is probably unnecessary for the military to have other powers *vis-à-vis* motoring offences, such as the power to enforce regulations relating to drinking, unless they are completely substituting for the Police and it is felt important that such regulations should be enforced. The military need to have the power to check, as of right, vehicle and driving documents and to arrest where these arouse suspicion, or to order the production within a certain period of vehicle documents that cannot be produced immediately. This need is based on the principle that motor vehicles are, first, a fundamental part of the urban, industrialised way of life; secondly, essential tools of the terrorists' trade, and thirdly, one of the best documented and most rigidly controlled aspects of our life, much more so than individuals. This means that terrorists are exceptionally vulnerable to being detected and having their clandestine cover broken through their motor vehicles. The checking of driving and vehicle documents by soldiers can hardly be discerned as a derogation of civil liberty in relation to the other derogations, such as the right to search dwelling-houses without a warrant, which is also necessary in countering terrorism.

Whenever a terrorist incident occurs, traffic control is involved, whether it be to divert traffic from the scene of a bomb or to stop vehicles in the hope of discovering terrorists in one of them. One of the easiest and least offensive ways whereby the military can relieve an overstretched Police force is by taking over their traffic control duties. One can imagine a situation in which, for example, the Police in London were involved day after day in controlling a series of disorderly demonstrations, perhaps specifically designed to have this effect of exhausting them. In October 1968, 9,000 police were deployed to cover the demonstration in Grosvenor Square,[4] yet the total strength of the Metropolitan Police at the end of 1973 was only 20,953.[5] It is easy to imagine the fatigue which a series of demonstrations would cause to the Police when all the other duties that they have to perform every day of the year are considered. The Army could do a great deal to help them by taking over certain manpower-intensive traffic duties, thus releasing Police to meet the public order threat, without the military ever being involved directly in the suppression of disorder. However, the military cannot give the Police even this mundane assistance without the requisite legal powers. It therefore seems sensible that whenever the military are deployed in aid of the civil power, they should be given the powers of constables to check driving and vehicle documents and to direct traffic.

The same considerations apply to the rights of the military and civil Police to check customs clearance documents and to enforce border control regulations in the special case of the frontier between Northern Ireland and the Republic of Ireland. It has been suggested from time to time that a physical barrier should be built along this completely open land frontier, or of deploying many more troops there, but up to the time of writing, the simple expedient of giving the soldiers and policemen the legal authority to exercise some control has not been tried. There is ample precedent for the military carrying out customs control tasks.[6]

This lack of authority for the police and military to assist in the enforcement of the customs regulations seems strange when the Customs and Excise Act 1952 states at sections 4 and 5:

Exercise of powers and performance of duties.
4. (1) Any act or thing required or authorised by or under any enactment to be done by the Commissioners or any of them may be done—
(*a*) by any one or more of the Commissioners; or
(*b*) if the Commissioners so authorise, by a secretary or assistant secretary to the Commissioners; or
(*c*) by any other person authorised generally or specially in that behalf by the Commissioners.

(2) Any person, whether an officer or not, engaged by the orders or with the concurrence of the Commissioners (whether previously or subsequently expressed) in the performance of any act or duty relating to an assigned matter which is by law required or authorised to be performed by or with an officer, shall be deemed to be the proper officer by or with whom that act or duty is to be performed, and any person so deemed to be the proper officer shall have all the powers of an officer in relation to that act or duty.

Assistance to be rendered by police, etc.
5. It shall be the duty of every constable and every member of Her Majesty's armed forces or coastguard to assist in the enforcement of the law relating to any assigned matter.

It therefore seems that nothing more is required than the authorisation by the Commissioners of Customs and Excise of the military and Police to enforce the customs regulations.

The need for these measures was mentioned in the Gardiner Report:

A number of other proposals were made to us concerned with the regulation of cross-border vehicular traffic, the control of motor vehicles, the control of detonators and certain fertilisers used by terrorists. ... However, we strongly recommend that these studies should be pursued thoroughly and urgently.[7]

It is an indication of the failure to provide in Northern Ireland some of the measures that are needed to win an anti-terrorist campaign that this sort of statement had to be made in the report of a Parliamentary Commission five-and-a-half years after the Army were first deployed to suppress civil disorder in the province.

The military will be ineffective in the suppression of insurrection and terrorism or in supporting the Police unless they are given the powers necessary to carry out these functions. It is suggested that, subject to overall contingency legislation for the suppression of disorder, the exact police powers that the military may exercise should be specified in the Royal Warrant that authorises their deployment for this purpose.

(b) Proposal to give the military and police clear legal authority to suppress riots

Another particular power that the military urgently need is concerned with the suppression of riots. The military in suppressing a riot are required to use only as much force as is necessary and reasonable. But what is reasonable and what will alarm a person of reasonable firmness and courage? Or, more relevantly, what will be thought to come within and without these vague definitions? As a guide to action, as a guide to the awesome responsibility of using a lethal weapon against a fellow-citizen with the possibility of a murder charge, let alone assaulting the self-same fellow-citizen with rubber bullet or baton, these definitions are inadequate.

In suppressing a riot, the serious problem is to prove afterwards that there was a riot of a degree of violence that justified the use of the force that was used. The existence of the riot has to be proved to the law courts, both as a defence to a possible charge against the military of murder or manslaughter, and to secure convictions against rioters who are charged with rioting. It is no very great offence to throw a stone in the street, but it is a serious crime to throw one in combination with others as part of a riot which has as its purpose the overthrow of the constituted authority of the state. Rioters will not be deterred from rioting if on conviction they are fined £1 or £2 for throwing stones instead of being sent to prison for rioting because the Crown failed to prove the existence of a riot. It is moreover extremely difficult, given the hurly-burly of a riot, to produce weeks later in court unshakable evidence as to the actions of the accused in particular. Often the most that can be proved is the presence of the rioter at the place where he was arrested, which will result in an acquittal.

Considerations of this nature led me to purchase a videotape camera for my battalion which was used to prove a case against a rioter for the first time ever in the Belfast Magistrates' Court on 20 August 1973 resulting from a riot outside the Springfield Road Police Station on 5 August 1973. It was possible to prove with the videotape record of the riot not only the part of the accused but also the existence of a riot, both of which could be seen by the court on film. Not the least advantage of this was that it was no longer necessary to try to arrest rioters at the time of the riot, a singularly unprofitable activity, both in terms of arresting the leaders rather than just anybody who happened to be in the way, and because an arrest scene is nearly always bad publicity for the Security Forces, since only the moment of arrest is seen on television and not what has led up to it. On this occasion of its first use, one-third of the active rioters were charged in court, having been seen and arrested sometimes weeks after the event, but the record of their conduct at the riot was still available on the videotape.

The other group to whom the existence of a riot and the reasonable use of necessary force must be proved is the news media and through them public opinion. The result of Bloody Sunday as seen through the media was to swing public opinion, particularly outside Britain, away from the *status quo* and behind the aspirations of the IRA. The disapproval by public opinion of the events of Bloody Sunday was probably the major factor that persuaded the British Government to end the Stormont Government, to embark on direct rule of the province, and to call the 1972 ceasefire with the IRA. All this happened because the Army were unable to 'prove' to public opinion through the media that on Bloody Sunday there had been a riot and shooting which made the response by the Army necessary and reasonable. Neither the Army nor the Civil Government realised at that time just how necessary it was to 'prove' this case to public opinion, or how quickly the judgement would be made.

What then can be done to improve the situation? It appears essential that an element of clarity should be reintroduced into the matter of suppressing riots, so that not only the soldiers may know with some certainty what they are required to do, but so that ordinary citizens—both rioters and bystanders—may also know what they should do and what the military will do. The present legal confusion leads to the dangerous unpredictability of all parties to a riotous situation which can lead of itself to clashes unwanted by both sides.

This clarity could be restored by reviving something resembling the Riot Act, 1714.[8] It seems that the repeal of this act in 1967 was a grave error, and one which has contributed significantly to the near-continuous and apparently uncontrollable street tumult in Northern Ireland since that time. Section 3 of the Riot Act read:

Persons so assembled and not dispersing within an hour to be seized. Here follows a list of peace officers.

3. AND ... if such persons so unlawfully, riotously, and tumultuously assembled, or twelve or more of them, after proclamation made in manner aforesaid, shall continue together, and not disperse themselves within one hour, that then it shall and may be lawful to and for every justice of the peace, sheriff or under-sheriff of the county where such assembly shall be, and also to and for every [1 high] or petty constable, and other peace officer within such county, and also to and for every mayor, justice of the peace, sheriff, bailiff, and other head officer, high or petty constable, and other peace-officer of any city or town-corporate where such assembly shall be, and to and for such other person and persons as shall be commanded to be assisting unto any such justice of the peace, sheriff or under-sheriff, mayor, bailiff, or other head officer aforesaid (who are hereby authorized and empowered to command all his Majesties subjects of age and ability to be assisting to them therein) to seize and apprehend, and they are hereby required to seize and apprehend such persons so unlawfully, riotously, and tumul-

And if they make resistance, the persons killing them, &c. to be indemnified.

tuously continuing together after proclamation made as aforesaid, and forthwith to carry the persons so apprehended before one or more of his Majesties justices of the peace of the county or place where such persons shall be so apprehended, in order to their being proceeded against for such their offences according to law; and that if the persons so unlawfully, riotously, and tumultuously assembled, or any of them, shall happen to be killed, maimed, or hurt in the dispersing, seizing, or apprehending, or emdeavouring to disperse, seize, or apprehend them, by reason of their resisting the persons so dispersing, seizing, or apprehending, or endeavouring to disperse, seize, or apprehend them, that then every such justice of the peace, sheriff, under-sheriff, mayor, bailiff, head-officer, high or petty constable, or other peace-officer, and all and singular persons, being aiding and assisting to them, or any of them, shall be free, discharged, and indemnified, as well against the Kings Majesty, his heirs and successors, as against all and every other person and persons of, for, or concerning the killing, maiming, or hurting of any such persons or persons, so unlawfully, riotously, and tumultuously assembled, that shall happen to be so killed, maimed, or hurt as aforesaid.

[1 office of High Constable abolished (E.), 32 & 33 Vict. c. 47].

The beauty of the Riot Act was that it gave clarity to all concerned as to when a riot was officially taking place, and indemnified those who suppressed it for any actions when doing so that would otherwise have been illegal. This clarity, inherited from an age more familiar than ours with riots, seems to have been rather casually thrown aside, to the nation's considerable disadvantage. It is true that the Riot Act did not remove all problems and confusions from riot control; of this the Gordon Riots give sufficient evidence. Nevertheless, all parties knew that, an hour after the proclamation had been read, any continuing tumult would be held by the courts to constitute a riot and that the law enforcement agencies had lawful authority to use whatever force was needed to disperse it. Not only would this be of legal value in proving a riot, but it would also be of great value in 'proving' to public opinion that the Security Forces had acted reasonably. For it could be shown that the rioters had been given a formal warning to disperse within one hour in accordance with an Act of Parliament, and that they had not done so. Any rioter killed or injured after that could only be considered to have courted his fate.

Some attempt to give statutory authority to an order to a crowd to disperse was made in Section 21 of the Northern Ireland (Emergency Provisions) Act, 1973:

(1) Where any commissioned officer of Her Majesty's forces or any officer of the Royal Ulster Constabulary not below the rank of chief inspector is of the opinion that any assembly of three or more persons may lead to a breach of the peace or public disorder or may make undue demands on the police or Her Majesty's forces he, or any of those forces on duty or any constable may order the persons constituting the assembly to disperse forthwith.

This section has seldom been invoked in Northern Ireland, and on the only occasion when it was used in my presence, it lacked all credibility. This lack of credibility lay in the absence of any special authorisation to disperse the riot or any special indemnity for doing so. I was the person who should have taken some action in face of the total failure of the rioters to obey the order to disperse, but I did not do so because I knew for certain that, had I ordered the extremely severe steps required to disperse the riot, I would have been liable to suffer severely both in court and on the media. It also lacked credibility because of the absence of a formal notification of a time at which to disperse. The order to disperse immediately was simply absorbed into the string of incidents that formed the riot. To have been able to say, as the Riot Act would have allowed, 'Disperse in one hour or be shot dead', would have quickly put an end to all rioting in Northern Ireland.

CONCLUSION

No Government can expect to succeed in defeating terrorism and disorder unless, as first requirements, it has the right constitutional arrangements and the right policing rules.

The constitutional arrangements are in effect the management organisation for the counter-insurgency operations. These need to co-ordinate in one mutually supporting effort all aspects of Government and as many elements of the social fabric as possible outside Government. There needs to be a clearly defined civilian chain of command with adequate authority over all military, Police and civil organs of Government.

It is necessary to ensure that the Security Forces and citizens in general, whether disaffected or not, know as clearly as possible the rights and duties of the Police, of the military and of citizens in the suppression of disorder. As far as possible, the actions of the Police and military should cease to be flexible and uncertain, and become automatic and predictable.

The measures needed to counter insurgency and terrorism should be considered in depth and be enacted in dormant legislation, only to be invoked when needed in emergency. Moreover these measures need to be the ones that will in reality enable the Police and military successfully to detect and prosecute terrorists and the disorderly, rather than dramatic powers carrying a severe political penalty that have only a marginal effect on the outcome of the counter-insurgency campaign. The two vital powers are those to identify the population and those to produce informers from among the terrorists.

A state that is affected by widespread disorder and terrorism must realise that it is in mortal danger and that it may itself perish if it fails to master this threat. It is unlikely to achieve this unless it has a constitutional organisation and policing laws that make this mastery probable.

To avoid misunderstanding, I wish finally to state my personal position. If asked to describe my own political views, I can only reply that I am an unshakable adherent to the principles of constitutional democracy and the rule of law, as enacted by our Parliament. I also much admire the American Constitution and the capacity for correcting unlawful and unconstitutional conduct through the checks and balances supplied by its system of dividing among three bodies the supreme powers of the state.

One of my objects in writing this book has been to call attention to the anomalous and potentially dangerous state of the legal and constitutional arrangements for dealing with terrorism and disorder as so sharply revealed to me in Northern Ireland. If the book should stimulate some debate on how they might be improved with such proposals as the one I have made for dormant emergency legislation, I shall be well satisfied.

I do not advocate, never have advocated, and never will advocate the use of the military within the United Kingdom for any purpose connected with counter-terrorism or public order; these are properly tasks for the Police. The purpose of the military is external defence. Nor do I at the present foresee any likelihood of the Army being required to become involved in the maintenance of public order in mainland Britain. Nevertheless, at the time this book goes to press the Army is, inescapably, involved in the maintenance of public order in one province of the United Kingdom—Northern Ireland. This has recently happened in other similar constitutional democracies such as Canada and the United States,[1] and it has happened in England, Scotland and Wales in the past. It is moreover important to remember the time-scale involved. The law I am discussing is essentially more than two centuries old, and it is seventy years since Parliament examined these laws. It is possible that in seventy years or less from now, situations that could unavoidably drag the Army into the maintenance of public order in mainland Britain might arise.

They might arise, moreover, in connection with issues we have not thought about yet, when the issues that currently excite us may be as dead as those which divided Disraeli and Gladstone seem now. I believe that the best time to update the law on this subject is in quiet times such as the present, when it is unlikely to be invoked, and not in the middle of some crisis fifty years hence. Perhaps I can legitimately draw a parallel with the timing of India's independence. Who can now doubt that it was wise for the United Kingdom to grant independence to India before a war of liberation had begun rather than after it had been lost?

I repeat, therefore, that I do not support military involvement within the United Kingdom unless it is absolutely unavoidable, but I do recommend that the constitutional and legal control of such involvement should be more carefully thought out than it is at present, just in case it might be required for some reason that we cannot now foresee.

NOTES

Introduction

1. *Manual of Military Law*, Part II, 'Employment of Troops in Aid of the Civil Power', 1968 (Army Code No. 14470 [Section V]).
2. Cmnd. 3297, para. 30.
3. Emergency Powers Act 1920 as amended by the Emergency Powers Act 1964.

Chapter 1—*Shortcomings in the Constitutional Structure for Suppressing Civil Disorder and Terrorism*

1. Report of Scarman Tribunal, April 1972, Cmnd. 566, para. 20.1.
2. Cmnd. 566, para. 19.3.
3. Cmnd. 566, para. 19.8.
4. Report of Select Committee of the House of Commons on the Employment of Military in Cases of Disturbances, 16 July 1908, para. 12.
5. Cmnd. 566, para. 5.
6. Confirmation of this kind of thinking is given in the statement of Mr Oliver Napier, leader of the joint Protestant–Catholic Alliance Party, on 27 August 1975: 'Soon we will be at a stage where the ordinary Catholic could be forced out of sheer necessity to look to the IRA as his only means of protection.'
7. Robert Taber, *The War of the Flea*, St Albans 1970, p. 28.
8. Report of Select Committee on Employment of Military, op. cit.
9. Op. cit., page 11.
10. [1838] 4 Bing (NC) 574.
11. *Attorney-General for New South Wales* v. *Perpetual Trustee Co. Ltd.* [1955] AC 457 at p. 489.
12. [1930] 2 KB 364.
13. *Manual of Military Law* (hereafter referred to as *MML*), Part II, Section V, 1968, 'Employment of Troops in Aid of the Civil Power'.
14. Op. cit., para. 3.
15. *R.* v. *Pinney* [1838] 5 C&P 254.
16. R. F. V. Heuston, *Essays in Constitutional Law*, 2nd ed., London, 1964, p. 137.
17. Article by Professor Claire Palley, *The Times*, 13 February 1973.
18. [1968] 2 QB 118 at 137.
19. *The Guardian*, 25 September 1975. The difficult extension of this is to decide what authority a Chief Constable or senior policeman possesses to give orders to

subordinate policemen on law enforcement. The problem is deployed in an article in the *Criminal Law Review*, June 1975, by Chief Inspector I. T. Oliver, LL.B., entitled 'The Office of Constable'.

20. Charge to the Bristol Grand Jury on 2 January 1832 by Tindal C.J., 5 C&P 261.

21. Popham's Rep. 121.

22. *MML*, paras. 3 and 4.

23. *The Queen's Regulations for the Army* 1961 (Army Code No. 13206), para. J1164a—amendment 92 of March 1975. Referred to below as '*QR*'.

24. [1841] C&M 314.

25. L. Radzinowicz, *A History of English Criminal Law*, Vol. 3, London, 1956, pp. 93–6.

26. Report of Select Committee on Employment of Military, op. cit.

27. Op. cit., answers to Questions 10, 11 and 12.

28. HL Deb, 16 January 1974, col. 1052.

29. *Stone's Justice's Manual*, 1973, page 2972.

30. Administration of Justice Act 1973, s. 1 (9).

31. Report of Select Committee on Employment of Military ... 1908, answer to question 368.

32. Report of the Royal Commission on the Police, 1962, Cmnd. 1728, para 35.

33. Burke and Walsh (*ed.*), *Current Law Statutes Annotated*. London, 1956.

34. Capt. K. O. Fox, 'The Tonypandy Riots', *Army Quarterly*, October 1973.

35. Report of the Cameron Commission on Disturbances in Northern Ireland, September 1969, Cmnd. 532, para. 168.

36. C. J. N. Townshend, 'Military Rule in the Search for a Settlement in Ireland 1919–1921', unpublished D.Phil. thesis, Oxford University, 1973.

37. Report of the Widgery Tribunal into Events in Londonderry on 30 January 1972, 18 April 1972, HL 101, HC 220, paras. 10, 11 and 12.

38. Report of the Diplock Commission to consider legal procedures to deal with terrorist activities in Northern Ireland, December 1972, Cmnd. 5185, para. 17.

39. *The Times*, 19 September 1973.

40. Widgery Report, op. cit., p. 6.

41. Cf. note 18 above.

42. [1973] 1 QB 241.

43. Heuston, op. cit., p. 71.

44. [1968] AC 997.

45. C. J. N. Townshend, op. cit.

46. TLR, 5 December 1974.

47. Bernadette Devlin, *The Price of My Soul*, London, 1969, p. 14.

48. Report of Scarman Tribunal, op. cit.

49. Charge to Bristol Grand Jury, op. cit.

50. Bernadette Devlin, op. cit., p. 205.

51. Report of the Compton Committee to enquire into allegations of brutality by the Security Forces in Northern Ireland, November 1971, Cmnd. 4823.

52. Diplock Report, op. cit., para. 29.

53. [1803] USA 1 CRANCH 137.

54. The Yellow Card was a set of instructions issued to each soldier in Northern Ireland by the military authorities to give him guidance on when he could shoot to kill. It was a complex document that required amendment from time to time and at one time contained 23 fairly elaborate paragraphs.

55. [1968] 2 QB 118 at 137.

56. K. Boyle, T. Hadden and P. Hillyard, *Law and State: The Case of Northern Ireland*, London, 1975. p. 10.

57. Op. cit., p. 10.

58. Op. cit., p. 23.

59. Report of Select Committee on Employment of Military, op. cit., answer to question 104.

60. [1900] Cape of Good Hope Supreme Court Reports, 561.

61. HC Deb., 5 July 1973, cols. 746 and 747.

62. HC Deb. 28 November 1974, col. 719.

63. *Daily Telegraph*, 11 September 1975.

64. The writer was present in court.

65. *The Times*, 16 July 1975.

66. Maria McGuire, *To Take Arms*, London, 1973, p. 75.

67. Charles Foley, *The Memoirs of General Grivas*, London, 1964, p. 77.

68. *Daily Telegraph*, 26 August 1975.

69. Report from the Select Committee on the Petition of Frederick Young and others, *Parliamentary Papers* (1833) Vol. 13, pp. 407 and 522.

70. Common Article 4 of the 3rd Red Cross Convention at Geneva of 12 August 1949 relative to the treatment of Prisoners of War.

71. [1921] 2 IR 241.

72. [1902] AC 109.

73. [1921] 2 IR 329.

74. S. A. de Smith, *Constitutional and Administrative Law*, Harmondsworth, 1971, p. 498.

75. Restoration of Order in Ireland Act 1920.

76. D. L. Keir and F. H. Lawson, *Cases in Constitutional Law*, 5th edn., Oxford University Press, 1972, p. 250.

77. *MML*, Part II, Section V, op. cit.

78. A. J. Hayter, 'The Army and the Mob in England in the Generation before the Gordon Riots', unpublished D.Phil. thesis, University of London, 1973, p. 253.

79. Scarman Report on the Red Lion Square Disorders of 15 June 1974, February 1975, Cmnd. 5919, para. 26.

80. Army Act 1955, Section 224 (1).

81. Army Act 1955, Section 225 (1).

82. John Darby and Geoffrey Morris, *Intimidation in Housing*, research paper authorised by the Northern Ireland Community Relations Commission, published February 1974, pp. 102 and 103.

83. *History of the Second World War*, United Kingdom Civil Series, London: HMSO, 1955, T. H. O'Brien, *Civil Defence*, p. 418.

84. Article in the *Magazine* of the Royal Victoria Hospital, Belfast, League of Nurses, April 1975.

85. *The Times*, 22 July 1972.

86. Scarman Report on Red Lion Square Disorders, para. 129.

87. *The Times*, 20 August 1975.

88. Cf. Scarman Report on Red Lion Square Disorders, para. 80.

89. *QR*, para. J894.

90. *QR*, para. J886(a).

91. *MML*, 1972, note to Army Act 1955, s. 34.

92. *The Times*, 28 August 1973. It was incorrectly reported that the riot had taken place outside the Hastings Street Police Station.

93. Simon Winchester, *In Holy Terror*, London, 1974, p. 175.

94. *The Times*, 14 August 1971.

95. Barry Zorthian (of *Time-Life*), speech to US Naval War College quoted in *Military Review* (USA), April 1972.

96. *Canadian Defence Quarterly*, Autumn 1973.

97. Darby and Morris, *Intimidation in Housing*, op cit., p. 73.

98. Op. cit., p. 76.

99. Lieut.-Col. P. W. Graham, in *Royal United Services Institution Journal*, September 1974.

100. Russell Stetler (ed.), *The Military Art of People's War* by General Vo Nguyen Giap. New York, 1970.

101. Review Body on Local Government in Northern Ireland under Mr Patrick MacRory. Its report (26 June 1970) was in general accepted, and implementation began in 1972. See *The Times*, 28 September 1971.

102. Darby and Morris, op. cit., p. 101.

103. Diplock Report, op. cit., para. 109.

104. Richard Clutterbuck, *The Long Long War*, Cassell, 1966, p. 4.

105. HC Deb., 12 March 1975, col. 530—Mr Merlyn Rees.

Chapter 2—*Shortcomings in the Laws Controlling Counter-insurgency Operations*

1. F. E. Kitson, *Gangs and Counter Gangs*, London, 1960, p. 47.

2. Michael Blundell, *So Rough a Wind*, Weidenfeld, 1964, p. 116.

3. D. A. Thomas, 'Police Powers—II. Arrest: a General View', *Criminal Law Review*, 1966, p. 644.

4. Royal Commission on the Police, 1962, Cmnd. 1728, paras. 26 and 27.

5. D. A. Thomas, op. cit., p. 659.

6. Opinion Research Centre Survey, 4th May 1973, which showed that the Police enjoyed more public confidence than any other major institution in Britain. Cf. also Royal Commission on the Police, op. cit., p. 103: a survey revealed that 83 per cent of those interviewed expressed great respect for the Police.

7. See Simon Winchester, op. cit., p. 75.

8. Richard Clutterbuck, *The Long, Long War*, London, 1966, p. 5.

9. Report of Commissioner of Police of the Metropolis for the year 1974, Cmnd. 6068, p. 19. Author's italics.

10. Charles Foley, *The Memoirs of General Grivas*, Longmans, 1964, p. 74.

11. Foley, op. cit., p. 120.

12. David Wilkerson, *The Cross and the Switchblade*, Oliphants, 1968, p. 46.

13. *Regina* v. *Mealey* and *Regina* v. *Sheridan*. TLR, 30 July 1974.

14. *Daily Telegraph*, 18 February 1975.

15. Cf. works previously cited by Frank Kitson and Richard Clutterback; also Penelope Tremayne, 'Guevara through the Looking Glass: a View of the Dhofar War', *RUSI Journal*, 3 September 1974.

16. Gardiner Report, op. cit.

17. *The Times*, 23 July 1973.

18. Diplock Report, op. cit.

19. See General Jacques Massu, *La Vraie Bataille d'Alger*, Paris: Plon, 1971.

20. Scarman Report on Red Lion Square Disorders, para. 80.

21. Cameron Report, op. cit., p. 84.

22. [1907] 2 KB 853.

23. Diplock Report, para. 45.

24. D. A. Thomas, op. cit.

25. HC Official Report of Standing Committee B, 19 June 1973, col. 539.

26. See HL Deb., 25 September 1975, col. 591—Lord Brookeborough.

27. D. L. Keir and F. H. Lawson, *Cases in Constitutional Law*, 5th edn., Oxford University Press, 1972, p. 177.

28. Army Act 1955, s. 192.

29. Army Act 1955, s. 209.

30. E.g. see the figures between March 1972 and September 1974 quoted in K. Boyle, T. Hadden, P. Hillyard, *Law and State: the Case of Northern Ireland*, London, 1975, p. 142.

31. HC Deb, 6 November 1974, col. 1069—Mr Merlyn Rees.

32. In the interests of brevity the complicated processes of how soldiers were ordered to make statements have been somewhat simplified. This was usually done by the soldier and his officers being told that all soldiers had to make statements and that they had no right to refuse. This was usually enough to ensure that the soldier did not insist on being specifically ordered to make a particular statement, which would have increased the chances of it not being admitted in evidence in court. However, I personally challenged this practice and was specifically told by the Legal Branch at Headquarters Northern Ireland that soldiers had to make statements if asked to do so by military investigators under their general duty as citizens, and that they could only remain silent once the investigator had made up his mind that he would charge them. When I further challenged this view of the law with the Legal Branch in the Ministry of Defence, I was told that, while my notion that a citizen had a general right to remain silent when questioned by an investigator might be correct, this did not affect soldiers, because a military order to make a statement overrode this general right to silence, and that this was the basis of the practice in Northern Ireland of Military Police investigators compelling soldiers to make statements and asserting that they had no right to remain silent. I was further told that any soldier who refused to make a statement to a Military Police investigator would make himself liable to being charged under Section 34 of the Army Act 1955 with disobedience to a lawful command.

33. Lord Parker in *Rice* v. *Connolly*, [1966] 2 QB 414. This sentiment was reiterated by Lord Widgery in *Dibble* v. *Ingleton*, [1972] 1 QB 450.

34. L. H. Leigh, *Police Powers in England and Wales*, Butterworth, 1975, p. 224.

35. This is confirmed at para. 87 of the Gardiner Report.

Chapter 3—*Proposals to Rationalize the Constitutional Status of the Military Engaged in Countering Insurgency within the United Kingdom*

1. Anthony Deane-Drummond, *Riot Control*, Royal United Services Institute, 1975, p. 78.

2. Police Act, 1964, section 5.

3. See Charles M. Clode, *Military Forces of the Crown*, London, 1869, Vol. 2, p. 127: 'Under the Militia Act 13 Car II the duty for the public peace was laid on a military officer, the Lord Lieutenant and under 14 Car II and 22 Car II he could call out the military to collect customs and suppress conventicles.'

4. 1 William & Mary, Cap 5 of 1688.

5. C. M. Clode, op. cit., Vol. I, p. 499.

6. Clode, op. cit., Vol. II, pp. 132–5. In the early eighteenth century employment of the troops in support of the civil power was only on the warrant of, variously, the King, the Secretary at War and the Privy Council.

7. A. F. Wilcox, *The Decision to Prosecute*, London, 1972, p. 27.

8. R. F. V. Heuston, *Essays in Constitutional Law*, 2nd edn., London, 1964, p. 195.

9. S. A. de Smith, *Judicial Review of Administrative Actions*, 3rd edn., London, 1973, p. 425 and ch. 10 passim.

10. [1958] 1 QB 571.

11. Sir Francis Vallat, *Current Legal Problems*, 1964.

12. See a letter entitled 'Justifiable Force' published in the *Criminal Law Review*, March 1975, by Lieut.-Col. J. C. Wakerley (retd.), p. 186.

13. [1971] 2 All ER 254.

14. Diplock Report, op. cit.

15. Letter from Lieut.-Col. J. C. Wakerley, op. cit.

16. *Heddon* v. *Evans.* 35 TLR, p. 645.

17. D. L. Keir and F. H. Lawson, *Cases in Constitutional Law*, 5th edn., Oxford University Press, 1972, p. 231.

18. 41 Geo III C. 104.

19. HL Deb., 28 July 1975, col. 931.

20. Sir Robert Mark, Commissioner of the Metropolitan Police, in a lecture, ('Minority Verdict', Police Federation Occasional Papers, 1973, p. 8) pointed out that about 50 per cent of the cases that reached the higher courts ended in acquittals and that in some Welsh counties the acquittal rate was as high as 90 per cent.

21. Cameron Report, op. cit.

22. [1956] 1 QB 220.

23. The direction is in Chapter V, para. 91, of the *Manual of Military Law*, 1972:

91. (*a*) The Judges' Rules are not rules of law but were prepared for the guidance of the civil police. Rule VI, however, provides that persons other than police officers charged with the duty of investigating offences or charging offenders will comply with the spirit of these Rules as far as is practicable. *Principle to be observed in applying the Judges' Rules*

(*b*) The principles enunciated in these Rules should be applied by persons concerned with the arrest and custody of persons accused of offences against A.A. 1955, bearing in mind, however, the differences between service conditions and those pertaining to civilians. For instance, a person subject to military law may be ordered to attend the office of R.M.P. (S.I.B.) and the fact that he had been so ordered would not render a statement made there inadmissible. If, however, a person, when there, asked for an officer to be present while he was questioned and the request was refused or he was ordered to answer questions, a court might well regard his answers as being involuntary and inadmissible. Courts-martial must distinguish between an order to attend an office and an order to make a statement. In normal circumstances for all serious offences S.I.B. assistance should invariably be requested, and regimental personnel should not find it necessary to invite suspected persons to make statements under caution. Where, however, S.I.B. assistance is not available or serious delay would be occasioned in obtaining it, with the result that regimental personnel are required to undertake any investigation, they also must comply with the Rules so far as is practicable.

(*c*) Provided that the spirit of the Rules is observed, any statement obtained will undoubtedly be admissible, unless positive evidence is given that some threat or inducement was held out. Even if the Rules are not followed, the statement will still in law be admissible, if the prosecution is able to satisfy the court that it was made voluntarily, notwithstanding the breach of the rule.

24. 'Administrative Directions on Interrogation and The Taking of Statements'. Appendix B to Home Office Circular 1964, no. 31, January 1964, entitled 'Judges' Rules and Administrative Directions to the Police', para. 71.

168   *Peace Keeping in a Democratic Society*

25. Army Act, 1955, Section 77 (4).
26. As recommended by Mr Maxwell-Hyslop, HC Deb, 28 November 1974, col. 720.
27. *Daily Telegraph*, 19 March 1975.
28. *Reid v. Covert*. 354 U.S.1, 36 (1957).
29. Emergency Powers (Defence) No. 2 Act of 1 August 1940.
30. [1921] 2 IR 386.

Chapter 4—*Proposals for a System of Civilian Control to Manage and Coordinate the Whole of Society in One Campaign to end Disorder and Terrorism*

1. See volumes in the *History of the Second World War*, United Kingdom Civil Series (London, HMSO): T. H. O'Brien, *Civil Defence* (1955) and Richard Titmuss, *Problems of Social Policy* (1950).
2. O'Brien, op. cit., p. 153.
3. O'Brien, op. cit., p. 612.
4. O'Brien, op. cit., p. 303.
5. The authors were John Darby and Geoffrey Morris.
6. Titmuss, *Problems of Social policy*, op. cit., pp. 272–96.
7. Translated extract from 'Le Préfet de Région et la Défense', *Administration*, November 1971.
8. Jean Ravail, 'La Participation de l'Armée à la Défense Civile', *Revue de la Défense nationale*, July 1972.
9. Richard Clutterbuck, *The Long, Long War*, London, 1966, p. 57.
10. O'Brien, op. cit., p. 308.
11. HC Deb, 5 July 1973, col. 747.
12. HL Deb, 25 September 1975, col. 591—Lord Brookeborough.

Chapter 6—*Methods of Population Surveillance*

1. *R. v. Roberts* (Unrep), *Manchester Guardian*, 25 March 1953, per Devlin, J.
2. See case of Mr William Laing, *Daily Telegraph*, 7 and 21 March 1975.
3. L. H. Leigh, *Police Powers in England and Wales*, London: Butterworths, 1975, p. 200.
4. Diplock Report, op. cit., para. 17.
5. HC Deb, 26 June 1975, col. 818.
6. Leigh, op. cit., p. 198.
7. Leigh, op. cit., p. 204.
8. Leigh, op. cit.
9. *Sunday Times*, 1 December 1974 ('Spectrum' article).
10. HC Deb., 28 November 1974, col. 908.
11. Gardiner Report, op. cit., para. 94.
12. Richard Clutterbuck, *The Long, Long War*, London 1966, pp. 37 and 38.
13. HC Deb, 28th November 1974, col. 722—Mr Maxwell-Hyslop.
14. Philip Goodhart, MP, *The Climate of Collapse*, Petersham, 1975, p. 5.
15. [1968] 1 All ER 874 at 888.
16. [1743] 17 State Trials 1139.
17. [1970] 3 All ER 593.

Chapter 7—*Proposals for Encouraging Information from Within the Terrorist Ranks and for the Infiltration of Their Organisations*

1. Compton Report, op. cit.
2. See Michael Blundell, *So Rough a Wind*, London 1964, p. 194; F. E. Kitson, *Gangs and Counter Gangs*, London 1960, pp. 124 and 173.
3. *Starritt Report into the Case of Kenneth Joseph Lennon*, 31 July 1974, p. 3.
4. M. R. D. Foot, *History of the Second World War—Special Operations Executive in France*, London, 1966, p. 124.
5. HC Deb, 17 April 1973, col. 388.
6. *Daily Telegraph*, 20 September 1975.
7. Parker Report on Interrogation Procedures in Northern Ireland, March 1972, Cmnd. 4901, paras. 18–26.
8. Parker Report, Minority Report, para. 20.
9. Gardiner Report, op. cit., para. 14 (c).
10. [1965] NILR 138.
11. Parker Report, op. cit., p. 20.
12. Sir Geoffrey Jackson, *People's Prison*, London, 1973, p. 103.
13. Noel Barber, *The War of the Running Dogs*, London, 1971, p. 269.
14. Richard Clutterbuck, *The Long, Long War*, op. cit., p. 99.
15. Starritt Report, op. cit., para. 31.
16. Noel Barber, op. cit., p. 166.
17. Clutterbuck, op. cit., p. 104.
18. L. H. Leigh, *Police Powers in England and Wales*, London, 1975, p. 141.
19. HC Deb, 28 November 1974, col. 901—Mr Stainton.
20. Diplock Report, op. cit., para. 79.
21. Leigh, op. cit., p. 248.
22. HC Deb, 28 November 1974, col. 903—Mr Roy Jenkins.
23. Smith and Hogan, *Criminal Law*, 3rd edn., 1973, p. 597.
24. *Regina* v. *Mealey* and *Regina* v. *Sheridan*, TLR, 30 July 1974.
25. [1969] 2 All ER 1131.
26. Clutterbuck, op. cit., pp. 104–5.
27. *Regina* v. *Turner and Others*, TLR, 25 March 1975.
28. Written reply in HC on 8 February 1971—Sir Peter Rawlinson, Attorney-General.
29. K. Boyle, T. Hadden, P. Hillyard, *Law and State: The Case of Northern Ireland*, London, 1975.
30. Gardiner Report, op. cit., para. 153.
31. Northern Ireland (Emergency Provisions) (Amendment) Act, 1975.
32. R. F. V. Heuston, 2nd edn., *Essays in Constitutional Law*, London, 1964, pp. 66–75.

Chapter 8—*Additional Police Powers for the Military to Make Them Effective Against Insurgents*

1. Diplock Report, op. cit.
2. Gardiner Report, op. cit., chapter 4.
3. Keith Devlin, 'Arrest and Detention', *Justice of the Peace and Local Government Review*, 13 March 1971.
4. Richard Clutterbuck, *Protest and the Urban Guerrilla*, London, 1973, p. 34.

5. Report of the Commissioner of Police of the Metropolis for the Year 1974, Cmnd. 6008, p. 8.

6. Charles Clode, *Military Forces of/the Crown*, Vol. 2, 1869. On page 127 he points out that one of the first duties of the new Standing Army in the seventeenth century was to collect customs dues.

7. Gardiner Report, op. cit., para. 92.

8. I Geo I.

Conclusion

1. Deployment in 1957 at Little Rock, Arkansas, USA, of regular Army 101st Airborne Division in substitution for the local Police and National Guard to enforce the admission of black pupils to previously all-white schools. Deployment of Canadian regular troops in October 1970 in Quebec Province and the Montreal area in response to FLQ terrorist kidnappings and murders. These troops were given the status of 'Peace Officers' by the Canadian Parliament.

SUBJECT INDEX

Acts of Parliament: Bill of Rights (1688), 18, 19; Riot Act (1714), 13, 78, 157-9; Army Act (1955), 11, 26, 36, 44, 80, 85, 88, 99, 101, 103; Police Act (1964), 103; Criminal Law Act (1967), 5, 77, 147, 154; Northern Ireland (Emergency Provisions) Act (1973), 62, 66, 75, 76, 80, 82, 87, 88, 95, 99, 120, 122, 125, 145, 159; Prevention of Terrorism (Temporary Provisions) Act (1974), 117, 145; Northern Ireland (Emergency Provisions) (Amendment) Act (1975), 106

Algeria, 75

Alienation of parts of Northern Ireland from effective British rule, 33, 49, 50, 81

Armed propaganda, 38

Army: Constitutional Status, 3, 9, 11, 15, 17, 19, 21, 22, 91, 93, 94; danger of its becoming an instrument of tyranny, 92, 93; effect of inexperience in policing, 97, 106, 153; inactivity, 35, 37, 78; initial involvement in N. Irish troubles, 6; legal status, 3; weakness in personal position of soldiers in upholding law, 95; need for soldiers to be able to confirm legality of orders in court, 25, 31, 94, 96; need for soldiers to be informed of their legal rights, 102; power of arrest, 154; predictability, 3, 21, 78, 93; unlawful acts in Ireland, 17, 27

Arrest, 64, 120

Border problems, 84, 156

Borneo, 48

Capital punishment, 5, 62, 83

Cases: *Attorney General for New South Wales* v. *Perpetual Trustees Co. Ltd.* [1955], 9; Charge to Bristol Grand Jury on 2 January 1832 by Lord Chief Judtice Tindal, 9, 22; *R.* v. *Commissioner of Police of the Metropolis ex parte* Blackburn [1968] 10, 18, 26; *R.* v. *Mealey* and *R.* v. *Sheridan*—TLR of 30 July 1974, 71; *R.* v. *Murphy* [1965], 139

Catholics of N. Ireland, 48, 60, 93, 129, 151

Census, *see*—Population Surveillance

Citizens—common law duty to suppress disorder, 3, 36, 122, 131

Civil Affairs Advisers, 53, 54

Civil Authority for the suppression of disorder, 3, 13, 17, 19, 52, 116

Civil Government: comparison with France, 109, 110; competition between terrorists and established government, 48, 50, 57; confusion in N. Ireland, 49, 55, 57, 58, 113; coordinated counter-terrorist campaign, 3, 52, 59, 108, 111, 113; inadequacy in Catholic areas of N. Ireland, 51, 52, 54, 56, 59; incident Centres, 113; involvement of the Army in civil government in N. Ireland, 48, 53, 54, 59; proposals for a system to cope with civil disorder, 4, 108, 111, 112, 113, 115; regional